HILARY A

The LION of the WEST

A biography of John MacHale

VERITAS

Published 2001 by
Veritas Publications
7/8 Lower Abbey Street
Dublin 1
Ireland

Email   publications@veritas.ie
Website   www.veritas.ie

ISBN 1 85390 572 0

British Library Cataloguing
in Publication Data.
A catalogue record for
this book is available
from the British Library.

Cover design by Bill Bolger
Printed in the Republic of Ireland by Betaprint Ltd, Dublin

Veritas books are printed on paper made from the wood pulp of managed forests. For every tree felled, at least one tree is planted, thereby renewing natural resources.

To my mother

Margaret Freeman

who first told me about 'the Lion of the West'

ACKNOWLEDGEMENTS

In writing this book, I owe thanks to many people. I should first of all like to thank the MacHale family of Laherdane, especially Sr Mary MacHale who gave me a great deal of information about John MacHale's family. I should also like to thank Liam and Nuala Doyle, who showed us round their home, the birthplace of MacHale, and allowed us to use their portrait of him for the cover of the book.

Thanks are due to Fr Brendan Kilcoyne for allowing me access to the Tuam archive, and I was pleased to be able to use the Heythrop Library in West London, the Catholic Central Library and the British Library.

I am grateful to all those who encouraged me in the early stages of the book, particularly Elizabeth Gowans, Sheila and Michael Phelan, and my sister, Cecilia Hatt. I should also like to thank Fr Paddy Carroll for his help with the Irish language, and my niece, Katharine Lewis, for continually looking for books for me. I am also grateful to the older members of my family, Rose Marly and Margaret Graham, for recalling information about my great-grandmother, Margaret MacHale.

Thanks are also due to Kevin McNamara for writing the foreword.

Most of all I should like to thank my husband, Peter, and my children for their continuing patience, help and encouragement.

Hilary Andrews

CONTENTS

FOREWORD

THERE ARE SOME people who play an important role in the history of their country, who help to mould events and influence the political thought of their generation. They are important in their time, but because of the fashions of history, whilst not sinking without trace, they only occasionally appear in the footnotes of the history books and the biographies of others. This has been the lot of many of the nineteenth-century Irish nationalists; stereotyped and ridiculed by the revisionists for their nationalism, and scorned by the advocates of physical force for their insistence upon constitutional methods and parliamentary democracy. Such a leader was John McHale, Archbishop of Tuam, the first Irish Bishop since the introduction of the Penal Code to have been educated solely in Ireland. Remedying the poverty, despair and desperation of the people from whom he sprang in County Mayo, and of whom he was the spiritual leader in Killala and later Tuam, was to be the essence of his ministry. To him, emancipation, tenant rights, the abolition of the tithe, parity of religious education and repeal of the Union were as one, all part and parcel of his Catholicism, his Irishness and his spiritual mission.

Of the many parts that he played, MacHale would probably have wanted to be most remembered for his ordinary pastoral care of his people, and particularly for the devotion that he had to them and his local clergy. Speaking at MacHale's Golden Jubilee celebrations in June 1875, A. M. Sullivan said, 'But we saw him under another aspect when famine was mowing down the people of Ireland. There are at this day present in the homes in the West, old men and women who could tell a tale, otherwise unheard by human ear, or unseen by human eye, of the great Archbishop's labours during those dreadful years. If he had no other title to our love, it would be found to his heroism and devotion during the famine time . . .'

In rescuing MacHale from the footnotes of history, and using new material, Hilary Andrews has positioned him in the context of the

7

politics, passions and culture of his time. Frequently it is only many years after their deaths, when the rivalries, disputes and controversies of times have ceased to be current, that a proper detached view can be made of men and women who have made history. MacHale was not without his faults; determined, stubborn, some might say he was obstinate and over-principled. He was also forthright – no Roman cleric skilled in diplomacy was he. Perhaps he should have been more diplomatic, more careful, but if he had he would not have been John MacHale, priest, champion of the poor and the oppressed, Irish patriot, and deservedly bearing the title he won from O'Connell – 'the Lion of the West'.

Kevin McNamara MP

1

THE EARLY YEARS

'I once saw John MacHale' said Mr Kernan 'and I'll never forget it as long as I live.' (James Joyce, *Dubliners*)

JOHN MACHALE lived from 1791 to 1881, a long life that spanned some of the most turbulent years of Irish history. He was not only a great archbishop, involved in the religious and philosophical controversies of the day, but a great scholar and Irish nationalist, who played an important role in the movements for reform and the preservation of the Irish language. He was a contemporary of Daniel O'Connell and John Henry Newman, and became one of the best-known men in Ireland. He was certainly well known to the prime ministers of England and was renowned throughout Europe as a patriot and a great man. For the most part, MacHale's ninety years were spent in the west of Ireland, and if this man, who was hated by some and almost worshipped by many, is to be understood, it is necessary to look to the west.

John MacHale was born on 6 March 1791.[1] The MacHales lived in Tubbernavine, a village in the west of Ireland that derived its name from the Celtic hero, Fionn or Finn Mac Cumhaill. It means well or spring of the Fenians. Tubbernavine is in the district of Tirawley in County Mayo, surrounded by magnificent scenery. It is overlooked by the majestic Mount Nephin on one side, and looks towards the beautiful Lough Conn on the other. John's parents were Patrick and Mary (née Mulkieran), and John was the sixth of ten children. Patrick MacHale was known as Pádraig Mór, or Big Patrick, on account of his great height. He was well over six feet tall, with fair hair and deep blue eyes. He was said to have been strong and energetic, with a good sense of humour and a quick and practical intelligence. Patrick also seems to have been a man of some dynamism. He was an innkeeper with a small farm, who supplemented his income by his dealings in the linen trade. In late eighteenth-century Ireland, the linen trade was still flourishing. Patrick travelled as far as Dublin to buy dyes and yarns, and he would travel round his own neighbourhood, buying linens and selling them at a profit in the linen-hall of Castlebar. Mary, John's mother, whose family came from Donegal in the seventeenth century and subsequently lived near the MacHales, was described by a friend of the family, Ulick Bourke, as possessing a 'clear and comprehensive intellect' and 'firmness of character'.[2]

John MacHale was baptised at two days old, partly because he was a tiny, delicate baby and also because he was born on the Sunday preceding Ash Wednesday. The christening was held on Shrove Tuesday, as the MacHales would have been unable to have a lively christening party, with music and dancing, if they had waited another day. In eighteenth-century Ireland, the regulations for Lent were very strict. John was baptised in the inn kept by his parents by the local priest, Fr Andrew Conry, the pastor of Addergoole and a family friend.

The inn where John MacHale grew up was well placed on a busy post-road between Sligo and Castlebar, the capital of Mayo. The area at that time was quite populous for, in the late eighteenth century, the west of Ireland had a fast-growing population. The innkeeper's household was large, including, besides him and his wife and their children, farm labourers and servants. The environment would have been lively and interesting and the MacHale children would have overheard much news and information from travellers and been aware of differing points of view about the political events of the time. The inn would have also been a centre for story-telling, the reciting of the old Celtic legends, and the place where people would learn episodes from their history, such as the horrors of the Cromwellian era.

The language spoken by most people in the west of Ireland at that time was Gaelic, but Pádraig Mór was anxious that his children should also learn English. He was strongly opposed in this by the children's grandmother, Annie Moffet, who resisted the infiltration of a foreign language, but Pádraig seems to have been outward-looking and ambitious for his children and he persisted in teaching them English.

At the end of the eighteenth century, Ireland still had a separate parliament from England. This had been granted complete legislative independence in 1782 and, under the leadership of Henry Grattan, sought further powers and privileges for Ireland. All political power was in the hands of members of the Established Church, the Church of England, and the majority of the Irish population, the Catholics, had few political rights. However, in the second half of the eighteenth century there had been a stirring of intellectual, largely aristocratic Catholics in Ireland towards certain measures of reform. The Catholic Committee was formed in 1760 and it did achieve some measure of success. After 1774 Catholics who were willing to take the oath of allegiance were allowed to play a greater part in public life. In 1790 the Committee was working towards the admission of Catholics to both branches of the legal profession and for the right to vote in parliamentary elections. By 1793 Catholics were allowed to enlist at the lowest level in the militia and they were also allowed the vote if they were forty-shilling freeholders. The progress of the Catholic Committee was slow and the conservative nature of its members did not make for swift or forceful action.

In the north of Ireland in Ulster, the Presbyterians, the descendants of the Scottish Calvinists, like the dissenters in England, were also excluded from political influence, though they were exempt from the harsher religious laws that affected the Catholics. Despite their privileges, the members of the Irish Established Church were not, thereby, pro-English. They felt as a grievance, and as an impediment to their own prosperity, all the constitutional and economic limitations imposed by England. Added to this, those English who had been planted in the south of Ireland to suppress the Irish had, by the eighteenth century, become in the eyes of their former fellow-countrymen Irish too, and therefore subject to the traditional English contempt. Swift complains about this in many of his letters: 'We seemed strange and remote to them' and 'one impression was that they [the Irish] were a disloyal and turbulent people'.[3]

Nevertheless, despite all their disabilities, some sections of the Irish population prospered during the eighteenth century. This is reflected by the magnificent buildings of Georgian Dublin. During the two decades in which Ireland enjoyed an independent parliament, there was a healthy revival of Irish trade and industry. The linen industry was thriving. Irish mills supplied the calicos and muslins needed by the Irish market, and Irish glass was being exported from Cork and Waterford to the United States. However, while the middle classes prospered, poverty, the perennial problem of Ireland, continued. Ireland produced neither wood nor coal nor iron on which to develop industrially. Irish agriculture had not kept abreast of the agricultural movements in England. Capitalists were unwilling to invest in a country where unrest seemed likely. The greatest landlords were absentees, living in England, who drew what they could from their Irish estates without reinvesting. The main development in Irish agriculture had been the increased cultivation of the potato. The population had increased with the advent of the potato, but it was a population living at subsistence level. Edmund Burke, writing in 1747, said:

> Whoever travels through this kingdom will see such Poverty as few Nations in Europe can equal . . . . As for their food it is notorious they seldom taste bread or meat; . . . their cloaths (sic) so ragged that they rather publish than conceal the wretchedness it was meant to hide, nay it is no uncommon sight to see half a dozen children run quite naked out of a cabin, scarcely distinguishable from a dunghill, to the great disgrace of our country.[4]

The MacHale family, though by no means rich, lived in an inn and were not totally dependent on the land. They were moderately comfortable for the area in which they lived.

John MacHale, though weak and slow in walking for the first few years of his life, was reputed to have spent long hours in the fresh air to improve his health. This seemed to have been successful, since by five years old he was as strong as his brothers and eventually grew to be a tall, athletic young man.

John MacHale's education began in the hedge school at nearby Laherdane. These hedge schools were charity schools. They were informal and gave a very basic education, but kept alive the Gaelic language and traditions. MacHale described his first school thus:

> It was planned by the Author of the Universe, fashioned by Nature; its halls were most majestic; its dimensions magnificent; the blue vault of heaven was its canopy and the desk on which I essayed to write was the bosom of mother-earth; her lap the seat on which I reclined.[5]

The young John was seen to be intelligent from an early age and was able to serve Mass for Fr Conry at six years old. He read any book he could lay his hands on, whether in English or Gaelic, and loved particularly to listen to the local story-teller, Mr O'Callaghan, who told tales of history, folklore and adventure, particularly about the local area.

It was during the early childhood of John MacHale that the Irish rebellion of 1798 took place. This rebellion sealed the fate of the Irish Parliament. It was largely a Protestant rebellion, led by the revolutionary Wolfe Tone, a Belfast lawyer. Tone and his allies founded the Society of United Irishmen. They hoped that Irishmen would sink their religious differences and unite to force England to give Ireland complete freedom. These men were influenced by the ideas of the French Revolution. Although many Catholics, including some members of the Catholic Committee, supported the rebellion, the Catholics on the whole were not very sympathetic to the French Revolution and such infidels as Voltaire. In later life, MacHale often quoted the counsel of his parish priest, Fr Conry, who told the people to avoid an alliance with the French:

> For bad as the English are, they believe in God, but the French people, whom I know well have no faith in God; they have no religion; in name they are Catholic; infidel in act and life.[6]

John MacHale's uncle, the Rev Rickard MacKeal, like many young Irish priests and seminarians, had been studying in France during that time. Now, as the pastor of Ardagh, he would tell of the horrors of the French Revolution and regale his listeners with the story of how he had been hidden for three days by the Sisters of Charity in a box of lumber while Robespierre's men searched the convent for suspects.[7]

In May 1798 the Irish under Tone rose in an abortive rebellion. They had some success in the south-east, capturing the towns of Wexford and Enniscorthy and holding them for a few weeks, before the English commander, General Lake, defeated them at Vinegar Hill near Enniscorthy.

The French government had wanted to intervene in Ireland for some time and, on hearing reports of the insurrection, decided that the time was ripe and so, in August 1798, shortly before the rising collapsed altogether, the French General Humbert with three companies of grenadiers landed in County Mayo. Most of the local population fled in terror, hiding in the hills to avoid conflict and suspicion. John MacHale, then a young child, also hid, with his sisters and his cousins, and watched the arrival of the French soldiers from the mountainside. The French invaders entered the house of Fr Conry, the MacHales' parish priest. It is thought that they demanded hospitality but some say that he made maps to guide the French.[8] Fr Conry was court-marshalled at Castlebar and hung on the nearest tree. This was ordered by Denis Browne, the lieutenant of the county and the brother of the marquis of Sligo. This incident of cruelty and injustice was to have a marked effect on the seven-year-old John MacHale. He attended the funeral with his family and later said that he 'then and there resolved, that, if given life, ability and position, he would expose the misdeeds of those who ruled Ireland'.[9]

Despite the valiant efforts of Grattan in Dublin and Edmund Burke in Westminster, the Act of Union was passed in 1800. This abolished the Irish Parliament and the Irish MPs were now to take their place at Westminster. Both Catholics and Protestants were divided amongst themselves as to the advantages or disadvantages of the Union. While many Protestants welcomed the Union as cementing their ascendancy, others feared that it might precipitate Catholic Emancipation. Most Catholics, these eventually including O'Connell and MacHale, wanted the repeal of the Union, but many thought that they were more likely to win concessions from the Parliament in Westminster, as it had less to lose from Catholic

Emancipation than the Protestant Parliament in Dublin. Indeed, they did have cause to hope as the Prime Minister himself, William Pitt, was in favour of Catholic Emancipation. Their hopes were dashed by the fanatical opposition of King George III. Pitt resigned in 1801 and the King's opposition was continued by the Regent. The Catholics felt betrayed and it seemed to them that the purposes of Pitt and Castlereagh, the Irish Chief Secretary, were to do away with the troublesome phantom of Irish nationality.

However, despite the bigotry of the King, the toleration of the slave trade and the barbarous laws still on the statute book, there were signs of the beginnings of change in the British Isles. In 1802 a group of young men founded the *Edinburgh Review,* in which they sought to challenge some of the accepted beliefs of the time. One of these men was a young Anglican clergyman called Sydney Smith who, although he did not have much sympathy with the Catholic faith, hated intolerance and paved the way for a gradual change of heart in English society by his sermons and writings. After one of his early sermons on Catholic Emancipation, in the Temple Church in London, the congregation were furious, and one of them, Lord Henley, said that he deserved the 'star chamber' for it.[10]

Many people still hoped to absorb the Irish Catholic Church into the Protestant establishment. They believed that toleration of what they considered to be erroneous beliefs was not only wrong but dangerous. John Henry Newman, speaking some twenty years later, spoke of the movement for emancipation as 'the *symptom* of a systematic hatred to our church borne by Romanists, Sectarians, Liberals and Infidels'.[11]

The Reformation had had little effect in Ireland. During the reign of Henry VIII, English power was so circumscribed that his writs went unchallenged only in a small area near Dublin. The situation in Ireland was different from that of England in that Ireland had never had a close Church-State relationship and had a much greater administrative dependence on the monastic tradition. English rule in Ireland was centred on a group of families of Norman or English origin, but there was no gentry comparable with that of England to put the tenets of the Reformation into effect. The situation remained the same during the reigns of Edward and Mary. Papal appointments of bishops continued and the Crown had no means to challenge this. During the reign of Elizabeth there was some effort made to encourage the Reformation in Ireland, but very little means to put it into effect. The dissolution of the Irish monasteries created anger and resentment, and the reformed Church, preaching only in English and with English bishops, remained merely an English import.[12] Oliver Cromwell's rampages in Ireland did nothing to further the cause of the Established Church but left a legacy of horror and bitterness that was to take centuries to eliminate. The Church of Ireland was re-established in 1689 and then began the harsh penal code, which was designed to deprive Catholics of lands, wealth and the ministrations of their clergy. A Catholic had to forswear his religion if he was to inherit his father's property, a law that did little for the character of the Church of Ireland converts.[13] The bishops continued to be recruited from the English gentry. They were disliked even by the Protestant ascendancy for their unhealthy subservience to English political interests and for their arrogance. Their lavish lifestyle provoked much jealousy. Swift observed that two sorts of gentlemen gained Irish bishoprics: English clergymen who succeeded 'by the force of friends, industry, solicitation or other means', and Irishmen distinguished 'by an implicit readiness to fall into any measures that will make the government easy . . . '[14]

The Church of Ireland was further alienated from the nation by the continuation of the existence of tithes. This unfortunate system for the upkeep of the Established Church destroyed Ireland's social and political cohesion and excited the passions of the people. Every tenth sheaf of corn produced by the peasantry was taken for the upkeep of the Church, and many peasants, while worshipping in a barn themselves, had to pay for the repairs to the Protestant church. Swift wrote that the payment of tithes was

> subject to so many frauds, wrangles and difficulties, not only from papists and dissenters, but even from those who profess themselves Protestants, that by the expense, trouble and vexation of collection and bargaining for them, they are of all other rents, the most precarious, uncertain and illpaid.[15]

The defence of the tithe system by the establishment was based on two factors. One was the protection of property, and leading on from that was the idea that any agitation against tithes was subversive and a conspiracy to destroy the established basis of order. It was also felt that it was important for the Church to convert the island to Protestantism, as this was the only firm guarantee of loyalty to the Crown.

A commentator, a generation later than Swift, characterised the tithe as

> A tax more vexatious than oppressive, and more impolitic than either; vexatious because paid directly and in kind, at unequal and fluctuating rates, impolitic because it is vexatious – because a people, unanimous in this alone, declaim against it.[16]

The conscientious clergy of the Established Church were the most vociferous against it. They felt the alienation it caused and found it 'inconsistent with Christianity'.[17]

In the year 1700 the Catholic Church in Ireland might have seemed on the verge of extinction. A penal law was passed in 1703 that required that bishops and the religious orders depart from the kingdom and that parish priests be registered. It was expected that these priests would not be replaced when they died and that the people would begin to go to the churches of the establishment, and in this way the Catholic Church in Ireland would gradually die out.[18] However, the law proved relatively easy to avoid, and as long as the clergy respected the Protestant nature of the kingdom and did not attack the Established Church, they were in little danger. Gradually the Catholic Church began to function publicly and bishops and friars were once more in Ireland.

Although at the beginning of the eighteenth century the religious orders had not yet founded the vast numbers of Catholic schools that were to exist by the end of the century, and there was still no system of national education, there were some schools that gave boys a classical education. After spending some years at the hedge school at Laherdane, John MacHale was sent to school at Castlebar, seven miles away. Here, under the direction of Patrick Stanton, John began the study of Latin, Greek and English Literature, subjects he was to enjoy for the rest of his life.[19] He boarded during the week and would walk the seven miles home to Tubbernavine every weekend. It was during this period that Mary MacHale, John's mother, died. John was fourteen years old. It is thought that Mary MacHale had encouraged the young boy to embark on a clerical career and it would seem likely that John MacHale would have wanted to fulfil the cherished hopes of a beloved mother, now dead.

In 1807, with the influence of the Bishop of Killala, Dr Dominic Bellow, John was given a bursary for Maynooth College. The Royal College of St Patrick had been in existence since 1796. During the eighteenth century Catholic priests had been trained on the Continent, particularly in France, but in 1793 the French revolutionaries took over the College des Lombards in Paris, which had been the principal training centre for Irish priests. The Irish hierarchy then had to consider the possibility of training their priests at home. In January 1794 Dr Troy, Archbishop of Dublin, appealed to the Lord Lieutenant, Lord Westmoreland, recounting the difficulties faced by the Church after the closure of continental colleges and expressing reluctance to expose students 'to the contagion and sedition of infidelity' of France, and soliciting the royal licence for the endowment of seminaries for the training of priests. The appeal was at first rejected but eventually, with a new Lord Lieutenant, Lord Camden, the bill was introduced into the Irish House of Commons and passed without much difficulty on 23 April 1795. The bill received the reluctant sanction of the King, and the Duke of Leinster gave fifty-four acres in perpetual freehold to the new corporation. The cornerstone was laid by Lord Camden in April 1796 and the college began with fifty pupils. There was some discussion about the number of Protestants who were to be trustees, but on the whole the college was left alone to pursue its task of training young men for the priesthood.

Maynooth seems to have been fortunate in its first two presidents, both of whom were there during the time of MacHale. Bartholomew Crotty was a good, open-minded pastor who guided the college through difficult times, and Michael Slattery was a spiritual man who possessed great organisational skills. He was later described by John Henry Newman as 'a most pleasing, taking man'.

It was of some significance that for the founding of the Royal College of Maynooth the Irish Government negotiated openly with the hierarchy. Thus by 1800 the Catholic Church was not declining as had been expected and during the nineteenth century was to go from strength to strength in a phenomenal development.

John MacHale was accompanied on his journey to Dublin and Maynooth by his brother, Thomas. They went on horseback, taking some days, on what would have been seen as a long and momentous journey. It was an opportunity for the young men to see something of their country and they took a great interest in the local monuments and traditions. In Dublin the brothers saw a dispirited city. The grand buildings erected before the Union, the Parliament House, the General Post Office and the Custom House, still displayed their classic fronts, pediments and colonnades, but they were all now silent. As Dublin no longer had a parliament, its role as a capital city was diminished and it became less and less a place for the gathering of influential people. This loss meant that the power of the Irish politicians to fight for the trade concessions was reduced, and so commercial interest in Dublin declined. The Act of Union effectively killed off the linen industry, and this was reflected in Dublin by more empty buildings. Some of the prosperous suburbs of Dublin that had previously been inhabited by linen-weavers were now deserted. There was no longer any money to be made in Ireland, and so the people had gone to England.

Notes

1 Early information about MacHale's life comes mostly from Bernard O'Reilly, *The Life and Times of John MacHale* (1890) and Ulick Bourke, *The Life and Times of the Most Reverend John MacHale* (1883). The dates are O'Reilly's and are the most generally accepted. There is some dispute as to the date of MacHale's birth, as Bourke, who was a family friend, maintains that MacHale was born in 1789.

2 Ulick Bourke, *The Life and Times of the Most Reverend John MacHale* (1883), p. 16.

3   Jonathan Swift, *Journal to Stella*, quoted in Desmond McGuire, *History of Ireland* (1987), p. 80.
4   Quoted in Desmond McGuire, op. cit., p. 81.
5   Nuala Costello, *John MacHale* (1939), p. 13.
6   Ulick Bourke, op. cit., p. 30
7   Ibid., pp. 34–5.
8   From an anonymous poem, 'The Priest of Addergoole', *Local Songs, Poems and Ballads from the Shadow of Nephin* compiled by Tony O'Donohoe. There is no date on the booklet but it is printed by the 'Ballina Printing Co.'.
9   Nuala Costello, op. cit., p. 15.
10   Hesketh Pearson, *The Smith of Smiths* (1934), p. 104. The 'Star Chamber' was a court founded by Henry VII to provide a quick and effective way of putting down opposition.
11   Ian Ker, *John Henry Newman* (1988), p. 33.
12   Edward Garland Brynn, *The Church of Ireland in the Age of Catholic Emancipation* (1982), pp. 7–9
13   Ibid., p. 21.
14   Ibid., quoted in Brynn, pp. 32–33
15   Ibid., p. 137.
16   Ibid., p. 152.
17   *Kilkenny Journal* (1831), quoted in Brynn, op. cit., p. 155.
18   Desmond Keenan, *The Catholic Church in Nineteenth-Century Ireland* (1983), p. 10.
19   Bernard O'Reilly, op. cit., I, p. 29.

2

MAYNOOTH

'Jesus Christ is the Alpha and Omega of religion and of men, from whom all things proceed, and in whom all things must repose.' (John MacHale)[1]

JOHN MACHALE entered the seminary of St Patrick at Maynooth in 1807 and was to remain there for the next eighteen years, first as a student, then as a lecturer and later as a professor. These years seemed to have been happy ones for MacHale. He was popular as a student and as a teacher, and studying remained one of his favourite occupations, even when he was a very old man. At Maynooth John MacHale studied Theology, Philosophy, Literature, Maths and Science, and also English, French, Hebrew, Latin, Greek and later German and Italian. He was very talented in languages and had a great love of literature. His tastes were the popular ones of the eighteenth century: Addison, Johnson, Goldsmith, 'Junius', Gray, Hume, and Young, and the modern writers, Scott, Byron and Moore.[2] MacHale was particularly fond of Edward Gibbon. He read his works frequently and was said to have used Gibbon in his attempts to improve his English style.[3]

John MacHale was so successful in his studies at Maynooth that, after gaining his doctorate, he was given the chair of Dogmatic Theology while still only a sub-deacon. His professor, de la Hogue, himself a scholar of some distinction, had a high opinion of MacHale's ability, and when in 1814 the professor fell ill, MacHale was unanimously chosen to take his place in the faculty. In July 1820 MacHale became, officially, the Professor of Dogmatic Theology. The title of Emeritus professor was retained by Dr de la Hogue. A warm friendship was to grow up between the old man and his youthful successor.

MacHale's ordination to the priesthood was somewhat delayed owing to the death of the Bishop of Killala, MacHale's local diocese. MacHale was finally ordained by Dr Murray, the Coadjutor of Dublin.

While MacHale was at Maynooth the students enjoyed the company of many French refugees. The French revolution of 1789 was not very favourable towards religion, as the Church was seen as bearing some responsibility for the country's troubles. For some years following the revolution, therefore, France was not always a safe place for priests. In Maynooth, however, these refugees were popular with Catholic and Protestant alike. MacHale was a member of a theological club, a circle for debate. This gave him the chance of listening to and speaking with some of those who possessed the most brilliant minds of the day. MacHale remembered these debates with affection, especially the part played by his old professor, de la Hogue. If a speaker, on quoting authorities, failed to cite de la Hogue's own works, he would be reminded of the omission: 'Mais, Monsieur, qu'est-ce que mon opinion?'[4]

The members of the circle and the professors from Maynooth were often the guests of the local Duke of Leinster, who enjoyed many friendly disputes at his home, Carton House. They would discuss the ideas of Voltaire and Rousseau and they enjoyed the study of Natural Science. The young MacHale, however, although he seems to have been a popular companion, did not like to give up too much time to socialising. He devoted much of his leisure time to study, even remaining at Maynooth during the long summer holidays in order to further his knowledge. A friend who knew him at the time said that he did not have the appearance of a bookworm:

> 'his frame, though slender was muscular, and remarkable for manly strength . . . presenting withal a dignity expressive of superior influence and command'.[5]

He was very athletic and thought nothing of walking the fourteen miles to Dublin and back in a day and, being a good horseman, he frequently rode there on horseback.

MacHale was a much admired professor. He was encouraging to every student and no trouble was too great for him on their behalf. As a young Irish professor he had great understanding and sympathy for the young men under his authority. A letter from a former student confirms this innate understanding of the national character:

> above all, your belief in that peculiar and distinguishing characteristic of your countrymen – an Irishman is a lamb when stroked, a lion when provoked – have contributed, by awakening the national feeling, to cast an air even of sacredness about your character.[6]

We have evidence that MacHale's pupils were grateful for the efforts he made on their behalf. There are many letters to this effect – some written by former students at MacHale's jubilee fifty years later testify to this. A letter from a pupil says how MacHale encouraged his students to have a broad education. He says that MacHale did not banish Science and Literature from the studies of the students, even though, in some religious circles, these were seen as encouraging materialism and providing students with worldly temptations.[7]

We have many interesting examples of MacHale's advice to his students, particularly in the addresses he gave them at the end of the academic year, when he would compliment them on their hard work and achievements. In 1822 he commends them for a 'spirit of inquisitive, and yet tempered criticism, united to a respectful though intelligent doubt'.[8] His words to them are affectionate and friendly. He inspires them with a love of God and of the Church:

> We are the children of the Church and we are told that 'he that honoureth his mother is as one that layeth up a treasure'.

He gives them high ideals for the priesthood:

> It would be a preposterous idea to separate great labour from the function of the priesthood. The high places of the world may be consistently aspired to by its votaries for the purpose of moving through a wider range of dissipation. Not so in

religion. This reverses the principles of human ambition. And what Christ says. 'He that is the greatest among you must be as if he were the least' is rigidly true.

and

> In religion, the higher you rise, the more restraints it imposes. What may be allowed to an humble, is denied to a higher ecclesiastic. The nearer you approach the centre, the more glaring become your defects, and the narrower the circle of your enjoyments.

He advises them against 'profane and licentious conversation', telling them that it is sometimes necessary to discuss subjects of a delicate nature, but these occasions should be rare and the language 'cautious' and 'should licentious conversation presume to approach his sacred person . . . he must wear a cold severity of countenance'. He constantly tells them to serve the poor and not to hesitate in their instruction.[9]

In his 1823 address to the students, MacHale tells them not to relax after their studies but to continue in their thirst for knowledge and education. He goes on to talk about 'the intuitive and unremitting contest' between reason and the passions. He says it has been a problem for all time. Cicero speaks of the cruelty of Nature and refers to Nature as our 'stepmother'. The Church tries to explain it by the doctrine of original sin, but it is still a great mystery. He speaks of Christianity as a

> majestic system of religion, mysterious but harmonious in its mysteries . . . in which the attributes of the Divinity are reconciled, the contarieties of human nature are explained, and God and man appear without the shadow of contradiction.[10]

Throughout his life, John MacHale had a deep devotion to the sacrifice of the Mass. To his students he speaks of the Mass as a banquet of reconciliation to be shared by Jew and Gentile. . . . It recalls the memory of the passover and the covenant of Abraham, the history of man's fall and the promise and accomplishment of his redemption, thus conducting the contemplative mind through all that is elevated and interesting in the history of religion, until at length it rests in the presence of its God – not that awful presence clothed in terrors which forbids approach, but the presence of a God clothed in our own nature, inviting us to more familiar intimacy. . . . In Him . . . Jesus Christ, true God and true man, united to the one by His divinity, to the other by His humanity . . . reconciling all things unto Himself, and making peace through the blood of His cross. . . . Jesus Christ is the Alpha and Omega of religion and of men, from whom all things proceed, and in whom all things must repose.[11]

In the address of 1824 John MacHale talks to his students about their possible disappointments:

Let those, then, who may be disappointed console themselves with the approbation of Him whose vigilance never slumbers, whose judgement never strays, inviting us to a competition into which the spirit of jealousy never enters; holding out a reward for which all may strive, and which all may acquire.

MacHale continually tried to inspire the young men with lofty ideals. He asked them to pray constantly for one another and to see their role as a priest as that of a servant:

While therefore we are robed in the ornaments of the priesthood we ought to tremble, lest we should be like the victim led to the altar, unconscious that the waving honours, in which he prides, are the very symbols of his destruction.[12]

While MacHale was a student at Maynooth, controversy raged between the British Government and the Irish Catholic Church about the right of the Government to have a veto on the appointment of bishops in Ireland. The Government tried to get Pius VI and Pius VII to agree to the Irish bishops being salaried servants of the British Government. This was resisted by the Pope and the Irish bishops but, in 1814, in return for the sympathy of the British Government during his imprisonment by Napoleon at Fontainebleau, the Pope agreed to the Government's right of veto on the appointment of Irish Catholic bishops. This was known as The Quarantotti Rescript, as Cardinal Quarantotti had sanctioned the measure during the Pope's absence, but it was so consistently resisted by the Irish bishops that it proved impossible to implement. Many English Catholics had supported the rescript, hoping that it might bring emancipation nearer, but if it had been accepted by the bishops it would probably have prevented MacHale from ever becoming an archbishop.

During this period, Ireland was emerging from a time of enforced intellectual starvation. The Irish language and literature had been proscribed since the Reformation, and the Catholic Church in Ireland was aware of the educational needs of its communities. It had no school system, apart from some hundreds of charity schools, which it had no real way of supporting. Many Catholic children had attended the schools of the Kildare Street Society, a charitable institution set up for the education of the poor. This society had been endowed by the Government in 1814 to assist schools with grants and to establish Model Schools for the training of teachers. They were to be non-denominational, and all religious teaching was to be excluded, but a Bible, without notes or commentaries, was allowed for the higher classes. These schools had been seen as being sufficiently neutral in religious matters as to make possible the attendance of Catholic children.

However, the situation changed with the rise of the Evangelical movement, the claimed 'Second Reformation' in England and Ireland. This movement had begun in the early eighteenth century in North America, where it was called the 'Great Awakening'. In the 1730s in Pennsylvania and other 'middle colonies', some Presbyterians enlivened the old Calvinist ways with their preaching, while in New England others revived the religion of the Puritans. One of the most popular preachers of the time was Jonathon

Edwards, who was distinguished by his emotional style of preaching. While this movement did not affect the well-educated founding fathers of American Independence, it did influence many of the settlers who were spreading out over the North American continent. Its characteristics – a love of the Bible, an enthusiasm for personal improvement and a belief that Christians must be 'born again' – began to be associated with the American identity and were transported into the wilderness as the American frontier moved west.[13]

In England this revival found expression in the preachings of John Wesley, George Whitfield and the emergence of Methodism. Wesley never intended Methodism to be a separate denomination from the Church of England, but this became inevitable as the characteristics of Methodism became increasingly distinct from the Established Church. These characteristics included preaching in the open air, praying extempore, forming societies and accepting the assistance of lay preachers. Many people were attracted to the new movements because of the worldliness of the Church of England and in particular of the Established Church in Ireland. Wesley himself visited Ireland twenty-one times.

By the end of the eighteenth century, the popularity of the Methodists and also the rise of the evangelicals within the Established Church was increased by the public reaction to the French Revolution and the Napoleonic wars. Catholic and Protestant alike were shocked by the atheism of the revolutionaries and by the horrors of the revolution and the subsequent wars.

In 1804 the British and Foreign Bible Society was founded for the printing and distribution of the Bible. This was run jointly by 'Dissenters' and members of the Established Church. It produced vigorous debate, and many churchmen were afraid of the fundamentalism of the evangelicals. As early as 1768, six students were expelled from Oxford for holding evangelical views, and Samuel Johnson remarked, 'A cow is a very good animal in a field but we turn her out of a garden'.[14] Jane Austen was suspicious of the evangelicals' claim that God inspired their many utterances and arranged every detail of their lives to their spiritual advantage, and she disliked their lack of sensitivity and reserve.[15]

In Ireland, Daniel O'Callaghan, an enthusiastic Church traditionalist, condemned the Bible Society, and in 1827 he described its new spirit of zealous proselytism:

> When they issue their marching orders to a regiment of bibles, to reinforce the garrison of a particular town, the march is preceded and followed by a numerous rabble of irregulars, composed of handbills, – newspaper squibs – speeches revised and reported – pious tracts – evangelical essay – serious reviews, and more serious magazines, in all which popery and its priesthood are described as the most abominable of all possible abominations, and clothed with the choicest attributes of hell and Satan, while the members of the holy alliance of proselytising fanatics, are held out as ministering angels, descending from heaven on errands of mercy. These are dropped on the roads, scattered in the field, given to good children, read in stagecoaches, forgotten at public houses . . . [16]

The Established Church in Ireland was in a difficult position. Many of its members, like O'Callaghan, thoroughly disliked the Dissenters and their proselytising. The Dissenters even attacked the Established Church. It was called 'an outwork of the great fortress of Popery'. Many Anglicans did not want to antagonise the Catholics, and Richard Whately, who became the Anglican Archbishop of Dublin in 1831, opposed the growing influence of the evangelicals. However, the Anglicans feared the increasing strength of the Catholic Church and the evangelicals were very successful in proselytising among the lukewarm and ignorant of the Church of England. As time went by, doctrinal and juridical distinctions between the Protestant Churches became blurred and the Dissenters had much influence within the Established Church. Eventually, the 'New Reformation' became a national proselytising effort directly supported by the Church.

There then began a campaign against Romanism in Ireland, which gave the Catholic clergy much cause for concern. The Bible Society took over the running of the Kildare Street Society and set about the work of proselytism. The original rules about the teaching of religion were violated. The strength of feeling was such that news of the Kildare Street Society reached Rome and the Irish bishops received a letter from Cardinal Fontana warning them about the situation:

> Information has reached the ears of the Sacred Congregation that Bible schools, supported by the funds of Catholics, have been established in almost every part of Ireland, in which, under the pretext of charity, the inexperienced of both sexes, but particularly peasants and the poor, are allured by the blandishments and even gifts of the masters, and infected with the fatal poison of depraved doctrines.[17]

This threat of proselytism gave some impetus to the wishes of the priests to organise a system of Catholic education in Ireland. To achieve this end, MacHale engaged in a prolonged campaign. In 1820 he began a series of letters under the pseudonym of Hierophilos that appeared in many newspapers. In these letters, which were eventually to arouse the curiosity of the two countries, he denounced the activities of the Bible societies. A second group of letters, which were addressed to the English nation, were intended to bring out into the open the controversies that were raging at the time. In his introduction to the letters, MacHale says that he wishes to forget 'those prejudices which have taught the two nations to regard each other with jealousy'. In his first letter, MacHale begins with some interesting observations on the relationship between England and Ireland:

> Perhaps, in the history of the world, no two countries have exhibited such an anomaly as England and Ireland. Notwithstanding the proximity of their situations, which naturally seemed to invite to a cultivation of mutual intimacy, a spirit of sullen distrust has kept them ignorant of each other; and while the genius of knowledge and of enterprize has annihilated the vast space between England and the Indies, the Irish Channel has been like an impassable gulf, which, from a

dread of the enemies on the opposite coast, the spirit of benevolent curiosity has seldom ventured to explore.[18]

MacHale continues the theme of the relationship between the 'sister countries' in his second letter. He states rather ruefully:

> Whatever may be the vision of some romantic lovers of country, it is one of the soundest and most incontestable maxims of political science that there are some countries whose fortunes must ever be obedient to the destinies of others. This principle . . . seems peculiarly applicable to the condition of Ireland.

MacHale says that although he is proud of the ample resources of his native country

> it must be confessed that she seems to have been destined to be an appendage of the English nation. Though this reflection may be mortifying to our national vanity, we should still be consoled with the consciousness that we may securely repose under the protection of the British Empire.

Here, MacHale states clearly that he does not envisage any separation from the English Crown. MacHale, although he later campaigned vigorously for the repeal of the Act of Union, never wavered from this opinion:

> The people are too sensible of the advantage of British connexion to wish for a separation. They would consider as their worst enemies, those who would entertain the chimerical project of divorcing that connexion; and the only object they sigh for is, to draw closer its relations, by a fuller participation of its benefits.[19]

MacHale goes on to argue in his second letter that, far from encouraging disloyalty to the Government, the Catholic Church is a bulwark against revolution. He stresses the loyalty of the Catholic people to the Crown:

> The attachment of the Catholic to the person of the Sovereign is derived from a nobler source . . . and the loyalty he must feel, in common with every other subject, is hallowed by the peculiar instructions of his religion.

MacHale says that the revolutionary principles entertained by many modern thinkers do not belong to the Irish Catholic:

> The relative duties of sovereigns and subjects have been discussed in the sister country with a bold, and, perhaps, dangerous freedom of opinion. We know that some of its most eminent political writers have ventured to fix the boundaries where obedience would cease to be an obligation, and resistance would become a duty. These are discussions which, in the Catholic Church, are considered as questions of a delicate and dangerous tendency.

He continues by saying that 'with or without a right, a revolution will be the very last resource of the thinking and the good'.

MacHale states that the character of the Irish Catholic has never been revolutionary and he reminds the English people that the rebellion of 1798 was brought about by those who would have willingly 'exchanged the cross for the crescent'. MacHale finishes this letter by re-affirming his loyalty to the King.

The young MacHale was very successful in drawing attention to the aims of the 'would-be apostles of education', and many influential men like the Duke of Leinster and Lord Cloncurry withdrew from the Kildare Street School board.

After the *Hierophilos* letters, the Protestant archbishops of Dublin and Armagh openly seceded from the Hibernian Bible Society. MacHale continued his letters: 'Men of warm and benevolent feeling are often caught by delusive theories for promoting the happiness of the human race. That such are engaged in the Bible system, in justice to human nature, I must admit', but others are 'actuated more by deadly hostility to the [Catholic] religion than by compassion for the ignorance of the people'.

Although MacHale has often been accused of violence in his writings, in his letters as Hierophilos, he tried to put the Catholic case clearly, honestly and without bitterness. Many of his letters were answered by an opponent who called himself Bibliophilos, and MacHale seems to have appreciated the argument. In his introduction to the publication of the book of his letters, he says:

> During some portion of my discussion on the Bible societies, I had to contend with one of their acutest and ablest advocates; and now in taking my leave of him, probably forever, I feel pleasure in making the acknowledgement, that he has manifested a tone of urbanity and good feeling seldom exhibited in the annals of polemical disputation.[20]

MacHale says that it was a relief to have someone who could rescue religious argument from 'acrimony and dullness, thus proving that the discussion of the most solemn subject that can engage the attention of man, is not incompatible with the exercise of good temper, or the display of elegant acquirements'.

While MacHale was studying and teaching at Maynooth, he also took a great interest in what was happening in the world at large. This was the time of the battle for Catholic Emancipation. In England this was being fought first by Burke and then by Canning, and in Ireland by O'Connell.

Daniel O'Connell was born in August 1775 into a rich Catholic family in County Kerry. Daniel's father and uncle, 'Hunting-Cap O'Connell', had made money out of smuggling, trading and farming and managed to hold on to their lands, owning a large mansion at Derrynane. After being educated in France, O'Connell studied for the bar in London. As a Catholic he was unable to obtain the higher legal positions but he earned a great deal of money by taking small cases, for which he travelled all over Ireland. O'Connell was never a revolutionary, having been witness to some of the excesses of the French Revolution in his childhood. He disapproved of the Irish rebellion in 1798 and after its failure was more than ever convinced that this was not the way to succeed. He passionately wanted the repeal of the Union and felt that Catholic Emancipation was a way to achieve this end.

MacHale made the acquaintance of O'Connell while still at Maynooth and fully supported him in his efforts for Catholic Emancipation. He continued his support after becoming a bishop and was to remain one of O'Connell's life-long friends.

There was much sympathy for the Catholics and the Irish on the Continent and in England; Sydney Smith of the *Edinburgh Review* had been able to further the cause of Catholic Emancipation with a good deal of wit and humour. In 1807 he published his *Letters* written under the assumed name of 'Peter Plymley'. In them he attacked what he called 'Erinphobia':

> The moment the very name of Ireland is mentioned, the English seem to bid adieu to common feeling, common prudence and common sense, and to act with the barbarity of tyrants, and the fatuity of idiots.[21]

He satirised the Protestant fear of Catholics:

> . . . after a Catholic justice had once been seen on the bench, and it had been clearly ascertained that he spoke English, had no tail, only a single row of teeth, and that he loved port wine – after all the scandalous and infamous reports of his physical conformation had been clearly proved to be false – he would be reckoned a jolly fellow . . . .

and,

> I have often thought, if the wisdom of our ancestors had excluded all persons with red hair from the House of Commons, of the throes and convulsions it would occasion to restore them to their natural rights. What mobs and riots it would produce! To what infinite abuse and obloquy would the capillary patriot be exposed . . . some would say that red-haired

men were superstitious; some would prove they were atheists . . . in short . . . these unfortunate people . . . if they did not emigrate to countries where hair of another colour was persecuted, would be driven to the falsehood of perukes, or the hypocrisy of the Tricosian fluid.[22]

In Dublin the young poet Percy Bysshe Shelley, on a visit from England, spoke at a meeting and composed a pamphlet demanding the formation of an association of philanthropists for the regeneration of Ireland. They were to take as their immediate objects Catholic Emancipation and the repeal of the Union.[23]

The British people were also affected at this time by the sentiments of 'Moore's Melodies', the poems and songs of Thomas Moore, an Irish nineteenth-century poet who was immensely popular. His poetry was particularly important in that it penetrated the hearts and minds of upper-class Britain.

Between 1821 and 1824 John MacHale wrote twelve letters to George Canning, who became Foreign Secretary in 1822. Canning was seen to be a champion of Irish rights, though there was some disappointment in him later. MacHale writes to him: 'Your efforts in the cause of Ireland will not cease to be remembered'. In his letters he discusses various Irish grievances. He writes about the privileged position of the Established Church. He asks whether the end of the Church is to bring people to God or to 'cement the Union?' He says he does not want to subvert a long-established tradition, but 'my design has been to expose the presumption of those who would fain place any portion of society beyond the reach of legislative interference'. He says that Catholics were willing to contribute to public functionaries but it was an anomaly to be under an obligation to support a body of people 'on the presumption of religious relations which do not mutually exist between them'. He suggests that paying the ministers of the Established Church out of the Exchequer would remove such discontent.[24]

Earlier in the century, the Anglican Archbishop of Armagh, William Stuart, had tried to encourage reform of the tithe system. He suggested the eventual conversion of the tithe into annuities and, perhaps, land, but this was opposed by many churchmen and regarded as too radical by members of the Government. However, in 1823 a tithe act was passed which called for temporary, voluntary composition of the tithes, which had to be approved by the parish vestry committee. This, though a step forward, did very little and did not remove the grievance.

In a letter written in 1823, MacHale speaks of the failure of capitalists to invest in Ireland. He says that the English nation is the wealthiest in the world, but, as Lord Bacon remarks, 'wealth is like manure, which must be spread, in order to be productive'. Capitalists complain that they can't invest in Ireland because of the character of the inhabitants. The Irish are seen as indolent and inactive, but unless there is some industry in Ireland 'they are doomed to languish in inactivity . . . The English Government, instead of giving encouragement for the working of mines or the establishing of manufacturing industry, instantly checks them lest the trade of England is injured.'[25]

In many of his letters, MacHale stresses the need for Catholic Emancipation. He says that Britain boasts of its civil liberties and its spirit of justice and yet an 'entire nation are deprived of the liberties deemed the birthright of a British subject'.[26] In his letters MacHale once again states that he does not want to sever the connection with England. This was also stressed in the 'Maynooth manifesto' signed by MacHale and others. The manifesto came about as a result of some correspondence in the press. The Chancellor of the Exchequer, Mr Robinson, declared that it was his ardent wish to see the reunion of the Protestant and Catholic Churches. This met with the approval of the Catholic Bishop of Dublin, Dr Doyle, but in agreeing with Mr Robinson he stressed that the continuation of the penal code might lead the people and 'even the priests' to physical force. The professors at Maynooth were horrified, and on 4 June 1824 they said that in consequence of the recent allusion to the domestic education of the Catholic clergy, they considered it their duty 'solemnly and publicly to state that in our respective situations we have uniformly inculcated allegiance to our gracious sovereign, respect for the constituted authorities, and obedience to the laws'.

John MacHale's time at Maynooth was now drawing to an end. When in 1825 he spoke to his students about the swiftness of their time at college, he was probably thinking also about his own time at Maynooth; quoting Isaiah, he said, 'My generation is at an end, and it is rolled away from me as a shepherd's tent'.[27]

Notes

1   John MacHale, Address to theological students, 1823, *Sermons and Discourses* (1883), p. 476.
2   Nuala Costello, *John MacHale* (1939), p. 18.
3   Ulick Bourke, *The Life and Times of the Most Reverend John MacHale* (1883), p. 52.
4   Nuala Costello, op. cit., p. 19. 'But sir, what is *my* opinion?'
5   Ibid., p. 20.
6   Ibid., p. 20.
7   Bernard O'Reilly, *The Life and Times of John MacHale* (1890), I, p. 58.
8   John MacHale, op. cit., p. 457.
9   Ibid., p. 457.
10 Ibid. 1823, p. 476.
11 Ibid. 1823, p. 476.
12 Ibid. 1824, p. 478.
13 David L. Edwards, *Christian England* (1981), pp. 40–41.
14 Ibid., p. 76.
15 Ibid., pp. 95–6.
16 Edward Garland Brynn, *The Church of Ireland in the Age of Catholic Emancipation,* (1982) p. 413.
17 Bernard O'Reilly, op. cit.
18 John MacHale, *Letters of Hierophilos* (1822), pp. 1–2.
19 Ibid., p. 6.
20 Ibid., p. viii.
21 Hesketh Pearson, *The Smith of Smiths* (1934), p. 129.
22 Ibid., pp. 136–8.
23 Denis Gwynn, *Daniel O'Connell: The Irish Liberator* (1947) p. 106.
24 John MacHale, *Letters* (1847), Letter XXVIII, 1821.
25 Ibid., Letter XXIX, 1823.
26 Ibid., Letter XXIV, 1823.
27 John MacHale, *Sermons and Discourses* (1883), p. 505.

3

BISHOP OF MARONIA

'It is really lamentable that those who labour together for public good should waste their time in theological contention.' (John MacHale)[1]

WHILE MACHALE was at Maynooth, the health of Dr Waldron, Bishop of Killala, was not good. Killala was MacHale's home diocese and Dr Waldron had, on some occasions, asked the young Dr MacHale to represent him in Dublin. When his health further deteriorated he asked Rome for a coadjutor. Irish affairs in Rome were dealt with by the *Congregatio de propaganda fide* – The Congregation for the Propagation of the Faith, usually referred to as Propaganda. Following Dr Waldron's request for a coadjutor, a petition was sent to Rome requesting that Dr MacHale be appointed.

The new Pope, Leo XII, confirmed the appointment and created John MacHale as Bishop of Maronia and Coadjutor to the Bishop of Killala on 8 March 1825. This appointment meant that MacHale had the automatic right of succession to the see of St Muredach (Killala). Maronia was an area in Greece and such titles were used for coadjutor bishops. The consecration of the new bishop took place in Maynooth Chapel in June 1825 by Daniel Murray, Archbishop of Dublin.

Thus began John MacHale's return to the west and his lifelong crusade for the people of that area. In later years he was to provoke much criticism from Catholic and Protestant alike, but nobody ever accused him of a lack of love for the people or a lack of care for the poor. He used every ounce of strength he possessed towards this end and employed every means at his disposal, including his undoubted intellectual gifts, particularly his skill with words, to fight the cause of the poor of the west of Ireland.

The old Bishop Waldron asked MacHale to join him in his house. This was a very modest dwelling and the two bishops had just a room each. At that time in the west of Ireland priests led a sparse existence, as they were dependent on the poor for their survival. The young Bishop MacHale, who was the first home-educated prelate since the days of Elizabeth, was given for his support the parish of Crossmolina.

From the very beginning, Bishop MacHale maintained constant contact with the priests of the diocese. He regularly went to the most remote areas for Confirmation and visitations. The year 1826 was proclaimed a 'Jubilee Year' or 'Holy Year' by Leo XII, and in the course of that year MacHale spent ten days in each parish. During this period he lived a life of great self-sacrifice and piety. Bernard O'Reilly, in his biography of MacHale, states that 'truth burned in his soul'.[2]

The diocese of Killala was in the province of Tuam, and in the years before MacHale's elevation to the episcopate, the Catholic Archbishop of Tuam, Dr Kelly, had enjoyed a good relationship with the Anglican Archbishop of Tuam, Dr Trench. There were frequent famines in the West of Ireland and, in 1821, the harvest was poor, resulting in a bad potato crop. The two Archbishops had worked together during this famine and Dr Kelly had recorded his thanks to Dr Trench publicly. The local people had also been grateful and to show their gratitude they had harvested Dr Trench's crops and his peat. Dr Trench and many local Protestants had also contributed generously to Dr Kelly's fund for the founding of a new Catholic cathedral in Tuam. It was unfortunate that at this time relationships between the Churches were hardening, and in 1826 Dr Trench found it necessary to attack the Catholic Church and its 'damnable doctrines'. MacHale replied to the attack, saying:

> It is really lamentable that those who labour together for public good should waste their time in theological contention. To what a miserable condition is our country doomed, when they who would entirely devote themselves to promote its peace and propagate goodwill among mankind must be forced

to repel attacks upon its religion – attacks made by persons who ought to be peculiarly tender![3]

In October 1826 Bishop MacHale had to be examined by the Commissioners of Irish Education who were inquiring into his activities at Maynooth. They were investigating both his letters as Hierophilos and his letters to George Canning. MacHale's replies to his questioners are characteristically frank and fearless. The Irish had been painted by the Bible Societies as being steeped in crime and immorality. They had said that the circulation of the Bible would be a certain remedy. MacHale was questioned on his attacks on the Bible Societies. He replied that if the possession of a Bible was a criterion of morality, the English should be the most moral on earth, whereas during the ascendancy of the Bible Societies, crime had increased more in proportion to the population than it had done in Ireland. MacHale was asked what he meant when he referred in one of his letters to 'malignant laws'. He replied:

> Penal laws which prosecute Catholics and require of Protestants as a condition to obtain office to declare before God, that the religion of Catholics is 'damnable and idolatrous'.

MacHale was then questioned on his attitude to the hierarchy of the Established Church. He was asked when referring to Dr McGee and Dr Trench whether he intended to omit their titles. He replied that he did not and that he often referred to the Catholic Archbishop of Dublin as Dr Murray – 'I will cheerfully give them any title which the law gives them'. MacHale was then asked if he thought the law of the land competent to confer spiritual authority. MacHale replied that he did not, as the State was not the source of spiritual authority.[4] The authorities appeared to be 'satisfied' and so there was no further outcome.

While John MacHale was the coadjutor at Killala he began the building of a cathedral on the banks of the river Moy at Ballina. In the archdiocese of Tuam at that time there were 106 places for Catholic worship. Sixteen of these were slated and the rest were thatched. Many services were taken in the open air. However, towards the middle of the nineteenth century in Ireland, the Catholic people were becoming more confident and, together with the bishops and priests, they undertook the task of rebuilding. There was no shortage of stone, which was quarried locally, and the buildings were often large and ambitious, as apart from the primary purpose of the churches the projects answered the need for work and the desire of the people to proclaim their suppressed identity. Within a surprisingly short time practically every parish had its own church. Between 1826 and 1829 Bishop MacHale collected £1,800 and laid the foundations of the cathedral, which, like that of Tuam, was designed by Dominic Madden. He then wrote letters to hundreds of people in the diocese and outside, begging for money for the cathedral. The merchants of Ballina gave generously and an Englishman, Kenelm Henry Digby, gave him money for a marble altar executed by a Roman sculptor. In 1832 MacHale wrote to Rome begging for money. He collected £12,000 in all.[5]

The parish of Crossmolina, which had been given to Bishop MacHale for his support, adjoined the parish of Addergoole, which was MacHale's own native parish and the place where his family lived. During the time that MacHale was Coadjutor of Killala, he was able to visit his old home and family frequently. After his mother's death, his father, Patrick or Pádraig Mór, married again and had three more daughters by his second wife, Mary Martin.[6] Patrick lived to a ripe old age and most of his children and grandchildren still lived in Tubbernavine and its neighbourhood. During his family visits MacHale always spoke in the Irish language and took great interest in the education of his nieces and nephews. John MacHale loved music and was especially fond of the popular 'Moore's Melodies', and in order to play these he asked his young half-sister, Catherine for piano lessons. He also learned to play the harp. He took great pleasure in his native countryside and spent whatever time he could walking on nearby Mount Nephin.[7] He seems to have been a man of great physical strength and fitness. Mount Nephin is over two and a half thousand feet high and towers above Tubbernavine and the neighbouring village of Lahardane. Its name means 'Fionn's Paradise', as the Celtic hero, Fionn

MacCumhaill, is reputed to have climbed the mountain and at the top proclaimed 'This is heaven!'[8]

While MacHale had been at Maynooth he had been writing a book of Catholic Doctrine. There were very few books available for English-speaking Catholics and MacHale became increasingly aware of the need. It was for this purpose that he wrote his *Evidences and Doctrines of the Catholic Church*. MacHale prepared this book for publication at his father's house in Tubbernavine. In it he tried to

> deduce evidences of the Catholic Church from the primitive source of revelation and illustrate the speculative truth of its doctrines, as well as their practical influence on the happiness of society.[9]

The book, which was published in 1828, was eagerly welcomed in England and Ireland. It was also popular on the Continent and was translated into French and German, languages already rich in Catholic literature.

Years later, *The Times,* when discussing MacHale, wrote:

> When we look to Dr MacHale's works, such a book as *The Evidences of the Catholic Church* is a marvel for the production of a man who, a few years before was toiling at a potato plot. It shows great reading, a ready command of materials, some thought and a style quite equal to that of many theological writers who have enjoyed much greater advantages.

– somewhat condescending, but praise indeed from 'The Thunderer'![10]

During the early years of John MacHale's episcopacy, there was renewed political agitation in Ireland. By the 1820s the Catholic Committee, after achieving some useful reforms, had stagnated. In 1823 Daniel O'Connell and other young radical lawyers broke away from the Catholic Committee and formed the Catholic Association. This was initially a middle-class organisation with substantial membership fees. The following year O'Connell suggested that they should introduce an associate membership, making it possible for the poorest Catholics to join. He decided to organise the Catholic peasantry into a peaceful force, which, he believed, could be used to force the English to listen to Catholic demands. At the meeting when this was proposed, the numbers attending were so small that in order to get a quorum, O'Connell enlisted the help of two priests from Maynooth whom he found in a bookshop below the premises of the Association. This was to be the turning point for O'Connell's Association. The people were invited to contribute a penny a month. This became known as 'The Catholic rent' and O'Connell as 'The king of the beggars'. O'Connell persuaded the Catholic clergy to support him and allow him to use churches to collect the money and to recruit new members for the Association.

O'Connell organised mass meetings and used his powers of oratory and persuasion to give hope and encouragement to the depressed and suffering peasantry. The organisation was enormously successful. In late 1824 the average rent was £300 a week. In March 1825 almost £2000 was collected in one week.[11] The Association was banned by Parliament in 1825 as it was thought that the excitement it caused was a threat to public order, but as one organisation closed O'Connell would start up another and continue to collect the rent.

In England Sydney Smith continued his campaign for Catholic Emancipation and against the English misgovernment of Ireland. By this time he had put down his pen as 'Peter Plymley' and wrote in the *Edinburgh Review* under his own name:

> Such jobbing, such profligacy – so much direct tyranny and oppression – such an abuse of God's gifts – such a profanation of God's name for the purposes of bigotry and party spirit, cannot be exceeded in the history of civilized Europe, and will long remain a monument of infamy and shame to England.

He looked a century ahead and wrote:

> Ireland, in short, till her wrongs are redressed, and a more liberal policy is adopted towards her, will always be a cause of anxiety and suspicion to this country; and in some moment of our weakness and depression, will forcibly extort what she would now receive with gratitude and exultation.[12]

It was during this period that MacHale was writing regularly to George Canning in an endeavour to 'enforce the necessity of Catholic Emancipation'.[13] The situation looked promising when, after the death of Lord Liverpool, Canning became Prime Minister, but Peel and Wellington refused to serve under him, fearing the passage of a Catholic Emancipation Act. Canning himself died in 1827 and after a short period with Goderich as Prime Minister, Wellington came to power in 1828.

After a parliamentary campaign, 1828 saw the repeal of the Test Acts. These were a series of acts passed during the seventeenth century to ensure that only loyal Anglicans were appointed to positions of power in the civil service, local government and the legal profession. Part of this act or repeal stated:

> It is just and fitting to repeal such parts of the said acts as impose the necessity of taking the sacrament of the Lord's Supper according to the rights or usages of the Church of England as a qualification for office.[14]

But while the Anglican Parliament under the influence of its leaders, Peel and Wellington, was prepared to concede this repeal to the mainly Nonconformist leaders of the campaign, it was unwilling to concede legal freedom to Catholics, who were still suspected of being members of a foreign and anti-British Church.

In 1828 O'Connell stood as a candidate in the County Clare by-election and, not surprisingly, as the majority of voters, the forty-shilling freeholders, were Catholics, he won. As the law stood, he could not enter Parliament. Feelings ran high in Ireland and the Government feared open rebellion. Lord Anglesey wrote to Lord Gower in July 1828:

> I see no possible solution but by depriving the demagogues of the power of directing people. By taking Messrs. O'Connell. Sheil and the rest of them from the Association, and placing them in the House of Commons, this desirable object would at once be accomplished.[15]

Wellington and Peel had come to power determined to resist the demands for Catholic Emancipation, but in so doing they had lost the support of some members of the Tory party, and Peel realised that, as the Catholics had the vote, the events of the Clare election would be enacted in nearly every county in Ireland and so was convinced that it was now not safe for the Protestant interest in Ireland. (If the Catholics voted for a Catholic candidate who was not allowed to sit in Parliament, they would be likely to cause disruption and even rebellion.)

In 1829, therefore, Parliament passed the Roman Catholic Emancipation Act, part of which reads:

> And be it enacted, that it shall be lawful for any of his majesty's subjects professing the Roman Catholic Religion to hold, exercise and enjoy, all civil and military offices and places of trust or profit under his majesty, his heirs and successors; and to exercise any other franchise or civil right, except as hereinafter exempted.

The wealthier Catholic voters had gained a victory and O'Connell's success was an encouragement to other reform movements. His methods of peaceful, popular pressure groups were copied not only in Britain by movements such as the Chartists and the Anti-Corn Law League, but by groups all over Europe. It was unfortunate that Pope Leo XII, who had taken a great interest in Catholic Emancipation, had died before it was enacted.

September 1830 saw the accession of William IV. There were great celebrations and pageants all over the kingdom. William IV was an eccentric, rather simple man. He had previously supported his brother, George IV, in his opposition to Catholic Emancipation, but when he became King in 1830 it was already a 'fait accompli'. Dr MacHale took the opportunity to remind the new monarch of his duties – 'Thou shalt defend from all oppressions widows and orphans, the poor and the feeble'.[16]

Notes

1   John MacHale, *Letters* (1888), Letter XXXIII, 1826, p. 224.
2   Bernard O'Reilly, *The Life and Times of John MacHale* (1890), I, p. 101.
3   John MacHale, op. cit.
4   Commission of Irish Education Inquiry, eighth report. Quoted in Bourke, *The Life and Times of the Most Reverend John MacHale* (1883), p. 85. See also Healy, *Maynooth College: Its Centenary History.*
5   Bernard O'Reilly, op. cit., I, p. 116.
6   Family records. (These were given to the author by Sr Mary MacHale of Lahardane, a member of the MacHale family.)
7   Bernard O'Reilly, op. cit., I, p.116.
8   Tony Donohoe, *Local Songs, Poems, and Ballads from the Shadow of Nephin,* p. 23.
9   Bernard O'Reilly, op. cit., I, p. 123.
10 *The Times,* 11 June 1875.
11 Desmond McGuire, *History of Ireland* (1987), p. 112.
12 Hesketh Pearson, *The Smith of Smiths* (1934), p. 145.
13 Nuala Costello, *John MacHale* (1939), p. 25.
14 Repeal of Test Act 1828.
15 Letter, *Anglesey to Gower,* 1828. Quoted in Peter Lane, *British History 1760–1914* (1978), p. 190.
16 Bernard O'Reilly, op. cit., I, p. 162.

4

ROME

'Nec alia erit lex Romae, alia Athenis; nec vero per senatum
aut populum hac lege solvi possumus.' (Cicero, *de Republica*)

IN THE SPRING of 1831 there was famine in the west of Ireland. The harvest had partially failed in the autumn of 1830 and starvation began to threaten the people of the area. It was not that Ireland did not produce enough food for its population, but whatever food was produced was the property of the landlord first and then of the tithe-proctor, who represented the Protestant establishment. Butter, eggs, fowl, sheep and cattle all found their way to the English markets, leaving only what was left for the tillers of the soil. This was usually potatoes.

Although generous individuals and local authorities did their best to relieve the distress, they did not have the means to help the whole population.

In England, Earl Grey, the Prime Minister, was preoccupied with his Reform Bill. In April 1831 Dr MacHale wrote him an open letter, calling upon him to do something about the Irish famine:

> Important as the question of Reform is, the distress that now afflicts, and the famine that menaces, some portions of this country, are still more imperative topics. Reform itself might be adjourned with safety for a short time, whereas, should his Majesty's subjects become the victims of starvation, it is a loss which no ulterior measures can retrieve.[1]

Dr MacHale tells of a family in a distant parish of his diocese where

> in one instance the father, mother and three children were stretched out on the same bed, without a morsel of food,

without a penny to procure it, or a human being to go in quest of relief . . . .'[2]

The bishop went on to say that in Crossmolina there were 120 families who awaited a similar fate. Some had sent a petition to Parliament, stating that not only had their cattle and their oats been seized for rent, but even their last potato. MacHale demanded from the Prime Minister and the Government 'a severe and unsparing legislation' to effect a fundamental change in Ireland's system of land-tenure. The bishop continued by saying that while he was writing, 'the town of Ballina, in which three hundred families are crying out for food, is busy with the bustle of corn traders, and the public roads are crowded with conveyances bearing away their exports'. The situation was doubly tragic because the export of food from Ireland gave the impression to the English that the Irish had no shortage of food. 'The presumption of there being no starvation, while corn was exported, is a fallacy.'

MacHale also pointed out the added problems of the loss of the linen trade:

> The extinction of our linen trade is attested by the number of females whose cheerful and virtuous industry was once supported by the varied process of preparing flax, and who are now seen digging in the fields, for want of any domestic manufacture . . .[3]

MacHale's letters are filled with the passion he feels for the poor of his diocese. He calls upon the members of the Government to see for themselves:

> The gilded saloons of London are not the appropriate lecture-halls for studying the wretchedness of an Irish cabin . . . faces sparkling with mirth are not the fittest mirror for reflecting the sunken eye and gaunt visage of despair; a taste palled with the satiety of feasts and revels cannot well judge of the acuteness of the pangs of hunger. . . . It requires a heart as well as eyes to be affected by the wants of others.[4]

After MacHale's letter of 29 April, the Reform Bill was passed in England. The bishop thought that this was now a favourable time to ask for changes to the Irish land laws. He wrote once again to the Prime Minister:

> I respectfully and earnestly solicit the government to the conditions and prospects of the suffering poor. . . . Let and lease the land at an equitable rent. . . . Relieve them from arrears accumulated in bad seasons. . . . Salus populi suprema lex esto [let the welfare of the people be the supreme law].[5]

Dr MacHale laid before the Prime Minister the evils of rack-rents, of the forced exportation of farm produce, arrears hopelessly accumulating, the lack of seed grain and seed potatoes, and the incredibly usurious interest exacted for this by landlords and their agents.

> In the course of last spring, the tenantry of Tirawley were, for the most part, without seed oats, having been forced to dispose of their entire crop the preceding winter, to meet rent and taxes. Many of them were then furnished by the landlords, or their agents or subagents . . . with seed at 10 shillings a cwt., on credit until the next autumn or winter.
>
> When that time came they were obliged to thresh and sell their oats at 5 shillings a cwt.; so that whatever quantity they had got for seed, they were obliged to dispose of a double portion of their crop, which amounts to 100% of usury![6]

The bishop goes on to say that the consequence was that 'no harvest can save the peasant from starvation, provided the landlord pushes his claims to the extent to which the law entitles him'.

MacHale thanks the citizens of Dublin for their generosity to the starving and asks them to continue in their goodness and

> In the name of the distressed districts of the West, where men are seen digging out the slit potato-seeds recently put down, I

must return my thanks to the people of England, adjuring them in like manner, to persevere in their work of mercy.

But, he says 'it is a reproach to any government that a hardy and industrious people should be thrown so often into the humiliating attitude of mendicants for food'.[7]

Dr MacHale's pleas fell on deaf ears. Earl Grey and the members of the House of Commons were themselves of the landlord class. They were unwilling to imply that landlords were not fulfilling their duties.

Eventually MacHale set out for London, accompanied by various influential gentlemen from Mayo. He had an audience with the Prime Minister and explained the extent of the distress in the west of Ireland. His hopes were raised as the Prime Minister appeared sympathetic and many of the people in England were moved by the plight of the Irish. Some ladies in London had a sale of work and raised a hundred pounds.[8] However, nothing came of his visit to the Prime Minister and the bishop and his companions returned disappointed.

Undaunted, MacHale wrote again in July 1831. However much the bishop blamed the British Government for their insensitivity to the wrongs and sufferings of Ireland, he did not accuse or condemn the English people:

To that generous [English] people, I must express our obligations; I shall do many of them the justice to say, that it is owing to their ignorance of our state, they do not exert themselves as much to prevent famine by a system of sound legislation, as they do by their purse to mitigate its horrors.[9]

In another letter Dr MacHale talks about the lack of industry and commerce in Ireland. He speaks of the need for investment in that country:

Let the Government issue its fiat. Canada is traversed by canals for the circulation of its trade, while the Shannon, undisturbed by machinery and commerce, is suffered to roll in silence its unprofitable waters, through the land, an emblem, as it were, of the dull and sullen repose of its inhabitants.[10]

During this period, a wave of anti-Catholic feeling was spreading throughout England. Many people felt threatened by the Catholic Emancipation Bill, and the New Reformation or Evangelical group was gaining ground. Many people objected to the annual Government grant made to the Maynooth seminary. One of the objections to the Irish clergy voiced in the press was that they came from 'the humbler classes'. MacHale was quick to reply in a letter to the *Morning Chronicle* – 'I rejoice in the objection'.[11]

Towards the end of 1831, suffering from exhaustion, MacHale set out for Rome. He first went to London, where in September he attended the coronation of William IV in Westminster Abbey. He went on from there to Paris, Auxerre and Dijon, the birthplace of Bossuet. In October he arrived in Geneva and visited the bower on the shores of Lake Leman where Gibbon wrote the closing chapters of *The Decline and Fall of the Roman Empire*. He wrote many letters home describing his travels. At the beginning of the eighteenth century there were few travel books and so these letters were eagerly awaited. Indeed, many were published in the popular Irish newspaper, the *Freeman's Journal.*

MacHale crossed the Alps by stagecoach. He was particularly impressed by Savoy, then not part of France, and the vale of Chamonix. He stayed with the pastor of Chamonix and wished that the Irish could experience the peaceful life enjoyed by the inhabitants of that area. He went to Milan where he said Mass on the anniversary of the death of his brother, James, who had also been a priest.

In November he reached Rome. MacHale describes Gregory XVI, who had succeeded Pius VIII in February 1831, as a learned man and says that 'affectionate charity beams in every feature of the good Pontiff'.[12] MacHale's trip to Rome coincided with the visit of three celebrated Frenchmen, the Abbé Lamennais and his two young friends, the Count de Montalembert and the Abbé Lacordaire, who called themselves 'the Pilgrims of God and Liberty'.[13] Lamennais was a turbulent Breton priest who combined a modern liberalism with a conservative devotion to the Pope. He was the most powerful social prophet of his generation. He saw no inconsistencies in his views as he saw the cause of the People as being the same as that of the Pope, being that of Truth and Freedom against all pretentions of temporal princes and aristocracies. Thus Lamennais became the founder of liberal Catholicism as well as a champion of ultramontanism. Lamennais, together with Lacordaire and Montalembert, developed their liberal ideas in a paper of their own, the *Avenir*, to which Dr MacHale enthusiastically subscribed. The paper stood for the separation of Church and State, for the freedom of the press, for freedom of education from state control, for freedom of association and an extension of the suffrage. For the brief year of its existence – it was suspended in 1831 and officially condemned by the Pope in 1832 – it was the leading liberal paper in France and both Victor Hugo and Lamartine wrote for it. It was natural that the young MacHale should find the company of these men interesting and stimulating. He wrote of them later:

> Fortunately for Monsieur de Lamennais, he was thus accompanied by two young friends who loved him much, but who loved truth and religion more. Though not sinking under the weight of years, Monsieur de Lamennais appeared to be sinking under the pressure of far more crushing influences, but his companions appeared the very impersonations of Catholicity and freedom; and I am much mistaken if France will not have to acknowledge a deep debt of gratitude to the one and to the other.[14]

MacHale's views did appear to be borne out by events. Lamennais, disappointed by the Pope's unwillingness to take up the cause of liberalism and his revolutionary programme, eventually lost all his religious faith. Montalembert was elected to the Chamber of Peers in France and fought hard for religious freedoms and rights. His most notable achievement came in later years under the second Republic of Louis Napoleon when, together with Falloux, the Minister of Education, he was able to secure the passage of the Falloux law giving the Church the freedom to run its own schools, a cause after

MacHale's own heart. Lacordaire as a priest remained throughout his life a man of the left, but he was always absolutely obedient to his religious superiors. He was noted for his great sermons. His friend Ozanam said of him:

> Our temples, so long forsaken, see their solitude re-peopled, the Abbé Lacordaire thunders forth the Word of God over an assembly of six thousand men, crowded into the mighty nave of Notre Dame.

While he was in Rome, Bishop MacHale was asked to give two sermons, one on the 'Reprobation of the Jews' and the other on 'St Patrick'. The latter was given on 17 March 1832 in the monastery church of St Isidore, which was attached to the Irish Franciscans.

In his sermon MacHale traced the history of the Christian faith in Ireland. He spoke of the relationship between England and Ireland. About his allusions to the penal laws he says:

> Do I allude to these to stir up angry recollections? – God forbid. From the lips of a minister of the Saviour of the world no accents but those of charity should fall. The Church should always be an asylum in which a truce should be given to the passions of mankind.[15]

He spoke of the Saxon monks who came to Mayo thirsting for sanctity and knowledge:

> If the old Catholic spirit could only revive and brotherly love stretch forth from Great Britain . . . and heal by sweet, Christian charity the deep and ever-bleeding wounds, caused by political and racial hatred, – how Mayo and all the West, and the Green Isle from shore to shore would put on life and strength and joy!
>
> Cannot the Blessed souls around St Patrick and St Bede in heaven obtain by their united prayers, that this, new, moral and material springtide should dawn at length on this desolate West?[16]

MacHale's letters home are full of the joys of the beauty of Rome and of its art. He visited the small church of St Peter on the banks of the Tiber, where a slab of marble bears the names of O'Neill and O'Donnell and commemorates the flight of the Ulster earls when their lands were partitioned by James I among the English and Scottish colonists. He visited the 'Fons Bandusiae' and recited Horace's ode.[17] He visited Mount Vesuvius and was filled with horror at the lava and the hot rocks.

MacHale particularly enjoyed his visit to those places associated with St Benedict, Subiaco and Monte Casino. 'If I become a monk', he wrote to his friend, 'I shall embrace his rule.'[18] He was in the countryside near Monte Casino when he wrote:

> As the evening fell, I heard with no ordinary emotion the piping of the shepherds . . . recalled all the images of pastoral simplicity and innocence with which our earlier years were familiarized.[19]

It at first filled him with classical recollections and then emphasised the contrasts between the conditions of the peasantry of Italy and his own native Ireland:

> The sounds conveyed to me a deeper and more mysterious emotion . . . and the source of this saddening feeling was the contrast between these shepherds and the peasantry of my own country, from whom such strains were but seldom heard, though nutured in the midst of scenery and recollections fraught with the most musical inspirations.

Like John Henry Newman, who visited Italy in February 1833, John MacHale took great delight in the island of Sicily. He described it as 'a land of poetry' with 'singular and striking features':

> The land alternately sinks into valleys terminating in abrupt ravines, or rising into hills gently sloping so as to form conical summits, thus revealing the volcanic agencies out of which the present surface has arisen.[20]

Newman said that Sicily filled him with 'inexpressible rapture' and that 'it was the theme of every poet and every historian of antiquity'. He says, 'In it I read the history of all that is great and romantic in human nature', and he speaks about 'the sheer beauty of the island'.[21]

On the feast of the Assumption in 1832, John MacHale had an audience with Pope Gregory XVI, at which the Pope gave him a chalice. The young bishop seemed to have made a favourable impression on the Pope, which stood him in good stead in later years when the Pope was to take his part against his opponents. MacHale also had money given him for purchasing things for the new cathedral. He brought back vestments with him and ordered the stone altar with the money given to him by Kenelm Digby. It is interesting to read MacHale's letters at this time, in which he speaks of his efforts to avoid paying import duty on the goods he is bringing home.[22]

As MacHale journeyed home he travelled through the Tyrol, Switzerland and Germany. In Germany he visited Munich, where he met the young German historian, Ignaz Döllinger, who was a member of a group of young Catholic intellectuals. Döllinger later wrote to Lamennais regretting the fact that the Church in France and Germany had no bishop of the calibre of MacHale:

> cet excellent homme nous a fait sentir encore plus amèrement ce qui nous manque: des évêques qui aient l'érudition, le noble courage et l'esprit d'indépendence d'un prélat irlandais.[23]

MacHale collected information about the conditions of the rural population and social institutions, as he wanted to enlighten public opinion in Great Britain.

The most important aspect of MacHale's trip to Rome, however, was his opportunity to put before the Holy Father the situation of Ireland. He spoke to the Pope about his fears for the Irish clergy and the Whig plans to 'pension them off'. The Whigs had come to power in 1830 under Earl Grey and had aimed to subordinate the power of the crown to that of Parliament. When Bishop MacHale returned to Ireland in mid December, the Irish peasants, priests and bishops were pleased that he had presented the Irish situation to the Pope. It restored their pride and gave them hope.

Before MacHale set out for home in August 1832 he wrote to Earl Grey, as he had received intelligence from home of a threat of an arms bill or coercion law to repress the discontented peasantry. He heads his letter with a passage from Cicero:

> *Nec alia erit lex Romae, alia Athenis; nec vero per senatum aut populum hac lege solvi possumus.*[24]

In this letter MacHale stresses his admiration for the British Constitution. He says that he is saddened to notice the contrast between the 'excellence of our Constitution and the misery of our people'. He says that whatever criticisms we might level against the governments of the continental countries, 'There is not so wretched a peasantry to be found under any one of them as that of Ireland'. He says that he realises that many English people are surprised at the fact that there is still discontent in Ireland. They think that by the Catholic Emancipation Bill the Catholics of Ireland can no longer claim that they are treated unjustly. He points out that Emancipation only affected a small number of Catholics, those rich enough to vote. For them it opened the way towards 'wealth and honours', but the mass of the population were still oppressed by the invidious land laws, and the commercial prosperity of Ireland was still 'stupidly sacrificed to the monopolists of Great Britain'.[25]

It was now time for Bishop MacHale to leave Rome. He was already hearing rumours of the outbreak of cholera that was now beginning to strike the west of Ireland.

Notes

1   John MacHale, *Letters* (1888), Letter XXXVIII, p. 265.
2   Ibid., p. 265.
3   Ibid., p. 269.
4   Ibid., p. 272.
5   Ibid., May 1831, Letter XXXIX, p. 273.
6   Ibid., p. 281.
7   Ibid., p. 284.
8   Ulick Bourke, *The Life and Times of the Most Reverend John MacHale* (1883), p. 90.

9   John MacHale, op. cit., Letter XL, p. 285.

10   Ibid., Letter XLI, p. 295.

11   *Morning Chronicle,* 5 September 1831.

12   John MacHale, *Letters* (1847), 27 March 1832, LVIII, p. 280. Quoted in Bernard O'Reilly, op. cit.

13   E. E. Y. Hayles, *Pio Nono* (1954), p. 44.

14   Bernard O'Reilly, *Life and Times of John MacHale* (1890), I, pp. 191–2.

15   John MacHale, *Sermons and Discourses* (1883), p. 166.

16   Ibid.

17   Horace, *Odes III.*

18   Bernard O'Reilly, op. cit. I, p. 185.

19   John MacHale, *Letters* (1847), LX, 20 August 1932, p. 291.

20   Ibid.

21   Ian Ker, *John Henry Newman* (1988), p. 72.

22   Pádraic Ó Tuairisg, *Árd-dheoise Thuama agus Cartlann Choláiste na nGael sa Róimh sa naoú haois déag,* unpublished thesis, Tuam archives, p. 98.

23   Döllinger to Lamennais, 12 October 1832, *Le Porte-Feuille de Lamennais 1818–1836* ed. by G. Goyau (1930), quoted in Donal Kerr, *Peel, Priests and Politics* (1982), p. 24. 'This excellent man made us realise all the more acutely what we lack: bishops who have the learning, the noble courage and the spirit of independence of an Irish cleric.'

24   Cicero, *de Republica* – 'No! there must not be one law for Rome, and another for Athens; no, nor can any decree of the senate or of the assembled People dispense us from the obligation of that law.'

25   John MacHale, *Letters* (1847), LVIII, 27 March 1832, p. 280.

5

WHIGS, TITHES AND EDUCATION

'Anyone but him.'
(Lord Melbourne)

WHEN DR MACHALE returned to Ireland after his visit to Rome, he faced the aftermath of the cholera and a poor harvest. The burdens of the peasantry, the exaction of tithes, rack-rents and consequent evictions had brought about a wave of agrarian crime. Because the peasants had no legal redress for unfair evictions, and the weight of the wealthy and the powerful was stacked against them, the people found ways of meting out rough justice. This often consisted in threats of murder against those who would carry out an eviction. Various secret societies grew up for this purpose – the Whitefeet, Blackfeet, Terryalts, Lady Clares, Molly Maguires and the Rockites. The most important of these organisations began in Ulster and was known as the Ribband or Ribbon. It was started to protect the Catholics from the Orangemen. It eventually spread from the North to absorb the lesser organisations. It came to Sligo about 1820 and in the thirties became involved in agrarian crime.

In response to this, the British Government passed coercion acts. It was understandable that they should do so, as otherwise Ireland could have slipped into anarchy, but at the same time Parliament took no steps to apply remedies to the causes of agrarian crime. The House of Commons was full of landowners and country squires who, though enlightened enough in the running of their own estates, were unwilling to interfere with the rights of property. Added to this, they had no knowledge of Ireland. Nassau Senior noticed in his *Journals, Conversations and Letters relating to Ireland* that 'the great majority of each House – that is of the two assemblies which govern Ireland – know less of that country than they know of Belgium or of Switzerland'. Parliament did spend many hours discussing Ireland

57

but their knowledge was nearly always second-hand. Few people travelled in Ireland and saw the conditions for themselves.

After Catholic Emancipation in the early 1830s there was much discussion of Irish affairs by the newly reformed Whig administration. They were painfully aware that the acute poverty of the Irish was a cause of scandal on the Continent and worked against the supposedly liberal British Government. On 18 November 1832, Dr MacHale wrote to the *Edinburgh Review*. This was an organ of the Whigs and saw itself as a liberal paper. In October of that year the reviewer had travelled all over Europe and had used the October edition to impugn the Papal States with their lack of liberalism. MacHale in his open letter remarks that if they are shocked by the laziness of the monks and the amount of ecclesiastical property in Spain, how did it escape their notice that £3,000,000 was annually wrung from the poor of Ireland in tithes paid to the Established Church to pay for a clergy with hardly any duties to perform? He then goes on to describe the so-called liberalism of France:

> They talk of freedom, while their acts are most tyrannical. The press is persecuted; the poor, inoffensive Trappists are banished; and education is utterly proscribed, unless administered by a band of sophists . . . who labour to monopolise the human intellect, and to reduce man to the condition of a machine, that is, to move in blind obedience to all their caprices.

The Whigs tried to find ways of satisfying the Irish without losing their support in England. They had to contend with the newly elected Daniel O'Connell, a tireless campaigner for Irish rights. By that time O'Connell had become, not only the most famous man in Ireland, but renowned and admired throughout Europe, being popularly known as 'The Liberator'. O'Connell was a brilliant lawyer of immense physical vigour and power of concentration. He was a tall, attractive man with a strong musical voice and wonderful powers of oratory. He was never a man of violence and was generally prudent and ready for compromise, but his language was often extreme. One of the most contentious issues faced by the Whigs was that of the tithes paid to the Established Church by the Irish peasantry. In the south and west of Ireland, the Catholics were in a large majority and the concentration of ecclesiastical offices and rich livings in the over-endowed Anglican Church was a scandal that had few Irish defenders other than those who lived by its anomalies. During the eighteenth century the Protestant ascendancy had been strengthened, and positions in the Irish Church were looked upon as rich prizes, often awarded by parliamentary ministers for various services. Jonathan Swift claimed rather irreverently that while the Government elevated 'excellent and moral men' for Irish bishoprics

> It unfortunately happened that, as these worthy divines crossed Hounslow Heath on their way to Ireland, they [were] regularly robbed and murdered by the highwaymen frequenting that common, who seized their robes and patents, went over to Ireland, and were consecrated bishops in their stead.[1]

At the beginning of the nineteenth century the Anglican Archbishop of Armagh was William Stuart, an honest man of good principles who tried to bring about some reform in the Church. He was continually thwarted in his aims by unsuitable candidates being put forward for vacant bishoprics. Pressure was put on him to have George de la Poer Beresford, a member of a wealthy influential family, as Bishop of Kilmore. Stuart wrote:

> Mr Beresford is reported to be one of the most profligate men in Europe. His language and his manners have given universal offence. . . . I have six bishops under me. Three are men of tolerable moral character, but are inactive and useless, and two are of acknowledged bad character. Fix Mr Beresford at Kilmore and we shall have three very inactive bishops, and what I trust the world has not yet seen, three bishops in one district reported to be the most profligate men in Europe.[2]

Yet this system was allowed to remain a cause of unrest and insult to the Catholic clergy because English churchmen feared that an attack upon the system of raising money, and the amount of property owned by the established Church in Ireland, might result in a similar attack in England.

In 1832 the Government passed another tithe act, which extended the provisions of the 1823 act, making the composition of tithes permanent and compulsory and transferring payment from the tenant to the landlord rather than from the tenant to the Church. It relieved the poorest classes and cut down the number of those paying the tithe. This measure was regarded in England as an attack upon the Church and in Ireland as a trivial reform that had no effect on the root of the problem.[3]

The Whigs tried to appease both sides by introducing an Irish Church bill and a coercion bill at the same time. They proposed to abolish ten sees, to lay a tax of £60,000 a year on bishoprics, chapters and the richer benefices, and to set up commissions to manage the episcopal estates. Any increase in revenue as a result of more efficient administration would be applied to purposes chosen by Parliament. The coercion bill suspended the right of public meetings, partially suspended the Habeas Corpus Act, and applied martial law and a 'curfew order' in disturbed districts. The Irish Church bill had a difficult passage, particularly through the Lords, where it was considered that an important principle was at stake. John Henry Newman, on hearing of the Irish Church Reform Bill which had been narrowly passed in 1833 with the Coercion Act, commented:

> Well done, my blind premier, confiscate and rob, till, like Samson, you pull down the political structure on your own head, tho' without his deliberate purpose and good cause![4]

The act had made him 'hate the Whigs . . . more bitterly than ever'.[5]

Eventually, the cabinet was forced to give up the proposal to use the increased revenues for purposes unconnected with the Church. Because of this, O'Connell withdrew his support from the bill.

MacHale once again wrote to Earl Grey. He speaks of the 'powerlessness of Coercion to effect good'. He says:

> You may pass laws to have the hungry fed and the naked clothed . . . . Your laws will be of no avail without a development of the resources from which such necessary funds are to be drawn.[6]

He goes on to say that in the best regulated States of antiquity the laws were few and simple because

> They were the production of men who knew the wants of the people. . . . Members of Parliament chosen in England and Scotland who form the majority of the British Senate, have not sufficient knowledge of the wants of the Irish people, nor anxiety to relieve them.[7]

MacHale speaks of the 'patres Conscripti' of the ancient world. It was a name given to legislators who possessed 'fatherly solicitude' towards the people:

> No such name can ever attach to legislators who are filled with the idea of the ascendancy of one portion, and the abasement of another, of the subjects.

In his letter, MacHale argues vehemently for the repeal of the Act of Union:

> I have confidence in laws: but it is in such laws as proceed from men who are acquainted with the wants of those for whom they legislate, and who are fitted with a parental anxiety to promote their happiness. . . . It is these alone that can enact laws for the benefit of the Irish poor; direct their labour into remunerative channels; develop the hidden resources of the country; and then call forth all those noble creations of art, of literature, of science, and of civilisation, which without coercive laws, will bring home the absentees.

Although MacHale wanted the repeal of the Union, he was always loyal to the Crown:

And while the people shall cling, with characteristic heroic devotion, to the throne of the British monarch, they cannot be content with anything short of the vigilant, paternal, and presiding care of a National Legislature.[8]

The period of the early 1830s was a time of some disillusionment for the Irish Catholics. The Catholic Emancipation Act had been passed in 1829 amid much rejoicing. It had been forced on Wellington and Peel against all their inclinations and those of the Tory Government. With the advent of the Whigs and Earl Grey, O'Connell had felt that the time was ripe for reform of Irish affairs. He ultimately aimed for the repeal of the Union but kept quiet on that while he argued for the abolition of tithes and more justice for the Catholics in the legal system. He hoped to introduce repeal gradually, hoping that some Irish assembly might be introduced that would eventually resume the powers of the old Parliament. He was deeply disappointed by the Whigs. Although there were many reforming members of Parliament, the new reformed house did not return any more Irish members than hitherto, and the interests of the Established Church and the landowners proved just as formidable.

The English Catholics gained more from Catholic Emancipation than their Irish counterparts. There were more openings for them in Parliament and public life. At first they were profoundly grateful to O'Connell. Bishop MacHale enjoyed good relationships with many English gentlemen. Despite his attacks on the Government, he always sought to cultivate brotherly feeling for the English people. Lord Shrewsbury of Alton Towers wrote to him congratulating him on his book *Evidences and Doctrines of the Catholic Church*. On his return from Rome, MacHale stayed with a Catholic gentleman of London, Henry Barnewall of Bayswater.[9] However, as time went on, many of the English Catholics had difficulty in understanding the problems of Ireland. They saw repeal of the Union as radical and revolutionary and altogether unnecessary. They disliked O'Connell, regarding him as flamboyant and vulgar, and lacked sympathy for his continual agitation for the Irish. Bishop MacHale became known as a 'political prelate' and often received a bad press from Catholic and non-Catholic alike.

During John MacHale's years as Coadjutor Bishop of Killala, there was much discussion in England and Ireland about primary education. In France the Jacobins had stated that education should be 'universal, compulsory, gratuitous and secular'. In the British Isles virtually nobody agreed with this. Compulsory education appeared to them to interfere with the liberty of the individual. Gratuitous education would have meant the State control of education – something that was equally suspect, particularly to those who were not members of the Church of England. Education was seen as the province of religion. Until the 1830s elementary education in England had been provided by religious societies. This grew out of the Sunday School movement. The first intention of these schools was to teach children the catechism and the Bible, but as time went on more secular education was introduced. There was some rivalry between these societies, as one, the National society, was primarily Anglican in nature, whereas the other, the British and Foreign Bible Society, was Nonconformist and laid stress on the Bible and not the catechism. By the 1830s many people in England were concerned about the lack of education of the urban poor. In Ireland, too, the growing population presented new educational problems. MacHale remained convinced that the Catholic Church could educate its own children. Many of the bishops, although supporting MacHale wholeheartedly in his onslaught against the 'Kildare Street' method of using education for the purposes of proselytising, felt that the Church was financially unequal to the task of providing universal elementary education for its children. Consequently they were prepared to back a State system, which, although they did not consider it ideal, fulfilled certain conditions. In 1826 the Irish hierarchy agreed on the following principles as a basis for discussion:

1) Catholic and Protestant children could share the same school for the purposes of 'literary education', provided the religion of the Catholics was safeguarded and adequate time allowed for Catholic religious instruction.
2) The master or assistant master must be a Catholic, the appointment being subject to the Catholic bishop of the diocese.

3) Four Catholic model schools to be set up, at Government expense, one in each province for the training of Catholic teachers.
4) Books used should be approved by the Catholic bishop.[10]

In 1831 Edward Stanley, later to become Lord Stanley, Earl of Derby, was the Chief Secretary for Ireland. He stated that the policy of the Whig government was for the provision of

> a system of education from which should be banished even the suspicion of proselytism, and which, admitting children of all religious persuasions, should not interfere with the peculiar tenets of any.

A Board of National Education was set up and Archbishop Murray of Dublin was persuaded to sit on the board. He reported favourably on the liberal nature of the other members of the board and continued to sit on the board despite opposition, particularly from MacHale.

There were many objections to the scheme. It did not allow the display of Catholic emblems or the saying of prayers during class time. The Catholic bishops were not allowed to appoint teachers; they did not have a veto on which books were used and they were not allowed a Catholic training college. However, Oliver Kelly, the Archbishop of Tuam, wrote to MacHale while he was in Rome, praising the new system:

> The new board of education, so far as it has gone works well to the extent of the means placed at its disposal, which, as yet, are very scanty. His Grace, Dr Murray, who is a most efficient member, assures me that the dissenting members are very liberal. . . . if the present government holds its place, I have no doubt the Board will become permanently useful. But if the Tory party succeeds in ousting the ministry, it can easily be seen that the Kildare Street folk will again resume power.[11]

Some time later, Kelly again wrote to MacHale hoping that he would be reconciled to the board, but MacHale opposed the system as it did not incorporate the principles laid down as essential by the bishops in 1826.

In 1834 there was some upheaval in ecclesiastical circles owing to the deaths of two of its bishops. The first of these was Oliver Kelly, Archbishop of Tuam, who died in April. Shortly after this, in May, Peter Waldron, the aged Bishop of Killala, met his death while winding his clock. On Waldron's death, John MacHale automatically became Bishop of Killala, a job he had been virtually doing for nearly ten years. The search then began for a successor to Oliver Kelly.

The position of Archbishop of Tuam was an important one in Ireland. Tuam was one of the four provinces of the Irish Catholic Church, the others being Dublin, Armagh and Cashel. The names of three candidates were sent to Rome to Propaganda. John MacHale's was one of them. Dublin Castle and the British Government under Lord Melbourne, who had succeeded Earl Grey in 1834, were filled with consternation at the prospect of MacHale filling this position. Palmerston, the Foreign Secretary, wrote to his brother:

> I am sending off a messenger suddenly to Florence and Rome, to try to get the Pope not to appoint any agitating Prelate, Archbishop of Tuam.[12]

Melbourne himself addressed the Pope, asking for 'Anyone but him'.[13] The British Government, mindful of the short-lived Quarantotti Rescript, still had aspirations about influencing the Pope's choice of Irish bishops. After the Act of Union they had tried to link the possibility of Catholic Emancipation to a clause giving the Government a right of veto on the Irish bishops. But O'Connell, backed by the Irish bishops, had continually held out against it.

All the bishops of Tuam voted for MacHale, and Archbishop Murray, though disagreeing with MacHale, particularly on the education issue, explained to Propaganda:

> I must confess indeed, most eminent Lord, that prelate, otherwise most worthy, sometimes uses too sharp a style, as it seems to me, when he writes about political matters.

It must be remembered nevertheless that he is surrounded by poor persons languishing in want and misery, and if he adverts to the causes of this misery more sharply than I would wish, I think it should be attributed to his sense of duty towards the poor and to a zeal which burns for religion, although for a little while it went beyond the limits of prudence, as some believed. . . .

I am very happy to be able to add my testimony to the votes of the bishops of the Province of Tuam concerning that prelate, learned, pious, eloquent, and deserving well of religion.[14]

Archbishop Murray was a man respected by everyone for his kindness and holiness, but he represented the older class of bishops, educated on the Continent. They were very wary of upsetting the Protestant establishment. Murray wished to avoid anything that would offend Protestant sensibilities. He forbade the Sisters of Mercy to display crucifixes or rosary beads in the street and would avoid outward shows of Catholicity such as processions. John MacHale was the first Irish bishop to be completely educated in Ireland and he represented the new, more confident Irishman, ready to speak out for the rights of the Irish Catholics and fearless of the consequences.

Gregory XVI chose John MacHale to be Archbishop of Tuam on account of 'the distinguished fame of your learning and your zeal in defence of the Catholic religion'.[15] The people in the west of Ireland went wild with joy. Bonfires were lit on the hilltops and ballads were composed for the occasion. However, the people of Killala were very sad at losing their hard-working young bishop who had displayed such gentleness and devotion to the people. On his departure they expressed the extent of their loss:

Were we only to reflect on the loss we sustain, our expressions would be those of unqualified sadness: nor could we easily reconcile our respective flocks to the deep sense of bereavement. We are, however, consoled by the thought that, though removed, your removal is not to a great distance; and that it places you in a higher position, where your zeal and virtues will have a wider range, embracing even our own diocese.[16]

The priests say they will not mention MacHale's merits as they are 'national property' but they will remember his 'nearer virtues', which they have all felt and witnessed.

Your unwearied zeal in visiting the remotest districts, and imparting the light of your instructions to every portion of your flock; your constant solicitude for the wants of the poor, and your unceasing exertions to obtain sympathy for their condition; your paternal advice to your clergy, with whom you took a special delight to mix rather as a friend than as a superior, not lording it over them, but preventing all occasions for the exercise of authority by the efficacious examples of your own life.[17]

The clergy also appreciated MacHale's efforts in the building of their new cathedral. They presented him with 'a travelling carriage' as they did not want to be outdone by the students who had presented him with a silver cup when he left Maynooth.

Though you are going from among us, the influence of your virtues shall ever remain; and be assured that you bear with you the hearts and affections of the clergy and the people of the diocese of Killala.[18]

Before he left Killala, MacHale spent some time with his family in his birthplace of Tubbernavine. At this period, his father was still alive. He lived until 1837, aged 88. After his wife's death he had married Mary Martin with whom John MacHale had a good relationship. He seems to have been particularly fond of his young half-sisters, Margaret, Eileen and Barbara. He also had a great many nieces and nephews. Throughout his life John MacHale maintained a powerful affection for his family and also for his native area.

It is a feeling akin to that filial reverence which the Almighty has planted in our hearts towards our parents, that extends itself also to the place where we first came into being.[19]

There in his old home he enjoyed some rest before he began the enormous task that awaited him in Tuam. Bernard O'Reilly mentions his delight in the local pipers and harpists. MacHale always maintained a love of the simple Celtic melodies. John MacHale's father was still alive at this time and O'Reilly describes the moving farewell between the two men, 'There were few eyes without tears as the Prelate lifted up his aged father from his kneeling position and clasped him to his heart'.

When MacHale finally left the diocese of Killala the people escorted him from Ballina as far as the division between the two lakes, Lough Conn and Lough Cullin. There they left him to proceed on his way to his new Archdiocese of Tuam.

Notes

1 Jonathan Swift, quoted in Edward Garland Brynn, *The Church of Ireland in the Age of Catholic Emancipation* (1982), p. 13.

2 Stuart to Henry Addington, 27 November 1801, Hardwick MSS, 35771/152, quoted in Edward Garland Brynn, op. cit. (1982), p. 46.

3 Llwellyn Woodward, *The Age of Reform 1815–1870* (1938), p. 344.

4 Newman, quoted in Ian Ker, *John Henry Newman* (1988), p. 64.

5 Ibid.

6 MacHale, *Letters* (1888), p. 481.

7 Ibid.

8 Ibid.

9 Bernard O'Reilly, *The Life and Times of John MacHale* (1890), I, p. 214.

10 Ulick Bourke, *The Life and Times of the Most Reverend John MacHale* (1883), p. 104.

11 Bernard O'Reilly, op. cit., I, p. 196.

12 Bernard O'Reilly, op. cit., I, p. 243.

13 Charles Greville, *The Greville Memoirs*, III (1948).

14 Murray to Pedicini, 16 August 1834. Quoted in Donal A. Kerr, *Peel, Priests and Politics 1841–1846* (1982), p. 25. Translation in Appendix, p. 359.

15 Bernard O'Reilly, op. cit., I, p. 249.

16   Ibid., p. 260.
17   Ibid., p. 260.
18   Ibid., p. 261.
19   Ibid., p. 256.

6

TUAM

'Mercy to the poor, which is the duty of all, is one specially incumbent on the ministers of religion.' (John MacHale)

THERE WERE GREAT celebrations in Tuam at the inauguration of the new Archbishop. On Monday, 13 October 1834, the people began to stream into the town well before dawn. There were festivities throughout the day, culminating in a banquet in the evening at which a new triptych was produced, which had pictures of St Patrick, Mount Nephin and Tubbernavine, and Croagh Patrick. In a speech in the evening MacHale said that he wished to serve God and the poor, a theme that he reiterated the following day in his sermon at the inauguration. 'Mercy to the poor, which is the duty of all, is one specially incumbent on the ministers of religion.'[1] He was installed as Archbishop in the 'chapel', as the cathedral was not yet opened.

Dr MacHale felt that one of his first duties as Archbishop was to save the faith of his people against the proselytisers. In the early 1830s the Protestant Bible Societies were very powerful and the strength of the new Evangelical groups was increasing. An example of a man of this new, reforming fervour was Edward Nangle, who was born in Meath in 1799. He was described by his biographer, Henry Seddall, as 'God's chosen vessel to hold aloft the torch of truth for the benighted Romanists on the western coast of Ireland'. He said that Nangle

> became fully alive to errors and superstition of Romish system; and determined that, with God's help, he would henceforward use all his energies to counteract the influence of that system.[2]

70

The proprietor of Achill Island gave him some land, and with much difficulty Nangle and his associates induced the tenants to give up 130 acres. They sought the encouragement of Dr Trench, the Protestant Archbishop of Tuam, and in 1833 a schoolmaster and a scripture reader were sent to Achill. Seddall describes how Nangle met a popular Evangelical minister in Dublin, who advised Nangle against going to Achill, saying that it was a 'wild goose chase'. Nangle replied, 'I wish to lift the standard of the cross among its inhabitants.' The minister said that the Catholic priests would 'blow him into the Atlantic', to which Nangle replied, 'God is stronger than priests.' To Nangle's horror the minister exclaimed 'Bah! I hate cant!'[3] Nangle was undaunted and arrived in Achill in 1834. He and his followers were determined to infiltrate into the Catholic west and they bought much land for churches and schools. They continually denounced the 'superstitions' of the Catholics and described the Masses as 'blasphemous fables and dangerous deceits'. Many of Nangle's activities were criticised by Catholic and Protestant alike, particularly his woodcut for his newspaper, the *Achill Herald,* which consisted of a mouse devouring a wafer watched by two ecclesiastics. Much money was sent by people in England to Nangle, who described in the English newspapers the 'superstitions' of the Romanists and exaggerated versions of his conversions. MacHale wrote to Lord John Russell to complain about him in 1835:

> The wretched inhabitants of the west of Connaught, exhausted with hunger, supplicated for bread, and those tender-hearted missionaries attempted to drown the cries in the louder and more protracted echoes of the charge of their idolatry.[4]

Archbishop MacHale also determined to do battle against the privileges of the Established Church, especially with regard to tithes. In December 1834 the new Archbishop wrote to the Duke of Wellington in the newly formed Tory ministry. He called upon him to disestablish the Church in Ireland, to do away with the tithe system and to regulate the laws on the principles of justice. He informed Wellington that he himself had leased a farm and had no intentions of paying tithes on it.[5]

The following year there was another General Election. MacHale became very concerned about the amount of bribery that went on. He saw elections as a time of serious moral danger for the Irish people. They were very poor and a bribe to vote for the landlord's candidate was an attractive prospect. The Archbishop wrote a strong pastoral letter in the defence of Truth, urging his flock to use their votes honestly. After the election of the Whig government he wrote to the Home Secretary, Lord John Russell, telling him of the plight of the Irish peasantry after recent famines. He spoke of accusations against the Irish clergy. They were accused of being political agitators for simply describing the conditions of the people. Russell acknowledged MacHale's letter but nothing was done. MacHale then wrote a public letter in which he claimed that the political parties always had money available for bribes but never any for the relief of famine.

Later in the year MacHale visited Westport, where he made a speech about banks, a fairly new phenomenon for the west of Ireland. He commended them on affording facilities for trade, sheltering industries and providing money for education, but he did not like the excessive charging of interest:

> I am not so familiar with business methods to be able to say whether or not a banking establishment is an advantage to a community – you are the best judges – but banks have brought ruin, bankruptcy and poverty.[6]

He pleaded with them to let interest be fair, not usurious, to a starving peasantry.

Soon after Dr MacHale's accession to the see of Tuam, there began, for him, a very unhappy episode. The priests of Killala met in Ballina to elect a new bishop. The name of a Fr O'Finan was put forward and MacHale supported the recommendation. Fr O'Finan, a Dominican, was from the local area originally but, like many Irish Catholic priests of that era, had been educated abroad. He had left Ireland in 1792 and had not really returned for any length of time.

He was known to be an exemplary and accomplished priest. O'Finan was subsequently elected and he returned to Ireland. It soon became clear that Fr O'Finan was not fully aware of the conditions of the Church in Ireland. He cherished the idea of building a great Catholic university in Mayo dedicated to St Thomas Aquinas. He also wanted to revive and restore the diocesan chapter to full canonical existence. The diocesan chapter had been in abeyance for centuries, since the see of Killala had been taken over by the Church of England. The Catholic Bishop had had no cathedral, no residence and no revenues. As Bishop of Killala, MacHale had improved the situation, particularly in the building of a cathedral, but the area was poor and O'Finan's plans impracticable.

Things became difficult in Killala when O'Finan appointed the Rev John Patrick Lyons as Vicar-General. Archbishop MacHale says in a letter that he was 'puzzled' by the appointment of Lyons but thought that he must have been recommended by Fr Burke, the Dean.[7] Lyons subsequently showed himself to be an avaricious man who possessed a violent temper, was inclined towards constant litigation, and was quite prepared to have difficult parishioners thrown into gaol. There grew up a problem about 'episcopal dues', which were larger in Killala than other dioceses. Many of the clergy signed a remonstrance against these. Bishop O'Finan had spent many years in Lisbon, where the people had a great fear of democracy and 'liberalism'. The bishop saw in the clergy a lawless band of radicals. Encouraged by Lyons, he set about removing from the parishes all those who had signed the 'remonstrance'. MacHale received many letters from priests and bishops, horrified at the appointment of Lyons. The Archbishop wrote to O'Finan to try to sort things out. They agreed to meet in Dublin, but in the meantime O'Finan appealed to Rome. The Pope appointed an apostolic visitor, Dr Crolly of Armagh. The Dominicans tried to supersede Dr Crolly, but Rome would not allow it. In case after case Crolly judged against O'Finan and his Vicar-General. There was even a public quarrel and MacHale and Crolly were subpoenaed to attend a civil court. MacHale wrote constantly to Rome and especially to Dr Cullen, the Rector of the Irish College, about the unfortunate situation.

There was scarcely an account in the supposed libel that was not true. In his passion he flung books from the altar at his flock. In his rage he spat in the face of one of them on Sunday. In his cooler moments one of his chapels was the ordinary receptacle for his cattle, and perhaps what was without precedent in the annals of priestly avarice I found at one visitation six score poor women, married women of honest repute, left unchurched on account of the rapacious demands of this priest . . . nothing will arrest the pride and presumption of that individual who will strive to . . . wrest the crozier out of the feeble hands of his infatuated dupe.[8]

Finally the Holy See accepted MacHale's advice and an administrator, the Rev Thomas Feeney, was appointed to run the diocese and it was temporally in the hands of the Dublin diocese. Dr O'Finan retired to Rome.

There is not a great deal of information available about the personal life of John MacHale, but in his biography of the Archbishop, Bernard O'Reilly tells us something about his daily habits. Throughout his life MacHale seems to have been an indefatigable worker, who despite tremendous exertions was always a student, being continually eager to gain more knowledge, read more books or to write himself. He rose early in the morning and devoted his first half-hour to mental prayer. Before he went to bed, he always read the subject for the following day's meditation. He celebrated daily Mass in the cathedral, which was preceded by an hour in the confessional. There was always a crowd of the poor waiting for the confessional. This practice continued until he was very old, when the people would wait for him at the door of his house to help him into the cathedral and to hold his umbrella for him. For MacHale, the love of the poor was a passion that he retained all his life. He was patient and gentle to all, but especially to the poor. When he went on visitations, his confessional was besieged and he would be in the confessional for four or five hours at a time. For the poor, he wrote instructions, catechisms and devotional works, all in the native dialect. He was especially concerned with the education of the children and encouraged them to speak two languages. He told them that it was no burden to learn and speak two languages: 'Keep the Irish which is your own and learn the English. . . . You will be more learned than the neighbouring gentry, who, as a rule, speak but in one tongue.'[9] He also translated parts of the Bible into Irish to make it available for the people. In the law courts, MacHale insisted that the lawyers speak in Irish, as he was concerned that if they did not use Irish the people would make mistakes. He argued that in Jersey the lawyers all had to speak French, so in Ireland they must speak Irish.

The Archbishop would preach every Sunday after the nine o'clock Mass. These sermons became famous and were largely for the benefit and education of the poor. He did not want their piety to be blind and unintelligent. In the west of Ireland in the eighteenth century, poverty was an almost continual phenomenon. Despite constant alms-giving, MacHale was said never to be annoyed or wearied by the requests for help. He was especially concerned about those people who did not ask for help, those whose families had got poorer and poorer with each generation, who did not want to make their distress known. With these families MacHale would use all his ingenuity and delicacy to find out their condition and try to help them without their knowing. Although MacHale, whenever possible, devoted a proportion of each day to study, he was always courteous to those who interrupted him and his hospitality was proverbial.

As well as being renowned for his charity to the poor, John MacHale was known for his kindness towards his priests. He was careful to make sure that no one ever felt overlooked or neglected. When visiting in his diocese he always declined the offer of hospitality by the local gentry, but stayed instead with the parish priest, however uncomfortable his house might be. He had a great affection for his priests and they trusted him. If reliable information reached him about a priest's misconduct, he would go to that priest, rather than call him to Tuam. He would find a natural opportunity to call upon him and hope that the priest would confide in him. MacHale did not hold it against his priests if they disagreed with him. In fact, he often went out of his way to be kind to those who held different opinions. He was inflexible about faith or principle but tolerant in matters of opinion. At first sight John MacHale looked austere, distant and reserved, but his austerity was only for himself. He was yielding and indulgent to others. He could on occasions throw aside his restraints and be full of wit and humour. Above all MacHale was a man of God. The recitation of the Rosary was a daily household custom and his observances of the fasts of Lent meant that by Holy Week he was very weak.

For recreation, he loved music and literature, particularly that of his native land. He loved Moore's melodies and translated them into Gaelic. He continued to learn the piano and the harp and often invited pipers to St Jarlath's. He had many friends whom he visited and who visited him. He numbered amongst them many Englishmen as, although MacHale was a fierce opponent of the English Government, he was always anxious to show kind feelings to the English people. One of the closest of these English friends was Charles Waterton, a naturalist and a rather humorous, eccentric aristocrat.

The issue of education remained a problem throughout the middle of the eighteenth century. As time went on the idea of universal education became more and more desirable, both to the people of England and to Ireland. However, both countries still considered education to be primarily in the province of religion. The first priority of elementary education was to teach children to know the catechism and/or to read the Bible. This meant that it could not be just a matter for Government legislation. In England the situation was more straightforward, in that the Established Church, the Church of England, was in fact the denomination of the majority. The Nonconformists and the Catholics accepted that if they wanted denominational education, they were to make their own arrangements. As the situation for Catholics became more relaxed, the Catholic Church encouraged the return of the religious orders particularly for this end. At the beginning, most of the schools were fee-paying, but as time went on the Church began to provide free Catholic education.

In Ireland, the majority of the population were not members of the Established Church and so the Government did feel obliged to provide some kind of non-denominational education. They could not be seen to be providing Catholic education, as this would have met with tremendous opposition, both from public opinion in England and from the Established Church. However, non-denominational education did not mean purely secular education. Nobody would have agreed with that. This meant that the National Schools were for the most part Protestant schools, which allowed a proportion of Catholic involvement. Two Catholics were allowed on to the National Board. Archbishop Daniel Murray sat on this board for many years despite the opposition of many Irish bishops, including MacHale. Archbishop Murray was universally regarded as a good man and a holy priest. There have been many different evaluations of his character. He was called a 'castle bishop' by many, a term of abuse that implied that Murray wanted to be on good terms with the wealthy, the aristocratic and the powerful to further his own ambitions or because he was flattered. This would seem to have been untrue. It is more likely that Murray was a peace-loving man, who thought the best way forward for good relationships between Catholic and Protestant, English and Irish, was co-operation and good will. Nevertheless, there seems to have been a certain naivety about the good Archbishop. While he was sitting on the education board, co-operating with Richard Whately, the Protestant Archbishop of Dublin, Dr Whately, was writing:

> The education supplied by the National Board is gradually undermining the vast fabric of the Catholic Church. . . . I believe that mixed education is gradually enlightening the mass of the people, and that if we give it up, we [the Protestants] give up the only hope of weaning the Irish people from the abuses of Popery . . . but I cannot venture to openly express this opinion. I cannot openly support the Education Board as an instrument of conversion.[10]

MacHale was never satisfied by the National Schools and continued to agitate either with the Government for more safeguards for the Catholic children in National Schools or with the Church and bishops for more Catholic schools. He wrote to Lord John Russell in February 1838 insisting that Government authorities had not the right to supervise Irish religious education. MacHale said he would organise his own schools in the province of Tuam. The National School system did spread throughout most of Ireland and in the three other provinces the system prevailed, even though it was disliked by many priests and bishops. In Tuam alone, owing to the influence of MacHale, the system did not succeed. In 1839 MacHale appealed to Rome to ask for support in his efforts for denominational schools. At this time, although Gregory XVI was sympathetic to MacHale, he did not want to intervene. He did not want the disagreements between the Irish bishops made public. It was suggested that the bishops meet and draw up a series of propositions on which they could all agree. Six bishops met, three who supported the National Schools and three who were against, and they agreed on various conditions similar to those adopted in 1826 for interdenominational schools. These propositions were sent to the Viceroy, Lord Clarendon, in 1840:

1) A Catholic priest should be a patron of a school where there are Roman Catholic children.
2) No books should be used for religious instruction without the approval of the archbishops.
3) Where the pupils are all Catholics, the bishop should have the power to dismiss or appoint teachers. The bishop and priests should have access to the school for religious instruction and the books used for religious instruction should be composed or selected by the Roman Catholic bishop of the diocese.
4) The Lord-Lieutenant is 'respectfully' requested to have two lay representatives from each province and one bishop on the Board of Commissioners.
5) The lecturer in the Model schools who instructs Roman Catholic teachers in the principles of religion and morals should be approved by the bishop.
6) There should be a Model school in each diocese for the training of teachers.[11]

Lord Clarendon refused to yield on any of the points. MacHale once again appealed to Pope Gregory. The Pope made various suggestions, which were on the whole favourable to MacHale, and in 1841 a

'Rescript' from Rome left it to the bishops in each diocese to decide whether or not they would temporise with the National School Board. From then onwards MacHale went to great efforts to erect his own schools. He invited various religious orders to come to Tuam, notably the monks of the third order of St Francis and the Christian Brothers. For the girls, there were the Presentation nuns and the Sisters of Mercy. MacHale ensured that in these schools, morning and evening prayer was said daily and also the 'Angelus' at noon. MacHale also saw to it that the schools preserved the Gaelic language and Celtic literature. He saw the National Schools not only as dangerous to the Catholic religion but as destructive of the national culture. One rhyme, often quoted to support this view, was in a set textbook for Irish schools:

> I thank the goodness and the grace,
> Which on my birth has smiled,
> And made me in these Christian days
> A happy English child.[12]

Cultural nationalists of the twentieth century have seen the State system of education as a deliberate agent of imposed cultural change. This is partially true, but the agencies involved saw themselves as pursuing a policy of 'improvement'. Their primary aim was to alleviate a perceived need among the poor and to 'improve' their moral and social values. The Irish language was merely one of the recessive attributes with which the system was committed to contend. The general aims of the curriculum were to inculcate knowledge that was standardised and useful. Thus, speaking the Irish language was punishable by the tally-stick and the limited classical education that had been provided in the hedge schools was abandoned for a rigid commitment to the teaching of the three Rs and such virtues as thrift, deference, punctuality, abstinence and self-improvement. Desmond McGuire in his *History of Ireland* says:

> These were the virtues that were so useful in creating a decorous industrialized proletariat in England. In Ireland the

absence of a general industrialized forum for the display of these virtues was to ensure that the literacy which education certainly created often contributed to the public articulation of values at sharp variance with the system.

Nevertheless, the decline of the Irish language continued. In 1800 about half the population of Ireland spoke Irish as their first language. By 1851 the number was down to less than a quarter, and so it continued. During the ensuing years there was to be much disagreement about education, not only about primary but also about secondary and university education.

In December 1834 the Whig government fell, largely due to disagreements on the Irish problems. The new government proposed to commute the Established Church tithe into a land tax payable to the State at a reduced sum. Lord John Russell, who succeeded Grey as Prime Minister, did not want the Government to maintain the revenues of the Irish Church and suggested that some of the revenues from the tax might go to other purposes. The question was then enlarged to include the partial disendowment of the Irish Church. Many cabinet members resigned over the issue, whilst O'Connell himself described the plan as 'most excellent humbug'.[13] Peel had a short administration and tried again to transform the tithe into a rent charge. Once again the discussions concerned the wider issue of the revenues of the Irish Church and once again the Government was brought down. In the modern age it would seem to be reasonable at least partially to disendow a church that catered for only a small fraction of the population in Ireland, but for the people of eighteenth-century England a principle was at stake.

O'Connell, who had helped to bring down Peel, supported the newly restored Whigs in what was known as the 'Lichfield House Compact'. This was an alliance of the different branches of the opposition that had met in the house of Lord Lichfield. O'Connell, though opposing the Whigs before, had decided to give them a chance.[14] In the years of the Whig ministry, 1835–41, a few acts were to be passed that would be of some benefit to Ireland, though O'Connell had hoped for better terms. They introduced the Poor Law into Ireland, reformed the corporations and settled the tithe question. The Poor Enquiry of 1833–36 began as a Government effort to curb the endemic violence in Ireland by an attempt to alleviate the condition of the poor. This resulted in a system that was largely the work of George Cornwall Lewis and George Nicholls. Lewis was assistant commissioner to the enquiry and his personal recommendations were preferred over those of the formal commission report. The responsibility for the final form of the system was given to Nicholls. Both saw the Poor Law as an attempt to aid the country through a transition period. Nicholls said that 'transition' was meant

> to indicate that season of change from the system of small holdings, allotments and subdivisions of land which now prevails in Ireland, to the better practice of day labour for wages, and to that dependence on daily labour for support which is the present condition of the English peasantry.[15]

The Government decided to apply the English system of workhouses. The Poor Law was not without some good effect, but it did give harsh landlords an excuse for eviction on the grounds that tenants could go to the workhouse, and it did not succeed in raising the living standards of a half-starved population.

The reform of the corporations took five years, owing to the opposition of the House of Lords. The initial proposals would have given all existing municipalities an elected representative council, but this was eventually narrowed down to the more important towns and the municipal franchise was limited to householders rated at £10 a year and upwards.

The tithe question was once again held up by the House of Lords, who were unwilling to deprive the Irish Church of any of their income, but finally in 1838 it was agreed that a rent charge, based on 75 per cent of the tithe, should replace the tithe. During the period of deliberation over the tithe bill, Archbishop MacHale was in continual correspondence with Daniel O'Connell. He asked O'Connell to refuse to accept the bill:

> I cannot express to you how great the dissatisfaction of the

people is . . . after the hopes so often held out to them of being released from the odious impost. The paying it to the landlord rather than the parson they do not conceive to be any benefit to them.

Though it cannot be expected that they should be all at once relieved from the encumbrance of the Protestant establishment, there should at least be a beginning . . . by getting rid of that encumbrance in the districts in which the Protestant clergy have no congregations. This was a feature in last year's bill. . . . The present Bill holds out no such encouraging prospect.[16]

O'Connell was in a difficult position, having promised to support the Whigs in the Lichfield House Compact. He also believed that the Whigs were the lesser of two evils and that nothing was to be gained from the Tories. He replied to MacHale, pleading with him to encourage local MPs to support the bill. He said it did have some advantages:

That this Bill at one blow strikes off 30% of the impost, affording a precedent for going further; and if such a bill passed, it would be the first law directly depriving the parsons in all cases of a percentage.[17]

MacHale was bitterly disappointed by the tithe bill of 1838. It was a less than dramatic outcome of centuries of agitation. O'Connell felt thoroughly exasperated with the results of his co-operation with the Whigs. The results from the Irish point of view had been meagre and the Government had spent months and sometimes years quarrelling over details and made no attempt to solve the really important issues. The Government's failure to deal with the agrarian problem was to have serious repercussions in the future.

During this period, owing to his compromise with the Whigs, O'Connell lost some of his popularity with the Irish people. They, like MacHale, wanted him to continue the policy of the repeal of the Union. MacHale sympathised with O'Connell and corresponded frequently with him, but would not be moved from his opinion that Irish politicians and representatives would achieve nothing for Ireland unless they stood together, independent of British political parties, and cast their votes only for the reformation of Irish grievances.

O'Connell, by his compromise, had helped to secure some reforms for the Irish and the benefits of these were enhanced by the appointment of Thomas Drummond as Under-Secretary for Ireland in 1835. Drummond had spent time in Ireland previously, working on the Ordnance Survey of Ireland, and was sympathetic to O'Connell and his demands. Drummond refused to govern Ireland by exceptional legislation and repressed Orange as well as Ribbon societies. He also forbade the packing of juries in the Protestant interest. Drummond achieved a great deal in the reorganisation of the administration in various fields. He reformed the police, the Board of Works, and changed the whole system of public communication and transport. He was also largely responsible for the report of the Irish Railway Commission, which suggested State aid for the construction of trunk lines in Ireland. This plan was not adopted, however, as English opinion applied English conditions to Ireland and, in England, private enterprise provided money for railways. Unfortunately Drummond died of overwork in 1840.[18] The Melbourne administration fell some months later.

From the beginning of his career as a barrister and public speaker and then as a politician, Daniel O'Connell had at the heart of his aims the repeal of the Act of Union. He saw this as being not just in the Catholic interests but in the interests of all Irish people, Catholic and Protestant. Indeed, the Catholics had been accused, with some justification in certain quarters, of supporting the Union, in the hope that it would bring Catholic Emancipation nearer. In an early speech to his supporters, O'Connell denies this:

> Let us show to Ireland, that we have nothing in view but her good; nothing in our hearts but the desire of mutual forgiveness, mutual toleration, and mutual affection; in fine, let every man who feels with me proclaim that if the alternative were offered him of Union, or the re-enactment of the whole

penal code in all its pristine horrors, that he would prefer without hesitation the latter, as the lesser and more sufferable evil; that he would rather confide in the justice of his brethren, the Protestants, who have already liberated him, than lay his country at the feet of foreigners.[19]

These sentiments were echoed by MacHale, if in a less dramatic way. He was at pains to stress that, though he wanted repeal passionately, he did not strive for Catholic ascendancy on the ruins of the disestablished Protestant Church. He wanted the two denominations to exist side by side, with each free to educate their children in the way they wished and to develop the political life of the country. During this period, MacHale's distrust of the British Government was continually confirmed. He felt that there should be no alliance with either Whigs or Tories, as either government wanted to decatholicise and denationalise the Irish Celts. They wanted control of the Irish clergy and the hierarchy and would seek to divide both clergy and Irish people. Bernard O'Reilly says of MacHale at this time that his misfortune

was to be in advance of his contemporaries, to see higher, clearer, farther in religious as well as in political matters, than the churchmen or statesmen who surrounded him, than Daniel O'Connell himself, than Archbishop Murray, than Cardinal Wiseman.

Notes

1   Quoted in Bernard O'Reilly, *Life and Times of John MacHale* (1890), I, p. 289.
2   Henry Seddall, *Edward Nangle: The Apostle of Achill* (1884), p. 38.
3   Ibid., p. 57.
4   John MacHale, *Letters* (1847), LXXVI, p. 375.
5   O'Reilly, op. cit., I, p. 305.
6   Ibid., pp.319–20.
7   Pádraic Ó Tuairisg, *Árd-dheoise Thuama agus Cartlann Choláiste na nGael sa Róimh sa naoú haois déag*, unpublished thesis, Tuam archives, p. 140.
8   Ibid., p. 149.

9   O'Reilly, op. cit., I, p. 400.
10   Jane Whately, *Life and Correspondence of Richard Whateley* (1866), p. 146.
11   Bernard O'Reilly, op.cit., I, pp. 424–5.
12   Quoted in Desmond McGuire, *History of Ireland* (1987), p. 109.
13   Llewellyn Woodward, *The Age of Reform 1815–1870* (1938), p. 346.
14   Ibid.
15   Desmond McGuire, op. cit., p. 108.
16   O'Reilly, op. cit., from MacHale MSS, 26 May 1837, I, pp. 484–5.
17   Ibid., 31 May 1837, p. 486.
18   Woodward, op. cit., pp. 347–8
19   Denis Gwynn, *Daniel O'Connell: The Irish Liberator* (1947), p. 85.

7

THE FIGHT FOR THE REPEAL OF THE UNION

'The fate of Catholic Ireland is now in your hands.'
(Daniel O'Connell)

DESPITE ARCHBISHOP MACHALE'S differences with Daniel O'Connell during the Whig ministries, he remained O'Connell's most influential and loyal supporter. O'Connell never failed to recognise this and in his correspondence with MacHale he is always respectful and warm.

The two men had very similar aims, in that they wanted the re-establishment of the Irish legislature, but at no time wanted to separate Ireland entirely from Britain. They both assumed that the destinies of the two nations lay together and both were entirely loyal to the Crown. Indeed, O'Connell was often mocked for a certain sentimentality when referring to the young Queen Victoria, and MacHale was always respectful and polite when speaking about her. O'Connell, although sometimes intemperate in his language, maintained a lifelong opposition to violence as a means to achieve political goals and, like MacHale, repeatedly condemned the secret societies.

In the late 1830s, in his attempts to prevent the fall of the Whigs, O'Connell suggested a 'Justice or Repeal Association', which became known as the 'Precursor Society'. He listed four demands – support by the State for the Catholic Church in Ireland, full corporate reform, the same political franchises as in England, and an adequate share of parliamentary representation for Ireland. O'Connell suggested that if these demands were not speedily granted, then he would resume his demand for the restoration of the Irish legislature.

Towards the end of the Whig ministry, in a letter to MacHale,

O'Connell pleads with him to join the Precursor Society. He says, rather dramatically, 'the fate of Catholic Ireland is now in your hands'.[1] Again in April 1840 he writes to MacHale 'in the strong wish to obtain the aid of your giant mind and national influence'. O'Connell declares rather ruefully, 'In this I have not been very successful. I got from you much excellent and very warm advice, but active co-operation you thought it fit not to give me.'

O'Connell's attempts to gain concessions for Ireland from Russell in return for his support did not work, and it soon became clear to O'Connell that repeal was the only route to justice for Ireland, and to this end he founded the Repeal Association. MacHale had no interest in supporting either party in power but he believed strongly in the repeal of the Union and his help for O'Connell was now forthcoming. The first great Repeal meeting was held at Castlebar on 26 July 1840. On 13 August, a Repeal banquet was held in Tuam. A variety of people attended this banquet, the local gentry, Catholic and Protestant, and representatives of the middle classes and the peasantry. O'Connell spoke at the banquet and Lord Ffrench, in proposing a toast to the Archbishop's health, mentioned that O'Connell had given MacHale the title 'The shining luminary of the West'. He went on to say, 'This is the wise appointment of Providence, a Paul was raised among the apostles and a MacHale among the Prelates of Ireland.'[2] In MacHale's speech in support of repeal, their aim was not, he stated, to try a new and hazardous experiment. The Union itself was only forty years old and a 'raw and crude experiment'.[3]

Both Archbishop MacHale and Bishop Browne of Galway publicly joined the Repeal Association and they were soon followed by Bishops Cantwell, Blake, Foran, Higgins and Feeny. O'Connell's success in winning over the bishops was by no means complete. Many, though agreeing with repeal, refused to take an active part in the movement. Some refused to be committed and some, like Archbishop Murray, while supporting repeal theoretically, had a great fear of revolution. In a letter to his vicar-general Murray says: 'It appears to me as certain as that the sun is now in the firmament that repeal can never be carried without such a convulsion as the great majority of its present supporters could not contemplate without horror.'[4]

Egan of Kerry told O'Connell that 'many are deterred from joining the Repeal Association through fear of revolution'.[5] William Crolly, Archbishop of Armagh and Primate of Ireland, who had previously supported O'Connell in the Precursor movement, also feared the Repeal movement, and in a letter to Murray says, 'I hope I have succeeded in guarding my clergy against that desperate and dangerous infatuation', but despite this he felt that

> the late atrocious manifesto published by the English Protestants, the intolerant menaces of our Irish Conservatives and the indignation of the persecuted Catholics afford at present a favourable occasion for exciting the people of Ireland to call for a domestic parliament.[6]

The manifesto that Crolly referred to was the address issued by the Protestant Association at its meeting at Exeter Hall on 6 August 1841, in which it denounced

> the Popish priests as being in too many cases . . . political incendiaries who abuse the power which superstition has given them over the minds of their benighted flocks in order to incite them to the commission of any crimes which may further their own factious ends.[7]

Crolly and some of the clergy may have been influenced by the intervention of the Roman Curia, who requested Crolly to dissuade priests and bishops from participating in politics. Despite his own fears about repeal, Crolly defended his clergy to Rome, saying that he did not want to cause divisions between the clergy and the people, and 'the greatest prudence is necessary lest we offend a faithful people by an unexpected separation from them'.

The British Government had no diplomatic relations with the Pope, but a certain sympathy had grown up between them during the French Revolution, when they were united against a common enemy. There was thus a temptation for the British Government to seek papal help when dealing with the Irish Catholics. In 1839 Cardinal Giacomo Fransoni rebuked MacHale for his speeches at political banquets. MacHale replied that he had always urged obedience to religious and civil authorities and explained to Fransoni that toasts such as 'To the people, the source of all legitimate power' and 'civil and religious liberty for the whole world' had not the same Jacobin overtones that they had on the Continent.[8]

Despite Fransoni's rebuke, MacHale had supporters in Rome. One appeared to be Cardinal Luigi Lambruschini, the secretary of state for the Pope. Lambruschini was rather a surprising friend for MacHale, as he was very conservative and anti-liberal in outlook. Lord Clifford recounts how he and Lord Shrewsbury were unsuccessful in persuading Lambruschini that MacHale was a radical.[9] MacHale also seems to have been supported by the Pope, who had welcomed MacHale in 1832. Gregory XVI was now seventy-eight years old. He was well known for his anti-revolutionary ideas and for being an upholder of legitimacy in Europe. He had condemned Lamennais's liberal Catholicism and refused to support the Poles in their struggles against the Czar of Russia. Gregory had some knowledge of Irish affairs, having been Prefect of Propaganda, and in 1837 he was reported by Nicholson as saying that 'O'Connell only looks for equal laws and equal justice'.[10] Paul Cullen, the Rector of the Irish College in Rome, and Kirby, the Vice-Rector, had access to the Pope and kept him informed of Irish affairs, and they reported him as being generally sympathetic to their points of view.[11]

O'Connell was concerned about the presence in Rome of Lord Shrewsbury, an English Catholic nobleman and an anti-repealer. It was one of the grievances of the Irish at this time that many of the English Catholics who had gained much from the labours of O'Connell in achieving Catholic Emancipation had now abandoned him and the Irish. In a letter to Paul Cullen, O'Connell warned that Irish Catholics were very much alive to any interference with their temporal concerns 'which are legitimately within the province of the laity as well as the clergy'.[12] O'Connell outlined to Cullen a memorial that he would use if he found it necessary. In this he used all his powers as an advocate to try to persuade the Pope that the repeal of the Union was to the advantage of the Catholic Church. O'Connell's memorial proved to be unnecessary as, although Cullen was on his way to Ireland when O'Connell's letter arrived, Kirby took up the case for repeal with the Pope. Kirby in a letter to Cullen says that the Pope

> expressed in the kindest way the conviction of Mr O'Connell's virtues, and merits and especially his love for religion, and wisdom in guiding the poor oppressed people of Ireland thro' such difficulties without the violation of the laws of the land. . . . His whole discourse was that of one who by no means disapproved of the legitimate and peaceful struggle of Mr O'Connell, the Irish Bishops and Clergy in the assertion of the rights of their oppressed country by such means.[13]

When the Repeal movement was at its height, Cullen told Murray:

> The Pope does not wish to interfere with the Irish clergy at present. . . . He said that the clergymen who have taken part in it should recollect that they have to preach 'Jesum Christum et hunc crucifixum'. However, he added, 'I would not condemn them, as in certain occasions, it is necessary to be on the spot, and to know all the circumstances of the case before you can say whether the thing is right or wrong'. [14]

In 1841 Daniel O'Connell was sixty-six years of age. His career had been remarkable and not even his enemies could doubt his continual capacity for hard work and his tireless devotion to his country. For many years he had toured Ireland as an advocate, unable to rise to the heights of his profession, to become a Kings Counsel, on account of his religion, but managing to amass a fortune by taking on hundreds of small, badly paid cases. His fortune not only enabled him to provide well for his large family (his wife Mary, five sons and three daughters), but made possible his political career. After Catholic Emancipation, O'Connell could have returned to the bar and continued in a more leisurely yet far more lucrative career. He chose instead to abandon the law courts for Parliament. To do this he was placed in the embarrassing situation of being totally dependent for his livelihood and that of his family on a 'tribute' paid as a subscription by the Irish.

O'Connell's fame spread much further than England and Ireland. He was known as 'The Liberator' not only in Ireland but throughout Europe and North America. Indeed, while his popularity might have waned from time to time in Britain and Ireland, there was more constant admiration for him as a liberal leader and reformer on the Continent. During the 1830s, owing to his support for the Whigs and the Lichfield House Compact and the meagre achievements for the Irish, O'Connell's popularity did diminish, but he remained the most popular man in Ireland and was seen as the only man who could effect change for Ireland and, in particular, the repeal of the Union.

During the late 1830s a group of younger men was rising in influence in Irish affairs. These were mostly upper-class and well educated. They were full of romantic ideals of nationhood and self-sacrifice. They gave themselves the title of 'Young Ireland', a name copied from Giuseppe Mazzini's 'Young Italy', a movement for the liberation and unification of Italy. They allied themselves with the revolutionary fervour of the Continent. This alienated them to some extent from the clergy and those Irish Catholics who had no truck with such thinkers as Voltaire and Rousseau.

The most famous of the Young Irelanders were Charles Gavan Duffy and Thomas Davis. They produced a journal entitled the *Nation*, which was the voice of their patriotic views and also of Irish culture and affairs generally. Duffy was from Ulster and Davis was a Protestant from County Cork. Duffy was the editor of the *Nation,* but Davis produced much of the writing. They brought forward a wide programme of national regeneration, including the revitalisation of the Irish language. They despised O'Connell as a procrastinator and a compromiser, particularly during the years of the Whig government. They were influenced by movements that never touched O'Connell and were impatient with his continual emphasis on the rule of law and the necessity for public order. Unlike O'Connell, they had not seen the terror and aftermath of rebellion in Ireland. They were also characterised by a hostility to England and wanted to be free 'even from the gratitude of the past'.[15] The Young Ireland movement was modern, cosmopolitan and secular. Despite their differences, however, and the fact that O'Connell referred to himself as 'Old Ireland', the two movements worked side by side for repeal. O'Connell had practical experience and the trust of the Irish people. They were to continue to disagree over the character that the repeal agitation was to take, but O'Connell insisted that meetings were orderly and that the people should not be incited to violence.

In September 1841 O'Connell's fears were realised when his old protagonist, Peel, formed his second ministry. Unlike Peel's first ministry, this was to run for five years and enact many reforming measures. His cabinet was a strong one and contained many talented ministers, five of whom would go on to become prime ministers. Peel himself was at the height of his powers and was acknowledged by all to be an extremely able and hard-working man. Gladstone later described him not only as the greatest man he had ever known, but also as 'the best man of business who was ever Prime Minister'. Peel had a warm, happy family life, but outside of this often appeared cold and reserved. He was the son of a rich Lancashire cotton-spinner and spoke with a slight Lancashire accent. Though aware of his great abilities, when mixing with the privileged, aristocratic Tories, he was very sensitive about his social position.

Peel's former experiences in Ireland and with O'Connell had not been good. In 1812, as a very young man of twenty-four, he went to Dublin as Chief Secretary for Ireland. The young O'Connell had already decided that the Irish people had no use for the young politician and he nicknamed him 'Orange-Peel'. In a speech to the Catholic Board, O'Connell described him as 'a raw youth squeezed out of the workings of I know not what factory in England . . . was sent over here before he got over the foppery of perfumed handkerchiefs and thin shoes'.[16] Peel read this description and it did not endear him to O'Connell. He realised that O'Connell was to be one of his most formidable opponents. The personal antagonism between the two men was an unfortunate beginning for the Peel ministry and ultimately for the cause of repeal.

Despite this antagonism, Peel had shown himself willing to listen and to change his mind if he felt, in all honesty, that it was right to do so. O'Connell hoped that he would be able to persuade Peel that the Union should be repealed. Peel was in a difficult position so far as Ireland was concerned, as he was the leader of a party that distrusted the Irish, were genuinely afraid of revolution and considered the defence of the Anglican Church a priority. Peel was also very slow to assimilate new ideas. Bagehot in his *Biographical Studies* says of Peel that he was converted to an idea only when the average person was converted and that he would have nothing to do with new ideas 'as long as they remained the property of first-class intellects, as long as they were confined to philanthropists or speculators'.[17] Peel appeared to want to help and conciliate the Irish but was determined to maintain the Union.

Meanwhile, the Repeal movement in Ireland was gaining momentum. Archbishop MacHale threw himself wholeheartedly into the movement. He believed that if the Irish were united in their wish for repeal and were not side-tracked by issues of party politics, they would be successful. He also believed that repeal of the Act of Union was the only way forward for Ireland. He realised that the English politicians, however sympathetic they might be, did not understand the nature of the Irish problems. They saw agricultural problems, landlord problems, industrial problems, religious problems, as comparable with the same problems in England. The politicians saw no virtue in travelling round Ireland, and if they did visit Ireland most of the English ventured no further than Dublin. Thus, Irish difficulties were not going to be solved by good will, even where it existed.

After the downfall of the Whigs, despite their opposition to the Tories, many Irish people, including MacHale, felt that it was an opportunity for O'Connell and his followers to form an independent group instead of sitting with the Whigs.

During the elections of 1841 Archbishop MacHale was active at the hustings in the west. Throughout his life MacHale had great respect for the workings of the British constitutional system. He recognised its strengths and virtues and so found its inability to offer justice to Ireland all the more frustrating. The cause was halted slightly by the death of Sir Wilfred Brabazon, a Protestant gentleman of Mayo who was an enthusiastic repealer. MacHale suggested Mark Blake for the seat. At the hustings MacHale denounced the Tories, saying that many of them had changed their name to Conservative but they were the same underneath, they wanted to 'conserve' oppression. MacHale was also very concerned about the Irish practice of 'place-hunting':

> Let all who give their support to our candidates leave these free to vote in Parliament as their consciences and honour dictate; let no supporter of theirs seek to bind and embarrass them by exacting promises of situation for himself or others. Let no man help to keep up or create a profligate and oppressive patronage through the establishment of new offices, destined to aid the minister in corrupting the servants of the people. . . . The Catholic freeholders are the tenants of the landlord; they are also the flock of the pastor; but they are not freeholders of either. Their freehold is their own given them by the constitution, in trust for the community to be exercised in accordance with the dictates of conscience. . . .
>
> One word to those who lived on Protestant ascendancy; your patent of monopoly is expired. The tide which bore forward the vessel of your political fortunes has receded, never to return. But lo! another tide is rising. It is the prosperity of a nation blessed with a legislature of its own. Do not allow this tide to ebb forever. Fit up and refloat your stranded vessel. Let it float alongside the Catholic bark. They are sister ships and should ride the waves together.[18]

During the early 1840s MacHale attended many public meetings and banquets and made many speeches in favour of repeal.

> We are told that the Union, which before was loose and precarious, has irrevocably been cemented by steam and railroads.
>
> I cannot understand what the laws of motion have to do with those of mind, or the moral responsibilities of legislature. . . . Because an Irish member of Parliament can now travel to London in the third of the time once taken by the journey, does it follow that Ireland should be content with a third of the Representatives to which she is entitled? . . . Improve the land and water passage as much as you can, bring out the latent

power of steam till you almost annihilate time and space, – the respective interests of both countries, and the necessity of providing for them by home legislation, will continue the same as before.[19]

At this time, Mayo had two representatives in Parliament for 270,000 people, whereas Wales had fourteen for a similar population.

The *Nation,* the journal of the Young Ireland movement, was launched in 1842. It quickly became the most widely read journal in Ireland and was circulated through the Repeal rooms – where members of the Repeal Association met – in provincial towns. Its enthusiasm and optimism were infectious and filled the people with hope. Bernard O'Reilly says that he was a young man, newly ordained, when the first number of the *Nation* reached him in Quebec. He says, 'How can he ever forget the delightful sense of near triumph for Irish nationality, which filled his soul and those of young and old around him, who, on the shores of the St Lawrence, still clung to their fondly cherished hopes of seeing Ireland a nation!' He also says 'God knows, so far at least as he can now remember, that never once was the hope of a near repeal of the Legislative Union mixed up with the idea of a total separation from Great Britain'.

During this period MacHale not only made use of the meetings and banquets for his speeches, but also of the newspapers. A letter addressed by him to O'Connell was published in the *Freeman's Journal,* the *Pilot* and the *Nation.* The editor of the *Nation* writes:

It is impossible to overrate the importance of the communication from Dr MacHale which appears in this day's *Nation* and which was read at the weekly meeting of the Repeal Association. It breathes the spirit of the most determined nationality. But the tone, although firm and unshrinking, is characterized by the toleration which is so appropriate to the sacred character and station of the writer.[20]

In the letter, MacHale presents O'Connell with money for the enrolment of 101 more priests in the Repeal Association. He speaks with optimism about 'the speedy triumph' of repeal and about how 'public opinion is propelling it forward'. He says to O'Connell, 'For this we are mainly indebted to your wise determination to stay in Ireland to guide your confiding countrymen in this loyal and peaceful movement.' He goes on to say

> There is only one vain fear which I am anxious to dissipate: it is the unhallowed phantom of 'Ascendancy' which the enemies of Ireland proclaim to be our only aim. Never was there entertained a more groundless apprehension. . . . The most indulgent exercise of charity toward those of different persuasions is compatible with the strictest and most scrupulous adherence to one's religious creed.
>
> It is not in a material indifference for the solemn sanctions of religion, nor in any unprincipled compromise of conflicting creeds, but in a faithful attachment to our conscientious convictions, and in practical kindness to those differing from us, that the best guarantee of toleration is to be found.
>
> Were the Repeal of the Union to take place tomorrow, and any enactment of wrong threatened as a consequence, I should be among the first to raise my humble voice against any invasion of the inviolable life-interest of any class; and I should advocate those measures of public policy which, irrespective of the ascendancy of any party, would mete out impartial justice to all Irishmen.[21]

By 1843 many people thought that the repeal of the Union was inevitable. Public opinion, especially in Ireland, was growing in its favour. O'Connell felt that it was only a matter of time and that Peel would eventually be convinced and would change his mind as he did on Catholic Emancipation. Other people were changing their minds. One of the most influential of these was Frederick Lucas. Lucas was an Englishman and a convert to Catholicism who became the editor of the *Tablet*. At first he was strongly opposed to repeal and argued vigorously against it in the press. Lucas's aim was to rouse the English people to treat Ireland with justice and humanity and so remove the causes for repeal. By 1843 he had changed his mind and had joined the Repeal movement. All over Ireland – Tara, Maryborough, Lismore, and in many other places – there were 'monster meetings', many of them attended by O'Connell and MacHale. The movement was gathering momentum. Even the Tory editor of the *Morning Herald* said that repeal was 'inevitable'. Archbishop MacHale was asked to speak at places all over Ireland. He did go to Skibbereen and Waterford but did not go to Dublin or Armagh as he did not want to be an embarrassment for the archbishops of those areas, but mostly he toured the west, and it was in the west that the needs of Ireland were most starkly apparent. He spoke at a monster meeting at Clifden in Connemara. He told the people there that they must have respect for the law but they must demand good laws. He said that the wilds of Canada were better known to their rulers than Connemara.

> To open the internal channels of communication in that distant province, to intersect it with roads and canals, hundreds and thousands of British capital, much of which has been wrung from Ireland, have been expended. What, during its long connection with Ireland, has been the amount spent by Great Britain in improving this province? . . . Nature has generously furnished Ireland with harbours capacious enough to invite the commerce of the world. But these are allowed to lie there neglected and abandoned, as if they belonged to a country but just discovered![22]

The Peel government could not ignore these enormous gatherings. In 1843 many European countries had suffered revolutions in recent memory. Many countries were simmering in preparation for further outbreaks. O'Connell took care never to incite violence. His meetings were orderly and disciplined. He was helped in this by a strong temperance movement that was at this time sweeping through Ireland. Started by a Catholic priest named Father Mathew, the movement was very successful and for a time almost eradicated drunkenness in certain areas. MacHale does not seem to have had much time for Father Mathew, however. The Archbishop did not agree with taking the pledge for life, and he objected to Fr Matthew travelling from diocese to diocese to address meetings, but his strongest objection was that Fr Matthew was determined not to become involved in politics and his temperance bands were pro-union. But there was no doubting Fr Matthew's success. Indeed, despite, or perhaps because of, the orderly nature of the gatherings, they demanded attention and compelled people from all over Europe to discuss the question of repeal. Peel, however, was determined to preserve the Union. He passed an arms act, drafted troops to Ireland, then made a warning speech that he would never concede repeal and would put down rebellion. In October 1843, O'Connell called a mass meeting at Clontarf. The meeting was immediately forbidden by the Government. O'Connell had to choose between insurrection and surrender. He surrendered. He called the meeting off and told his followers to obey orders. There was no rioting. The Government had won. To press the point home, O'Connell was arrested and, in April 1844, was tried before a packed jury on a faulty indictment, convicted and sentenced to a term of imprisonment in Richmond prison. The Repeal movement was over.

Notes

1   W. J. Fitzpatrick, *Correspondence of Daniel O'Connell: The Liberator* (1888), September 1838.
2   Bernard O'Reilly, *The Life and Times of John MacHale* (1890), I, p. 503.
3   Ibid.
4   Murray to Hamilton, 3 October 1840, Murray Papers, quoted in Donal A. Kerr, *Peel, Priests and Politics 1841–1846* (1982), p. 77.
5   Donal A. Kerr, op. cit., pp. 76–7, Egan to O'Connell, 28 September 1840, O'Connell Papers.
6   Donal A. Kerr, op. cit., p. 88, Crolly to Murray, 22 August 1841, Murray Papers.
7   *The Times,* 7 August 1841.
8   MacHale to Fransoni, 25 March 1839, cited in Broderick, *The Holy See* (1851), pp. 105–6.
9   Donal A. Kerr, op. cit., p. 94, Nicholson to Hamilton, Hamilton Papers, September 1839.
10 Ibid., 1 February 1837.
11 Peadar MacSuibhne, *Paul Cullen and his Contemporaries,* I, p. 246.

12 Quoted by Donal Kerr, op. cit., O'Connell to Cullen, 9 May 1842, Cullen Papers.

13 Kirby to Cullen, 16 June 1842, cited in Broderick, *The Holy See* (1851), p. 167.

14 Donal A. Kerr, op. cit., p. 97, Cullen to Murray, 11 June 1843, Murray Papers.

15 Llewellyn Woodward, *The Age of Reform* (1938), p. 349.

16 Denis Gwynn, *Daniel O'Connell: The Irish Liberator* (1947), p. 110.

17 Walter Bagehot, *Biographical Studies* (1881), p. 6.

18 Bernard O'Reilly, op. cit., I, pp. 519–20.

19 Ibid.

20 *Nation,* 16 May 1843.

21 Ibid.

22 Bernard O'Reilly, op. cit., I, pp. 538–9.

8

PEEL'S ATTEMPTS AT CONCILIATION

'A starving population, an absentee aristocracy, and an alien Church, and in addition, the weakest executive in the world. That was the Irish question.' (Benjamin Disraeli)

WITH THE IMPRISONMENT of O'Connell in 1844, the repeal movement lost its momentum. Despite O'Connell's successful appeal against his sentence, it was clear that the movement for repeal could not be renewed and that reform in Ireland must take a different route. With the end of repeal came the end of O'Connell's career. He was now seventy years old, and years of intense activity and the loss of his beloved wife had taken its toll. His trial and imprisonment finally broke him and he emerged in 1844 as a sick man. His emergence from prison was triumphant and O'Connell still held the hearts of the Irish people, but his relationships with the emerging 'Young Ireland' party were increasingly strained. They disliked his mob oratory and his assumption of authority and they detested his son, John, who took over the Repeal movement while O'Connell was in England.

O'Connell did try to rescue something from the ashes of Repeal by a suggestion of some kind of federalism. This had some support, even from the Orangemen, but it was denounced as unpatriotic by the Young Irelanders and surrounded by confusion and vacillation and eventually came to nothing.

The Repeal movement had, however, alerted the peoples of Europe and America to the plight of Ireland, and on the demise of O'Connell there was much sympathy from those quarters. There was also sympathy from the Whigs and Liberals, who recognised the unfairness of his trial. Peel himself, having done away with repeal, was anxious to conciliate Ireland.

He urged Sir James Graham, the Home Secretary, to 'look out' for suitable Catholics for office. 'We must discard that favourite doctrine of Dublin Castle – you cannot conciliate your enemies, therefore give everything to the most zealous of your friends.'[1] Graham joined Peel in pressing De Grey, the Lord Lieutenant, to appoint Catholics, but De Grey remained convinced that 'Conciliation is a chimera'.[2] Peel had almost to force the appointment of John Howley, a Catholic, as third sergeant-at-law, insisting that 'considerations of policy and also of justice, demand a liberal and indulgent estimate of the claims on the favour of the Crown of such Roman Catholics as abstain from political agitation'. This was a difficult demand on the Protestants of Dublin, who had been accustomed to seeing themselves as a superior class who had a monopoly on official appointments.

Lord John Russell began a series of debates on Ireland with a forceful speech that took for its theme 'Ireland is occupied not governed'.[3] The Whig leader and writer, Lord Macauley, accused the Tories of using Ireland for opposition purposes during the Whig ministry and fomenting religious hatred. The young politician Benjamin Disraeli gave a brilliant speech describing the problems of the English statesmen in understanding the Irish problem:

> One says it was a physical question; another, a spiritual. Now it is the absence of the aristocracy, then the absence of railroads. It was the Pope one day, potatoes the next.

Then he gave his own analysis:

> A starving population, an absentee aristocracy, and an alien Church, and in addition, the weakest executive in the world. That was the Irish question.[4]

Although Russell's motion in Parliament was defeated, it marked an important turning point. It was now accepted both inside and outside Parliament that something must be done for Ireland.

Peel wanted to make concessions but realised only too well the difficulties involved. In 1843 he had appointed a commission under the chairmanship of Lord Devon to study Irish agrarian questions. In

February 1844 he circulated to the Cabinet a memorandum on the fundamental issues of Irish reform, prefixing to it his own commitment to 'the great principle of maintaining intact the Established Church'. In advising concessions, he used the argument that, in the event of war, the position that they held towards Ireland would be important. He also stressed that it was essential to detach 'from the ranks of those who cannot be reclaimed or conciliated, all those who are not yet committed to violent counsels, and are friendly to the connection between the two countries'. After a week of debate, Peel once again stressed the need to detach 'from the ranks of Repeal, agitation, and disaffection a considerable portion of the respectable and influential Roman Catholic population'. Peel's reform programme was therefore geared in great part towards the Catholic clergy. He wanted to separate the clergy and the Catholic Church from political agitation.

To achieve his aims Peel passed three measures – the Charitable Bequests Act, an increased grant to the College of Maynooth and the setting up of university colleges in the north, west and south of Ireland. These measures were all intensely controversial and provoked angry responses on both sides of the Irish sea.

In Parliament Peel had laid stress on the timing of his reforms. He justified his conversion to reform on the grounds that he had maintained law and order by his victory over O'Connell and the concessions were granted from a position of strength, not from fear of agitation. One of the weaknesses of Peel's measures lay in the fact that, as often happened, the English Prime Minister had not looked at the situation from the Irish point of view. Their beloved leader, 'The Liberator', had been humiliated and imprisoned after an unfair trial. Their hopes of repeal and the mounting optimism had been dashed. The atmosphere was dispirited and not a favourable one for the grateful acceptance of concessions.

The Charitable Bequests Act sought to facilitate the endowment of the Catholic Church. In penal times the law did not allow the Catholic Church to receive charitable bequests, but in fact this law had fallen into disuse even before Emancipation, and the total amount of money bequeathed by the Catholics of Ireland for religious and charitable purposes was great.

By the new system, money was allowed to be bequeathed to bishops and priests but not to institutions, and on their death the money was to go to their heirs and not their successors in the ministry.

Peel's Charitable Bequests Act was fairly well-intentioned, but like other attempts at reform in Ireland, it was the usual half-hearted attempt to redeem an injustice without incurring the suspicion of too much partiality to the Catholics.[5]

An act of 1800 passed by the Irish Parliament established a board of commissioners to deal with charitable donations made in wills. This board had the power of 'cy-pres'; they had the discretionary power of judging certain bequests as inexpedient. No Catholic was allowed to sit on the board and the Church felt that they had a grievance, particularly when money was left to a Catholic charity. Peel's Charitable Bequests Act of 1844 was his reply to the complaint. The act did away with the old board, set up a new one of thirteen commissioners, of which three were judges and five were Catholics. The functions of the board were similar to those of the old board, with the notable exception that the much criticized 'cy-pres' powers were withheld from it. Catholic Emancipation had not removed the ban on religious orders and a proviso was laid down that the bill could not be constructed as repealing the sections of the 1829 Relief Act, which made bequests to religious orders illegal. The act also made invalid pious or charitable bequests of lands, if made by will or deed within three months of the testator's death. These should have been registered within three months of execution. The bill was an improvement from the Catholic point of view, as it included Catholics as commissioners and eliminated cy-pres. The main complaint from Catholic members of Parliament was one of lack of consultation. As Sheil pointed out:

> No reason has been offered for not consulting a single Roman Catholic Prelate upon a bill which related to property held for ecclesiastical purposes.[6]

The Government was prepared to accept amendments. The term 'minister' was abandoned, as Catholics disliked its Calvinistic overtones, and Clause 15 now referred to beneficiaries as 'any archbishop or bishop or other person in Holy Orders of the Church of Rome'. Although the territorial titles were left out, the clause was a real recognition of the bishop's spiritual functions. This limited recognition was as far as Peel and Graham would go, while maintaining the position of the Established Church.

O'Connell had drawn up another bill making a priest or bishop a 'corporation', which put the Catholic priests on the same footing as their Anglican counterparts, but it was left in abeyance when he was in prison. He denounced Peel's bill, saying it was a means of plundering the religious orders. MacHale agreed and said no Catholic should sit on the board. Frederick Lucas of the *Tablet* took up the cause, saying that if all the bishops refused to sit on the board the bill would become 'a dead letter'.

In November there was a meeting of the Catholic bishops to discuss the matter. All accepted MacHale's view, apart from Murray and Crolly, two most important archbishops. In the end it was decided that the matter be left to the decision of the individuals concerned.

MacHale wrote to Rome. He was furious when Murray and Crolly accepted seats on the board. The other Catholics were Anthony Blake, Sir P. Bellew and Dr Kennedy, the Bishop of Killaloe. Dr Kennedy felt uncomfortable on the board and withdrew, and Dr Denvir, the Bishop of Down and Connor, took his place.

In the Advent of 1844, both Archbishop MacHale and Archbishop Murray set forth their views on the Charitable Bequests Act in their pastoral letters. MacHale said that the act prevented any Catholic, on his death-bed, from bequeathing as much as one acre of land to charity, although he might bequeath all he wished to any profane or profligate purpose. It rendered bequests to religious orders null and void and made the commissioners – including the Catholic members – the legal executioners of the penal laws against them. MacHale also alleged that the Government was attempting, with some success, to detach some of the bishops from their brethren and make them dependent on the Crown. As a result, the hitherto united hierarchy was becoming disjointed, weak and deformed – an object of sorrow to the faithful but of triumphant derision . . . to the inveterate foes of Catholic Ireland.[7]

In a letter to Heytesbury, Graham said that he rejoiced 'on the advantage of the position which we have . . . won, when the heads of the Church, whose boasted strength is unity . . . break out into unseemly conflict'.

Shortly before Christmas, Archbishop Murray, in a pastoral letter to the Catholics of Dublin, replied indirectly to MacHale and his other critics. He praised O'Connell's bill as 'a perfect measure', of which the present act was an imperfect substitute, but although imperfect, he said the new act did bring substantial benefits to Catholic charities.

Peel, pleased with his success in the Charitable Bequests Act, proceeded further in his attempts to conciliate Ireland and in particular the Irish clergy. His next project was an increase in the annual grant to the seminary of Maynooth. The Maynooth grant had always been contentious, particularly as many deplored the fact that when the original grant was given in 1795, adequate provision was not made for State control. When Peel proposed raising the annual grant from £9,000 to £26,000 he was met with a storm of protest:

It is not Liberalism but Romanism which Peel is forcing on the nation. . . . It is not merely Popery; that is unpopular enough in England, especially Irish Popery; but it is Maynooth. It is a name and a thing above all others odious and suspicious to England.[8]

Edward Bickersteth went further:

paying money to undermine the Throne as much as if it had been spent in buying the barrels of gunpowder which were used by Guy Fawkes.

At this time in England there was much anti-Catholic feeling. The 'Oxford movement' was viewed with a great deal of suspicion as 'creeping Romanism'. Lord John Russell in a letter to the Bishop of Durham denounced 'Popery within and Popery without the Church' (of England).

Maynooth itself became a focal point of criticism. Many Protestants were convinced that Catholics were taught that the Pope could depose the monarch and that Catholics did not have to keep faith with oaths with heretics. Maynooth was also criticised as it was thought that since the students there were given a free education they would be from the dregs of society. Maria Edgeworth complained that the priests educated at Maynooth were 'so vulgar that no gentleman can, let him wish it ever so much, keep company with them'. Eugene O'Beirne, who had been expelled from Maynooth and had subsequently conformed to the Established Church, said that to secure training on the Continent it was necessary to muster about £100. For Maynooth, however:

> The rudest ploughboy, if he have but managed to obtain the interest of his parish priest, is infallibly certain of having the way smoothed for him. . . . The majority of Maynooth students for twenty years past, have been composed from the lowest grades of society.

De Grey made a similar criticism:

> They are born in poverty and want, they do not feel the misery of dirt and poor fare during their period of education. . . . An institution on a better footing in England . . . would never run the risk of being swamped with the sons of day labourers (an old woman at my gate earning a few shillings a week has her son a Maynooth priest).[9]

MacHale said he rejoiced in the humble character of the Maynooth priest. There was also much discussion about the contrast between the Maynooth-trained priests and those who were educated on the Continent. It was thought that those educated abroad were more socially polished and were less likely to cause trouble than the more confident Irish-trained priests. Archbishop MacHale added weight to this argument, as he was the first Irish bishop to be wholly trained in Ireland.

Maynooth was certainly in need of money. Appeals for an increase in the grant had been made from time to time. In 1823, the Maynooth president, Dr Crotty, had told Eneas MacDonnell, the London agent for the Irish Catholics, of Maynooth's financial difficulties and asked him to try to get the grant increased. In 1825 O'Connell had complained about a 'miserable penury' in the way Maynooth was treated, and in 1835 Lord Cloncurry had appealed to Melbourne for an increase in the grant. In the later 1830s the problem reached critical proportions. The college had drastically to reduce the number of free places and by 1841 had accumulated a debt of £4,600. At a meeting of the Irish bishops in November 1841, a motion was passed to seek aid from the Government. The motion was proposed by Dr MacHale and seconded by Dr Higgins.

The conditions at Maynooth were well known to the Government from the yearly visitations. Students were often sharing a room between four and sometimes between six. Indeed, after the increase in the grant, Clarendon was to describe the conditions:

> I saw the rooms. . . . They have three or four beds in them and are wretched comfortless and ill-ventilated, such as no one in England would ask a servant to sleep in for the night. . . . The single-bedded rooms are not much larger or better than those at Pentonville prison.

In his negotiations for the increase in the Maynooth grant, Peel did not make the same mistake of non-consultation that he made with the Bequests bill. A line of communication had been opened with an influential section of Irish Catholics. One of the most prominent of these was Anthony Blake, a leading Catholic layman who was on the Board of Government Commissioners for Primary Education. He was often criticised by MacHale as not being a good representative of the Irish Catholics as he was known to be rather luke-warm in religious matters. He was, however, a friend of Archbishop Murray and seemed to have played an important part in his negotiations with the Home Secretary, Sir James Graham, over the Maynooth grant. Virtually all the points requested by Blake were accepted and despite much discussion the bill made no serious attempt to gain control over the college.

In a letter from Heytesbury to Graham in November 1844 Heytesbury describes a meeting they had had with the bishops. Heytesbury had suggested changes concerning the trustees and visitors. When Murray agreed:

> . . . up started John of Tuam and declared that he would consent to no alteration whatever and in saying so, he spoke in the names of the bishops assembled in convocation.

Heytesbury had obviously enjoyed what he described as an 'amusing altercation' between the bishops.

Although he had the support of Graham and Heytesbury, Peel's measure was not a popular one within his own ranks. In January 1845 the young W. E. Gladstone resigned as President of the Board of Trade. Gladstone's reasons for resigning were not very clear, even to his own colleagues. He supported the grant to Maynooth but felt that the views expressed in a book he had written on Church and State made it impossible for him to vote for the measure or be a member of the Government. This created problems for Peel; in a letter to Lord Heytesbury, Graham says:

> It is true that Gladstone's scruples are placed by him not so much on the ground of political misgivings or religious qualms, as of written pledges . . . but still the general impression would be that he is a martyr to the Protestant cause.

When Peel finally did introduce his measure, the first protests, as expected, came from the ultra-Protestant press. The *Record* called for 'Resistance to the threat of Popery'. It urged Protestants to petition ceaselessly. On 6 February the Dublin branch of the *Record* deplored that 'idolatry was to be taught at a large increase of expense to the public purse'. At Exeter Hall, on 25 February, the Protestant Association set up a standing committee to organise opposition.

Many members of the Established Church, even those like Archdeacon William Wilberforce who regarded the measure as necessary, thought that it marked the beginning of the end of the special relationship between the State and the Established Church. He noted that Church and State were 'at the fag end of an old alliance'.[10] An anti-Maynooth committee had been set up at the London Coffee House in Ludgate Street and from there it urged Protestants of all denominations to stir up 'Protestant feeling and principle'. This committee contained Presbyterians, Congregationalists and Wesleyans, as well as Anglicans. Opposition to the Maynooth grant did not only spring from anti-Catholic feeling. The leaders of the Anti-Corn Law League were split. Cobden praised the grant as an educational measure, whereas Bright opposed it and appealed to Catholics to resist this 'hush money'. He said that the aim of the bill was to make their clergy 'as tame as the clergy of Suffolk and Dorsetshire'. Some members of Parliament opposed the measure as they disagreed with all form of endowment of religion. Outside the House of Commons the Duke of Newcastle called on all members of the 'almost persecuted' Church of England to resist this sinful endowment of a rebellious Popish seminary and to 'petition, petition, petition'.

The leaders of Irish Presbyterianism supported the grant. Henry Cooke, although opposed to the principle of aiding the dissemination of Popery, believed that 'if the thing is to be done it is not only as well to do it generously but it is better.' His rival, the Unitarian Henry Montgomery, sending on a petition from the Remonstrant Synod in favour of the bill, declared that:

We are shocked at the possibility of being identified for a moment with those degenerate Presbyterians who receive nearly £40,000 every year from the public purse for their own half million adherents and would withhold the mere trifle of £26,000 from seven millions of Catholics.

Some Presbyterians did oppose the grant, but the main opposition came from the Established Church and the Wesleyans. A colourful gathering of the anti-Maynooth campaign has been described, where various denominations joined together in a show of solidarity and

> Bands of Orangemen ranged round the room . . . with orange sashes over their shoulders, broad orange ribbons tied on sticks and held up in different parts of the room.

Despite the vehement opposition, Peel stuck to the measure and it was eventually passed. Although it was passed to conciliate the Catholics and as a result of requests from the bishops, it was at first received with suspicion. Laurence Renehan, Maynooth's bursar, wrote to Cullen in Rome: 'As yet we have no reason to dread any inconvenient interference with our government or internal arrangements of education or discipline'. But as the bill progressed, the nationalist newspapers expressed themselves as favourable to the bill. Even MacHale publicly praised the bill and Murray went to Dublin Castle to express his gratitude. However, the most useful gratitude came from Maynooth itself, and Peel was able to read to the House of Commons a letter signed by the entire Maynooth staff:

> The undersigned beg leave most respectfully to express our deep sense of gratitude for the very liberal provisions which you, as head of the government, have proposed for the education of the Roman Catholic clergy, and still more for the kind and gracious manner in which you have recommended the measure to the friendly consideration of the House.[11]

O'Connell also praised the bill. He wrote 'the ministry appear to be really sincere in their determination to do something for Ireland'. He hoped that the Government would build on the good will and do something for the Irish peasants. The evidence of the Devon Commission showed the terrible condition of the poorer peasants and gave urgency to O'Connell's pleas for reform.

During the repeal controversy and again during the discussions surrounding the Charitable Bequests Act, Peel and his Government tried to separate the Irish Catholic clergy from political agitation. One of the ways they used was trying to gain influence in Rome.

They used the services of an English Catholic, Charles Petre. The Roman cardinals did not initially trust the intentions of the British Government in their attempts to conciliate the Catholic clergy. They feared that the motive was to destroy the independence of the Irish Church. At the same time they did not want to alienate England, as she could do great harm to the Catholics in her colonies. Peel's Government continued to request that Rome denounce the political activities of the Irish bishops and clergy. They were encouraged by the support of Archbishop Crolly and Archbishop Murray, as well as the influential Catholic layman, Anthony Blake. They felt that they had achieved some success when Anthony Blake reported to Heytesbury that Archbishop Crolly had received a letter from Cardinal Fransoni criticising the political activities of bishops. Heytesbury wrote to Graham:

> It is supposed it [the letter] will induce many who were wavering, to abandon John of Tuam, and to rally round those of a moderate way of thinking.

It caused Heytesbury some surprise when the bishops accepted the document with 'respect, obedience and veneration' and pledged themselves 'to carry the spirit thereof into effect'. This motion was proposed and seconded by Browne and MacNally, two of the most outspoken supporters of Repeal. Browne then went with MacHale to speak at a Repeal banquet in Limerick. In a letter to Cullen, MacHale wrote of Cardinal Fransoni's letter:

> It was a private letter by the Cardinal-Prefect to the Primate containing vague complaints of some ecclesiastics and one or two bishops about intemperate speeches. . . . On this occasion it was evidently procured, nay extorted I am sure, by a malicious and calumniating importunity for the purpose of awing the prelates. . . . The vague document has reference to neither time, place or person.

The controversy was to reach a climax in the beginning of 1845 when fears of collusion between the Vatican and Westminster and of

'Goblin Concordats' (an agreement between the Church and the British Government that was secret and harmful to the Catholic Church in Ireland) resulted in the polarising of opinion and was not helpful to Peel's aims. The Roman Curia, alarmed at the charges of secret agents and concordats, became very cautious in their dealings with the Government.

Notes

1   Charles Stuart Parker, *Sir Robert Peel, from his private papers* (1899), Peel to Graham, 16 June 1843, III, pp. 53–4.
2.   Ibid., De Grey to Peel, 18 August 1843, p. 56.
3   Hansard, LXXII 684, 13 February 1844.
4   Ibid., 1016, 16 Feb.
5   Nuala Costello, *John MacHale* (1939), p. 57–8.
6   Hansard, 1528, 29 July 1844.
7   *Nation*, 14 December 1844.
8   *The Times*, 17 April 1845.
9   Kerr, op. cit. pp. 240–41. De Grey to Graham, 27 February 1844.
10   Kerr, op. cit., p. 271.
11   Hansard, LXXIXI 034, 18 April 1845.

9

THE GODLESS COLLEGES

'Wonder is not religion, or we should be worshipping railroads.' (John Henry Newman)

IN THE SPRING of 1845, Peel introduced his bill for a system of higher education in Ireland. He hoped that the bill would be well received, particularly by the Irish Catholics, but as with the Bequests bill, this did not happen.

To modern minds used to secular university education, the bill would appear sensible enough, and the opposition of MacHale and the majority of the Irish bishops unreasonable. Peel was aware of the lack of university provision for Catholics and Dissenters in Ireland. Trinity College, Dublin, though offering a high standard of education, was, like Oxford and Cambridge, only really available to members of the Established Church. Peel proposed to set up three university colleges, one in Belfast, one in Cork and one in the west that would offer a purely secular education.

Peel's measure was met with a furore from all denominations. On the continent of Europe the French Revolution had brought in much secularism, particularly in education, but in Britain and Ireland education was still firmly rooted in religion, and the experiences on the Continent only served to strengthen opinion that this must remain so.

In March 1834 John Henry Newman, then a young man at Oxford, wrote to the *British Magazine* to protest against a bill to admit Dissenters to the universities. It proposed to remove the obligation to subscribe to the thirty-nine articles, which was compulsory at Oxford on matriculating, and at Cambridge on taking a degree. Newman says:

113

The mere presence of Dissenters in a Collegiate University was objectionable anyway: assuming that the tutorial system had a pastoral dimension, would it not be necessary for 'dissenting pupils' to have 'dissenting tutors'? It was true that they might be improved by being educated by tutors the ethos of whose religion was founded on reverence rather than boldness and self-will, but will not the church pupils, nay the tutors themselves be injured?[1]

Newman remarked that the Dissenters would certainly 'be improved in the way of gentlemanly feeling, modesty and refinement' but there would be a danger of Anglicans lapsing into 'a mongrel faith, from the contact of laxer principles'. Later that year, after the bill had been thrown out by the House of Lords, Newman was again in 'great anxiety' as the heads of the colleges were proposing to relax the religious tests. Newman wrote:

But so fearful is the misery to the Church generally, and so shocking the thought that Oxford should be the place desecrated, that one should strain every nerve to prevent it.

Peel himself and the Tory party generally did not like the idea of education without religion. As early as 1825 there was a movement for a non-sectarian university in London. Lord Brougham (Lord Chancellor in Grey's Government), Russell and the poet Thomas Campbell formed a public utility company and raised money to build a college. In 1828 a college was opened in Gower Street with the title 'University of London', but religious opposition, the jealousy of Oxford and Cambridge and the medical colleges delayed the grant of power to give degrees. Churchmen feared the development of universities on secular lines, and so in 1829 King's College was founded on Anglican principles. In 1836 the two colleges were incorporated as the University of London, receiving the power to confer degrees. The issue of religion in universities provoked such intense feeling that Lord Winchilsea, a strong opponent of Catholic relief, accused the Duke of Wellington of using the plan to found King's College as a cloak 'for his insidious designs for the infringement of our liberties and the introduction of Popery into every department of state'. Wellington challenged Winchilsea forthwith and the two peers fought a duel in Battersea Fields on 21 March 1829, which was, incidentally, the last duel fought by an English prime minister.[2]

Peel, too, had opposed the Gower Street College, but State support for religious education was becoming increasingly difficult. He had felt obliged to support the non-denominational National School system in Ireland and was becoming influenced by the current glorification of education. Peel had already called down the wrath of Newman and traditionalists when he had opened the Tamworth Reading Room in 1843. He had declared that the individual 'in becoming wiser will become better'. He was accused of substituting knowledge and education for religion. Newman replied to his speech at Tamworth with some of his most biting satire. He says the idea that

> grief, anger, cowardice, self-conceit, pride or passion can be subdued by an examination of shells or grasses, or inhaling of gases, or chipping of rocks, or calculating the longitude, is the veriest of pretences which sophists or mountebank ever professed to a gaping auditory.[3]

In writing about science he wrote that, however wonderful nature might be, 'wonder is not religion, or we should be worshipping our railroads'.[4]

It was into this atmosphere that Peel introduced what Gladstone referred to as 'neutral colleges', in which all the usual branches of knowledge were provided for except theology. Peel did, however, suggest that lecture rooms be made available for religious instruction and the private endowment of theology classes. Graham instructed Heytesbury to discuss the arrangements with Cooke on the part of the Presbyterians, and with Murray, Crolly and Blake on the part of the Catholics. The negotiations with the Presbyterians proved difficult, as they wanted State endowment for a Presbyterian college of both theology and general studies. The Government rejected their claims, but after various negotiations and deputations they reached a compromise whereby a satisfactory connection could be effected between the intended Presbyterian faculty and the new college to be established at Belfast.[5] Despite Graham's instructions, Heytesbury did not consult Crolly. He did not consult Murray either but heard what he thought were his opinions second-hand through Blake. This was unfortunate for Peel as his proposals horrified Protestants and Catholics alike. An English MP, Sir Robert Inglis, called the system 'a gigantic scheme of godless education'.

Immediately after the introduction of the bill into Parliament an animated dispute broke out. O'Connell and his followers denounced the system using the pages of the *Freeman's Journal* and the *Pilot*. Frederick Lucas in the *Tablet* also opposed the colleges, whereas Davis in the *Nation* welcomed the system. Archbishop Crolly also moved quickly in an effort to unite his already divided hierarchy. He called a special meeting of the bishops to discuss the bill which, he wrote, appeared to be 'pregnant with danger to the faith and morals of the youth of this country'.[6]

Despite the short notice, the majority of bishops attended the meeting in Dublin on 21 May. On 23 May two resolutions were adopted, proposed by the Archbishop of Cashel, Dr Slattery, and seconded by Archbishop MacHale. They first of all put on record their gratitude for the 'kind and generous intentions manifested in the endowment of the College of Maynooth' but felt compelled to declare that:

> anxious as we are to extend the advantages of education, we cannot give our approbation to the proposed system, as we deem it dangerous to the faith and morals of the Catholic pupils.[7]

The second resolution was a 'respectful memorial' suggesting such amendments 'as may be calculated to secure the faith and morals of the students'. This memorial was presented to the Lord Lieutenant by Crolly, Murray, MacHale and Ffrench. In it, the bishops promised that they were willing to co-operate on the basis of 'such fair and reasonable terms' as they now put forward: a fair proportion of the professors and other office-bearers be Catholic; they should be appointed by a board of trustees that should include bishops; Catholic chaplains should be appointed, paid by the State, but dismissible by their bishops.

On the central issue of lectures, the bishops declared that Catholics could not attend lectures on history, logic, metaphysics, moral philosophy, geology or anatomy, without 'exposing their faith and morals to imminent danger unless a Roman Catholic professor will be appointed for each of these chairs'.[8]

Heytesbury pointed out to the bishops that the bill was only in outline and many other points might be eventually included. He said in a letter to Gladstone that Crolly, Murray and Ffrench seemed perfectly satisfied, but

> Dr MacHale, on rising to leave the room, observed that the memorial . . . had not been drawn up but after earnest and grave deliberation, and that it contained the minimum of the prelates' wishes. . . . A smile exchanged between the other members of the Deputation showed me that in this observation Dr MacHale had probably a little exceeded the limits of his commission.[9]

Graham told Heytesbury to maintain contact with Murray to see what was the 'real minimum which would satisfy the better portion of his brethren'.

The majority of the demands were turned down, however, with Graham giving a vague undertaking that a fair share of the professors would probably be Catholic. The *Tablet* proclaimed it as a flat rejection of the bishops' memorial, and indeed it did leave no middle ground for negotiation. Gladstone showed some understanding of the bishops' objections, remarking that:

> It would be monstrous for a majority of that House . . . to render, under the name of a boon, that which under other circumstances, would be no boon but a mockery and an injustice.[10]

Russell complained in stronger terms:

> I see no reason why the government should not . . . consult those distinguished Roman Catholics who . . . must have great influence with their countrymen on a question of this nature. I speak more especially of such men as Archbishop Murray – a man no less distinguished for his moderation of opinion . . . than he is by an unswerving fidelity to his own Church.[11]

Despite all the criticisms, however, the bill passed its second reading by an overwhelming majority. After the publication of the bishops' memorial and Graham's rejection of it, the goodwill built up by the Maynooth grant was dissipated. Archbishop MacHale wrote to Peel, saying:

> You fancied that, under the shadow of the Maynooth endowment, you could steal on the country a disastrous and demoralizing measure, which would have neutralized all the advantages of the other.

Once again Peel, despite probable good intentions, managed to aggravate Irish public opinion. It is interesting to note the views of Baron Stockmar, a friend and adviser to Prince Albert, not usually noted for Catholic sympathies. He writes in a letter to the Prince:

> That in the Irish question, – the vital one of all, – my good Sir Robert has had, relatively speaking, but a moderate success, troubles me. Again and again I ask myself to what this shortcoming is mainly due. I may be wrong, and my opinion I fear, may moreover appear to Sir Robert like presumption, still I cannot refrain from avowing, that to me the main reason of the inadequate result seems to be this, that a political question which is intimately mixed up with the essence of Christianity is handled by a Protestant Minister and a Protestant majority. By the nature of things Sir Robert cannot get out of his Protestant skin, and just as little can the Protestant majority of the House of Commons do so . . . . Were I an English Minister,

before I decided on adopting any . . . measure, I would cause
inquiry to be made by a Catholic . . . whether the measure
were really in substance and form calculated to meet Catholic
wants and feelings.[12]

The sentiments expressed here are somewhat different from those of
Heytesbury who, in a letter to Graham, said that he was unwilling to
see Murray 'because we must not lead Catholics to imagine they have
a right to be consulted on all such matters'.

Heytesbury did eventually meet with Murray after the passage of
the bill, but it is likely that Heytesbury read too much into Murray's
conciliatory attitude and that Murray made a severe error of
judgement in thinking that the other bishops would be satisfied with
minor concessions. Crolly, once again his ally in conciliation,
mishandled the situation, as he had condemned the colleges in May
as dangerous to faith and morals, and by August, after one or two
minor adjustments, without a word of warning to his fellow bishops,
he declared that the act was entirely satisfactory. He not only exposed
himself to the charge of inconsistency from MacHale and his
followers, but lost the possible support of the moderates.

Graham was pleased to see the disunity caused by the controversy.
Although not particularly sympathetic to the Catholic Church, he
did not have anti-Catholic motives. He wanted to see the end of the
repeal agitation, and the repealers, like others, were divided on the
issue. O'Connell had condemned the colleges. Davis had welcomed
them, but other Young Irelanders sided with O'Connell and
MacHale.

The Irish bishops once again appealed to Rome to give judgement
on the matter. The issue was complicated by a similar controversy in
France. Montalembert, who had met MacHale in Rome and had a
long-standing interest in Irish affairs, supported MacHale. MacHale
for his part was a subscriber to *Univers*, then under the direction of
Louis Veuillot, who was foremost in the attacks on the Université. It
was not, therefore, surprising to find MacHale, O'Connell and
Cullen citing the evil results of State education in France to support
their cause: *'Referimes itidem ad statum educationis Academicae in
Gallia ab omnibus catolicis lugendam'*.[13]

The Englishman Petre tried to put the Government's case in Rome. He sought the assistance of Cardinal Acton and wrote to Aberdeen that the Cardinal agreed with him

> that in Ireland political activity was the main source of the opposition and expressing deep sorrow at the language and conduct of many of the clergy and more especially of Archbishop MacHale.[14]

The opposition to the colleges was led by Dr Slattery. He was known to be moderate in his views and MacHale was content to let him take the lead. Cullen, who supported Slattery and MacHale in Rome, was anxious to have Slattery's testimony, as he did not have MacHale's controversial record to live down. The minority bishops' case was signed by Crolly, Murray, McGettigan, Ryan and Browne. They accused O'Connell and MacHale of causing dissension. Their main argument in favour of the colleges was the good faith of the Government. This was really the crux of the whole matter. The bishops all had the same end in view but Murray and Crolly were prepared to trust Peel's Government whereas MacHale was not. Murray was content with a Catholic presence in the educational system, whereas MacHale and his supporters wanted control. They believed that only with the control of the educational system could they adequately protect their flock.

This lack of trust largely stemmed from the attempts made by the Government and the Established Church to proselytise from the penal era, to the efforts of the Bible societies in recent years. For MacHale, the problems of proselytism, represented by the activities of Edward Nangle in his own province, continued to cause him irritation. Dr Trench, the Protestant Archbishop of Tuam, had died and Nangle found a much more ardent supporter in his successor, Dr Plunkett. A great deal of money was being poured into the Protestant mission on Achill by the people of Great Britain because they wanted to promote the Protestant cause, and many found it a cause for concern. The question was even brought up in Parliament during the debates on Maynooth. Lord Monteagle described the occasion when

Archbishop MacHale was saying Mass on the island, in the open air, with great crowds assembled. During Communion, the Protestant missionaries came among them, holding up the consecrated hosts and asking the people if that was God. There was a great rush of people against them, but they were rescued by the Catholic priests. 'Through the means of those very men whose religion had been so grossly and wantonly insulted, the public peace had been preserved.'

Some people came to Achill to see for themselves what was going on. The Reverend Stanley published a pamphlet, very adverse to the situation, and in the early 1840s Mr S. C. Hall came to Achill, as he wanted to visit 'a Protestant Colony'. Hall was an ardent Protestant, stating that 'we consider every conscientious accession to the Protestant Faith as a contribution in aid to the well-being of the state'. However, Hall's reports on Achill, later published in a pamphlet, were quite damning:

> Even if the plan and conduct of the mission were wise, humane and charitable – in a word, Christian – its purpose has been worked out in a manner not at all commensurate with the large amount of moneys expended on its formation and sustainment.[15]

Hall says that there were, in fact, hardly any converts, as the Protestant population mostly came from other parts of Ireland and England. He complains that the mission had been costing three thousand pounds a year and in 1840, 'considerably more'. However, Nangle was able to attract some by his money. He had a house built specially for priests who had left the Catholic Church. He composed a hymn for them, the chorus of which was:

> Lord, bless this house as a holy home
> For souls redeemed by thy Grace from Rome.[16]

The Irish Catholic clergy remained deeply suspicious not only of the Established Church but also of the Government, particularly a Tory government. Slattery also made the point to Cullen:

> But important as this question of Academical Education is, believe me . . . that in the present controversy another question of transcendent importance is also indirectly involved viz. whether the Catholic Church in Ireland is to be governed in future by the British ministry . . . through the agency of a few members of the Hierarchy as their Commissioners or by the great body of the bishops whom the Holy Ghost and the Common Father of the faithful have pleased to rule this portion of the flock of Christ.[17]

The majority of the bishops did resent the close collaboration of Murray and Crolly with the Government. It was during this period that the terms 'Castle bishop' and 'Castle Catholic' came into use, and they remained terms of insult as long as Dublin Castle was the seat of the British Government in Ireland.

By 1846 all parties concerned had other preoccupations besides the fate of the Irish colleges. Peel was concerned with the survival of his government. In Ireland, it was becoming clear that the effects of the potato blight were going to be horrific, and in Rome, Pope Gregory died suddenly on 1 June 1846. He was succeeded by Mastai Ferretti, who became known as Pius IX. The cardinals met on 13 July to discuss the Irish problem. Their decision was conclusive: the new colleges would be harmful to religion and the cardinals expressed their regret that some bishops had entered into negotiations with the Government without the agreement of the other bishops.

By June 1846 Peel was coming to the end of his office. In a farewell speech, he outlined the policy that his successors should follow in Ireland:

> There ought to be established a complete equality of municipal, civil and political rights . . . the favour of the Crown ought to be bestowed, and the confidence of the Crown reposed, without reference to religious distinctions. . . . The present social condition of the people in respect to the tenure of land, and to the relation between landlord and tenant . . . deserves our immediate though most cautious consideration.[18]

O'Connell remarked that Peel would 'take one turn more and bring in repeal'. Although no one would seriously have considered this as likely, it had seemed equally unlikely that Peel would have been the instrument of some attempt at the conciliation of Ireland. He had been able to make the situation better for Catholic charities, his grant to Maynooth had been generous and it had required courage to carry it through Parliament. Peel failed in his inability to consult the Irish and, in particular, the Catholic bishops, in measures that were of great interest to them. At the end of his term of office, Peel felt that his Irish policies had been misunderstood:

> I cannot say that justice has been done to our motives, nor has the position of the individual accepting a mark of favour from us been such as to encourage other Roman Catholics to receive similar proofs of confidence.[19]

In this he is referring to the archbishops, Murray and Crolly, whom he felt had also been misjudged. Murray continually strove to pursue a middle course in Irish politics and to do what he considered best for the preservation of public order. His attitude was often contrasted with that of MacHale. Murray was known to his followers as the 'St Francis de Sales of Ireland' on account of his humility and piety, whereas MacHale had been christened by O'Connell 'The Lion of the fold of Judah' or 'The Lion of the West'. Murray was twenty years older than MacHale and he never emerged from the shadow of the penal laws. It was said of him that his 'pathetic eagerness to accept whatever crumbs of conciliation flung him by the British Government was a natural result of early deprivation'. He was haunted by the fear that if he did not accept what was offered, the Irish would be subjected to more penal enactments. He hoped that by adopting a conciliatory attitude, greater benefits might ensue. MacHale, on the other hand, being the first bishop to be totally educated in Ireland, was typical of a new confidence both in the Irish Church and in Ireland itself. MacHale was not willing to accept second best or, indeed, anything that he considered unjust or insufficient. Peel's job was not easy. He was required to bridge the gap between 'what the people of England could be brought to consent [to] and what the people of Ireland would be content to receive'.[20]

Notes

1   Quoted in Ian Ker, *John Henry Newman* (1988), p. 101.
2   Llewellyn Woodward, *Age of Reform* (1938), p. 492.
3   John Henry Newman, *Discussions and Arguments* (1872), p. 261
4   Ibid.
5   Donal A. Kerr, *Peel, Priests and Politics* (1982), p. 299. Graham Papers.
6   Ibid., p. 303.
7   *Tablet,* 21 May 1845.
8   Catholic Directory (1847), *Memorial of the bishops to the Lord Lieutenant, 1845.*
9   Donal A. Kerr, op. cit., p. 304, Graham Papers, 25 May 1845.
10   Hansard LXXX 1261, 2 June 1845.
11   Ibid.
12   T. Martin, *The Life of his Royal Highness the Prince Consort* (1880), quoted in Kerr, op. cit., p. 306.
13   Lettera degli Arcivesovi di Tuam e Cashel e di altri sedici Vescovi d'Irlanda, 25 November 1845, Acta, Vol. 209 ff.289–93, Propaganda Fide Archives, p. 328-9.
14. Petre to Aberdeen, 10 December 1845, quoted in Kerr, *Peel, Priests and Politics 1841–1846* (1982), p. 332.
15   S. C. Hall. *Achill Mission* (1844), p. 1.
16   Henry Seddall, *Edward Nangle: The Apostle of Achill* (1884), p. 152.
17   Donal A. Kerr, op. cit., p. 341.
18   Hansard LXXXVII, 29 June 1846.
19   Ibid.
20   Charles Greville, *Journal* (1844), quoted in Kerr, op. cit., p. 116.

10

THE FAMINE

'Are the lives of the people of Ireland prized so low . . . that but fifty thousand pounds . . . is to be given for rescuing our people from certain death?' (John MacHale)

THE FAMINE OF 1845 to 1847 changed the course of Irish history. Ireland was used to famines. It was said that about 300,000 people died during the famine of 1739 to 1740. During the next hundred years there were to be lesser famines every few years. These were largely the result not just of poor crops but of an economic system run chiefly for the benefit of the ruling classes.

While John MacHale was a bishop, there was a famine in the early 1830s and another in 1842. He continually wrote to governments, informing them of the conditions in Ireland and particularly those in the west. He pointed out the lack of industry in Ireland and the lack of investment. The land remained undeveloped. Much of it was given over to pasture, as tithes were not paid on land used for pasture. There was no security for the tenant farmers and no incentive for them to improve their land. The absentee landlords made no improvements and had no care for their unknown tenants. The agricultural labourers depended more and more on the potato for their survival and watched the export of other crops. As well as writing to governments, MacHale sent out appeals for money to support the people of the west. In 1842 he received many donations in response to his appeal during the current famine:

£1 from the 'Protestant Tradesmen of Dublin'.

Hugh Byrne writes from Bolton, England: 'I send a Post-Office order for £1 joint subscription of myself and some other poor men of this town, toward the relief of the suffering poor in your Lordship's diocese.'

From Stonor, Henley-on-Thames, the Reverend Comerbach sent £5 in the name of a Miss O'Brien, 'a lady who supports herself by tuition'.

Lord Stourton of Allerton Park sent £150.

The Abbé Moriarty, Curé de Derchigny près Dieppe, sent £2.

John MacHale had become used to the business of appealing for money and distributing it to the poor. In a letter from a local priest, Fr Patrick MacManus, in 1842, we read:

I have just received your Grace's letter with £5 for the people of Innisturk . . . 800 of oatmeal sent to the island . . . a ton of meal sent to Clare island.[1]

After the 1842 famine, MacHale said that unless Ireland was the recipient of wise legislation, famine would come 'again and again, and be fraught at each returning visit with some new accumulation'.

Again and again he pleaded with the British Government to invest in industry in Ireland, to build roads, bridges, railways and canals. He complained about the protectionism practised by the English against any emergent Irish industry. Most of all, he asked for just laws for the tenant farmers. When it had become clear to him that the British Government were too far away to comprehend the problems of Ireland, he had campaigned vigorously for the repeal of the Act of Union in the hope that an Irish parliament would understand the nature of the problems of the suffering in Ireland.

In 1841 the census showed that there were just under nine million people living in Ireland. About half of these lived in 'windowless mud cabins of a single room'. These people scraped a living from the small plots that the agents of absentee landlords allowed them to rent. They paid the rent from the money they obtained selling potatoes, which was the easiest and most profitable crop to grow on the tiny plots. As the population grew, these plots were subdivided. The land was overfarmed, but there was no other employment. The land was taxed, the peasants having to pay tithes first to the Established Church and then later to the landlord. Peel set up a commission under the chairmanship of Lord Devon in 1843 to study Irish agrarian questions. After the Devon Report, Peel decided to give tenants a legal right to compensation for improvements they had made to the land. His proposals were modest. They recognised three types of improvement: fencing (which meant the removal of large and wasteful dykes that separated holdings), draining, and building. The amount of compensation was to be limited to £5 an acre. The opposition to the bill was so strong that it was withdrawn for alteration but within a short time the famine had begun.

The potato blight was first seen in North America in 1844. It was later felt in Belgium, Holland and Germany and as far east as Hungary. In Ireland the potato crop of 1844 was healthy and seed potatoes were confidently planted in the spring of 1845. In England the blight appeared in the summer of 1845 and by September it had spread to Ireland. The harvest of 1845 had promised well, but in the space of a month the blight seemed to spread throughout the land. An eye-witness reports: 'I myself saw whole tracts of potato growth changed, in one night, from smiling luxuriance to a shrivelled and blackened waste'.[2] The people were alarmed, but felt that the crop had been so good that it would balance out. To their horror they found that by winter the tubers were rotting in the pits and storehouses.

In Dublin O'Connell gathered round him those who might have some influence with the Government. In a speech to the Dublin Council he said:

> This is a time when the fullest confidence should be given to any Government that will act as it ought in such an emergency. I care not who the minister is, if he only comes forward decidedly to render assistance, he shall have my support and the support of every independent member for Ireland. I am not availing myself of this circumstance to raise more strongly the cry of Repeal, or to urge the agitation for Repeal. I am not mixing any kind of politics with our efforts to rescue the country from starvation.

The *Freeman's Journal* puts forward O'Connell's recommendations in October 1845:

> Restrain the export of food; Advance money for public works on the security of the Crown lands; Stop the distillers; Tax the absentees one half, and the resident proprietors one tenth of their incomes; Store provisions and distribute them in payment for labour.

Some of the members of the 'Young Ireland' group thought that O'Connell had gone senile at his recommendations for the immediate stoppage of distilling and brewing.

A deputation from a committee who met at the Mansion House went to the Lord-Lieutenant, Heytesbury. This was headed by the Lord Mayor, the Duke of Leinster, Lord Cloncurry, and Daniel O'Connell. The address contained the proposals of O'Connell and stressed that the famine and 'consequent pestilence' were imminent. It urged the Government not to hesitate:

> Whilst you hesitate, if hesitate you shall, the people of Ireland are about to perish in countless numbers.
>
> May we respectfully refer you to Lord Devon's report of last session, where you will find that the Irish agricultural labourers and their families are calculated to amount to more than four million of human beings, whose only food is the potato, whose only drink is water; whose houses are pervious to the rain; to whom a bed or a blanket is a luxury almost unknown, and who are more wretched than any other people in Europe.
>
> We call your attention to the fact that the foregoing description of the fate of the Irish peasantry was published long before there was or could be the least suspicion of the visitation of Providence in the destruction of the present crop. If then such was the condition of a large portion of the Irish people even in favourable harvests, you will, in your humanity, easily judge what must be the horrors of their situation, if the approaching famine be allowed to envelope the entire population.

> We implore you, Sir, not to allow yourselves to be persuaded that we exaggerate the horrors or certainty of the approaching famine. We have no motive under heaven for misleading or misinforming you. . . . Our only object is to impress on your mind what we know to be the fact, that famine and pestilence are at our door and can be averted only by the most extensive and active precautions.[3]

In his reply Peel states:

> I give full credit to the assurance in making this communication, your Lordship and those who are parties to it are influenced by no other motives than the desire to aid the government in the efforts which they are making to avert or mitigate the impending evil. . . . I beg to assure your Lordship that the whole subject is occupying the unremitting attention of her majesty's confidential advisors.[4]

The Mansion House committee felt somewhat let down by this reply, but Lord Cloncurry offered the whole of his revenue to alleviate distress and was determined to elicit from the Prime Minister some promise of help.

During the early months of 1846 the farmers worked doubly hard to raise money to re-crop the land. Bernard O'Reilly writes 'pawn-offices were choked with the humble finery that had shone at the village dance or Christening feast'.

The corn harvest of 1845 was also poor throughout Britain and Ireland and in many parts of Europe. In Britain at that time there was high import duty on corn to protect the interests of the English farmers. This meant that cheap foreign corn could not be imported and the price of grain and, therefore, bread, was kept artificially high. Peel, like all Tories, was a protectionist, who had resisted change to the Corn Laws. However, in 1845, the prospect of a starving population in England forced him to abandon the agricultural interest and to repeal the corn laws. He did not forbid the export of corn from Ireland and so the starving Irish had to witness the removal of their corn to the ports, often under armed guard, to be sold overseas. It was the misfortune of the Irish that their fate was decided at Westminster. Even if Peel had thought it wise to prohibit the export of Irish corn, it would have been difficult for him to do so while the English poor were suffering. The cabinet would have been accused of inconsistency if they had lowered the duties on corn while at the same time cutting off one of the normal sources of supply.

Peel did arrange for maize to be shipped from America to Ireland. This maize was unpopular at first and was known as 'Peel's Brimstone'. Public relief works were provided to give employment to the labourers to enable them to buy the imported food. Graham said that they had sanctioned the advance of 'no less than £448,000 to be laid out in public works'.

The harvest of 1846, like that of 1845, at first promised well, but Archbishop MacHale in his Lenten pastoral letter urged the people not only to pray but to save. He also told them to send 'strong remonstrances' to their rulers to stop the export of food from Ireland.[5]

In June 1846 Peel was voted out of office on account of his proposal for a coercion bill for Ireland. The real reason was that the Conservatives refused to support him because of the repeal of the Corn Laws. They felt that he had betrayed the party. Many members of the House of Commons at that time were country squires and landowners. The Whigs, led by Lord John Russell, took over the running of the Government in July 1846.

The transition from Tory to Whig added to the difficulties of meeting the emergency, and if the Tories were hampered by their continual protection of agricultural interests, the Whigs were impeded by their doctrinaire support of free trade. The prevailing mood was a distrust of interference with the normal course of trade, and every step taken to relieve Ireland had political or economic consequences in England, which raised serious controversy. The failure of the second year's crop was unexpected. By the end of July the blight had once more spread throughout Ireland. Archbishop MacHale wrote to Russell imploring the Government not to stop the relief measures until better ones were introduced:

I have read with dismay the report . . . announcing that the relief which, through the means of employment on public works, had been in some instances tardily meted out to the people, was . . . to be withdrawn . . . . You might as well issue at once an edict of national starvation, as stop the supplies which the feeble creatures are striving to earn with the sweat of their brows.

Allow me, then, in the name of a faithful and suffering people, to implore you, not only to stretch the present relief on an enlarged scale into the middle of September, but not to suffer the great council of the nation to rise without adopting prospective measures for the similar and severer calamities of the coming year.

Visitations such as that through which we are now passing are not always confined to one season. . . . That the disease of the potato is of that character, is now alas! too evident. Having recently passed through extensive tracts of country and made a minute examination into the state of the potato, I can bear testimony not only to the premature withering of the stalks, and consequent decay of the roots, but to the fact that, while the leaves were still green and sound, the tubers were diminutive in size and in a state of rapid decomposition.[6]

MacHale also suggested that the public works that were being undertaken could be of lasting benefit to Ireland:

It is not, then, on the miserable and peddling scale of levelling hills on a mail-coach road, that the physical wants of a numerous people are to be relieved, but by those extensive and necessary improvements which, while they mitigate distress, will afford to the government an adequate remuneration;– such as the erection of quays and piers along the southern and western coasts, by which the existing misery would be relieved, and courage given to the hardy natives to explore and develop their fisheries; this is a resource on which any enlightened statesman could draw for supplying the wants of the people.

These are public works which the people have a right to expect, in return for the ample revenues with which their industry enriches the Exchequer.[7]

Because of the slowness of reports, and the lack of contact the British government had with the West of Ireland, parliament thought the reports from Ireland were grossly exaggerated and sent £50,000.

Russell's Government was concerned to avoid the demoralisation of the destitute poor. The Government's chief civil servant who administered their policies was Charles Trevelyan. He shared the prejudices of his class and generation about the potentially morally corrosive effects of relieving the indigent, lest this corrupt the deserving poor who sustained themselves. However, the Government's overriding concern was to protect the free market at all costs. Russell was determined to avoid competition with private enterprise in the provision of public works. Thus the Irish countryside is still littered with roads that go nowhere and walls with no purpose, projects that did not compete with private enterprise and that preserved the market economy. It was estimated that three out of every four acres of potatoes were ruined, and that one-third of the oats crop was also lost. Approximately four million people in Ireland and about two million in Great Britain lived almost wholly on potatoes.[8]

At the end of August, MacHale wrote again to Lord John Russell:

Allow me respectfully to impress on your Lordship, that hunger and starvation are already at the doors of hundreds and thousands. . . . The British Empire boasts, and boasts with justice, of its measureless resources. Now is an opportunity of exhibiting as well the extent of its humanity. . . .

And what is the available sum that has been voted by the munificence of Parliament to avert the starvation of millions? FIFTY THOUSAND POUNDS!

Ten Placemen divide between them a larger share of the public money. Fifty thousand pounds for a starving people!

It is not many years ago since four times that sum was squandered on the pageant of the King's coronation. . . .

> Your Lordship does not forget when TWENTY MILLIONS were heaped out of the public treasury to give liberty to the Negroes of the West Indies. . . . Are the lives of the people of Ireland prized so low . . . that but fifty thousand pounds . . . is to be given for rescuing our people from certain death?[9]

Archbishop MacHale wrote again and again to the Prime Minister, pleading, urging, beseeching and agonising as he saw before his eyes the suffering of the people, especially those of his own area, the diocese of Tuam. On 7 October he once again pleaded with the Prime Minister:

> The people's hopes have been sustained by assurances of prompt and efficient relief. Their patience has been stretched to a degree of endurance to which human nature is seldom subjected. Yet when they find the enactments of Parliament . . . abortive of relief, it is to be feared that their suspicions of underhand intrigue will goad them on to violence and outrage. While we preach patience to them, it is our duty to adjure their rulers not to push their patience to its extreme limits. . . . The question is not now about the preference to be given to the constructing of roads or the most remunerative labour. The pressing, the imperative question, is about saving the lives of famishing thousands. . . . All the other speculations are unreasonable, nay cruel. . . . All your works, productive or unproductive, are only means toward saving the People's lives, which are more valuable than any property, and should not be sacrificed to these cruel speculators, who value property more than the people's lives. . . .
>
> Food is the first requisite, and then employment, productive remunerative employment if you can, but at any rate, employment to save the lives of the people.[10]

The administration of famine relief under the supervision of Trevelyan was a source of bitterness. Although managing Irish affairs, he had no wish to see the situation for himself. Russell described the disaster as 'a famine of the thirteenth century acting upon a population of the nineteenth'.[11] Although he acknowledged the extent of the disaster, however, he appeared to be powerless to provide adequate relief. His difficulties were great. The administrative machinery of the United Kingdom, not being familiar with famines of this scale, although officials who had had experience of famine in India were brought back to manage food depots, was unfitted to cope with a catastrophe of this kind. His Government's doctrinaire attitudes on free trade principles made many obvious solutions impossible. Peel's Government, though inadequate in its response, had been able to act with some pragmatic charity.

Russell's Government decided in January 1847 to give up new work programmes and concentrate on outdoor relief. They imported large quantities of corn, biscuit and salt meat for distribution. The new plan could not be put into effect at once, and meanwhile conditions were at their worst. Furthermore, it was felt that a system of free rations was open to abuse and it was necessary to prevent fraud. The sale of rations given in relief was checked by the distribution of cooked food, and, in order to encourage the resumption of ordinary agricultural work, no relief was allowed to those who held more than a quarter of an acre. This policy may have checked the abuse of relief, but it also left thousands of destitute families with a choice between abandoning their holdings and starvation.

At the end of 1846 a deputation from Achill, headed by the parish priest, Fr Monaghan, went to ask the government Commissary General, Sir R. Routh in Dublin for a supply of food from Government stores. They were told that they could not undersell the merchants as this was against the principles of political economy.[12] About this time Lord George Bentinck brought in a bill to allot £16,000,000 for the building of Irish railways. This was opposed and defeated by the Government. The relief measures were often ill-thought-out and abused by grasping officials.

Patrick McLoughlin from the parish of Islandeady had a starving wife and family. He applied for relief work. He was told that he could not get relief work until he got a relief ticket. He had to wait five days for the relief ticket. Then he went to work, but he had to work three days before he was paid. By that time his wife was dead. He then had to work two days to pay for her coffin and, helped by the priest, he buried her at night as he did not want to lose a day's pay to feed his children.[13] People were dying everywhere. They died by the roadside, in the workhouses, outside the workhouses waiting to gain entrance. Drivers of coaches often drove over bodies in the dark.

In 1847 the potato crop promised quite well, but many seed potatoes given in charity had been eaten. In the Castlebar Union of parishes, out of 160,000 acres, only 20,000 had crops; in Westport, out of 330,000 acres, only 16,000 had crops; and in Clifden, out of 189,000 acres, only 5,500 had crops.[14] Fever and dysentery spread over the land. The people ate the bodies of dead horses and dogs. They lived on grass and seaweed. The workhouses were overflowing. While workers were absent on relief works or in workhouses, their little cabins were emptied and destroyed. Many crops that were grown were seized for the payment of rent. Everything was seized, corn, cattle, pigs, poultry, even clothes and furniture. All over the country, but particularly in the west, tenants were evicted for the non-payment of rent. At Keel, in Achill island, forty families, one hundred and fifty people, were evicted at one time. They looked for a workhouse but they were all full. E. A. D'Alton wrote that laughter ceased in Connaught. There was no more music or singing. During 1847 every area had an horrific story to tell. In Ballina in one month there were between five and six thousand processes, besides a great many ejectments. In Castlebar there were sixteen hundred processes as well as ejectments. The famine affected Catholic and Protestant alike. In a speech in Conciliation Hall, O'Connell read a letter from Cork that gave the Protestant clergy returns for the deaths in that deanery; 5,000 were dead of starvation and 10,000 actually dying.[15] The clearances continued. Catholic and Protestant landlords vied with each other in their inhumanity. In 1847 an article in *The Times* read 'Let the people go and let beasts take their place', meaning that the population should be allowed to emigrate and the land used for grazing cattle, which would benefit the landowners.[16]

There were good landlords, however. Many bankrupted themselves to feed the starving and many went to the wall as their rents remained unpaid. George Henry Moore, an MP for County

Mayo and father of the novelist George Moore, asked for no rents during this period, and when he won some money on the race-course, he gave it to his tenants. There were 5,000 people on his estate and not one died of hunger.

The Society of Friends was one of the first groups to recognise the disaster; they saved thousands from death by their charitable work, particularly in the west. They were also imaginative in their relief works: they established fish-curing stations at Clifden and Achill. The sea around Achill was rich in herring and mackerel.

The priests of the area laboured night and day in their ministrations to the sick and the dying. They shared their food with the starving and many died themselves. This was particularly the case when the cholera took over.

Archbishop MacHale, besides his priestly work in the cathedral, his ministrations to the sick and the dying, his hours in the confessional, took upon himself, alone, without the help of a secretary, the immense work of receiving, acknowledging and distributing the alms sent to him. During the last three months of 1846 and the whole of 1847 MacHale spent many hours of every day receiving and registering money donations sent from every part of the world. They came from all parts of England, Ireland, Scotland and Wales, from all over Europe, from Canada and the United States, and even from India. He acknowledged every donation and used up whatever income he had himself. His nephew, Thomas MacHale, after examining the account books, said that he found that his uncle had given out £78,093 6s 8d in disbursements to the poor.[17]

Many of these donations came as just a few shillings or one pound. Individual people showed great generosity. People from every walk of life and from all religious denominations gave generously. Nonetheless, nearly a million people died from famine and disease and another million left Ireland during this period, mostly bound for North America. Of these, it is estimated that one in six died on the journey. The conditions on the emigrant ships, known as 'coffin ships', were horrific and disease was rampant.

The consequences of the famine and the subsequent clearances of land continued long after the 1840s and are still evident today. In 1800 the population of Ireland was a third of Britain and Ireland combined, i.e., there were five million in Ireland and about ten million in England, Scotland and Wales. Dublin was the second largest city. In 1841 the population of Ireland had risen to about nine million, over half the population of Britain and Ireland combined; England, Scotland and Wales had about sixteen million. Despite the massive loss of the famine years, the population of Ireland was six and a half million in 1851. By 1911 it had fallen to four and a half. Today it is just over three million, compared to fifty million in Britain.

Notes

1 Bernard O'Reilly, *The Life and Times of John MacHale* (1890), (MacHale MSS), I, p. 606.
2 Ibid., p. 609.
3 *Freeman's Journal,* November 1845.
4 Ibid.
5 Bernard O'Reilly, op. cit., I, pp. 612–14.
6 John MacHale, *Letters* (1847), 1 August 1846, p. 612.
7 Ibid.
8 Llewellyn Woodward, *The Age of Reform* (1938), p. 352.
9 John MacHale, op. cit., 21 August 1846, pp. 613–14.
10 Ibid., 7 October.
11 Quoted in Woodward, op. cit., p. 352.
12 E. A. D'Alton, *History of the Archdiocese of Tuam* (1928), p. 27.
13 Ibid., p. 28.
14 Ibid.
15 Edward Lucas, *The Life of Frederick Lucas MP* (1886), p. 246.
16 D'Alton, op. cit., p. 33.
17 Bernard O'Reilly, op. cit., I, p. 651.

11

AFTER THE FAMINE

'I would rather have one single word of praise from the present Archbishop of Tuam than a whole chapter of encomiums from English royalty itself.' (Charles Waterton)

IN THE EARLY months of 1847 it became clear that the health of Daniel O'Connell was declining rapidly. After his imprisonment in 1843 he never really regained his strength, either physically or politically, but to the Irish he was still the 'Liberator' and the embodiment of Irish hopes and aspirations. In January 1847, knowing that the end was near, he decided to make a pilgrimage to Rome, but never arrived, dying at Genoa on 15 May.

For John MacHale, at this time totally wrapped up with his dying flock, the news of O'Connell's death came as an added blow. MacHale had often disagreed with O'Connell. He had not supported him in his alliance with the Whigs and the Lichfield House Compact. O'Connell thought that the Irish language was an impediment to progress, whereas MacHale believed passionately in its use and preservation. However, John MacHale had believed in O'Connell as a true Irish patriot. He also believed that he had no successor. O'Connell had worked honestly and fearlessly for his fellow countrymen. He had achieved much. He had been largely responsible for Catholic Emancipation and had tried to gain, little by little, laws more favourable to Irish interests. MacHale had worked closely with O'Connell over the Repeal movement. Above all, MacHale admired O'Connell as a man of peace. Like MacHale, he was not a revolutionary. He did not encourage bloodshed and remained, throughout his struggles, loyal to the Crown and the connection with England.

In May 1847, on receiving the news of O'Connell's death, MacHale felt the loss to Ireland of an accomplished and experienced politician, but he also felt the personal loss of a friend. O'Connell had had great respect for the Archbishop and had always sought his approval. He had valued his help and had given MacHale the title 'Lion of the Fold of Judah'. MacHale did not like this title, as it was one given to Christ himself, but to most people MacHale became known as 'The Lion' or 'The Lion of the West'. When MacHale heard of O'Connell's death, he spent the day walking in the college close, praying for his friend. Those who saw him noticed the depth of his grief.

In May 1847 MacHale wrote a pastoral letter to his priests, asking them to say Mass for O'Connell. They were enduring terrible times in the midst of the famine, but MacHale asked his priests to keep to the principles followed by O'Connell: fidelity to God, allegiance to the throne and repeal of the Union. He told them to beware of those politicians who are 'clamorous for civil liberty' but 'would cheerfully bind in fetters the freedom of the Church'. He warned the priests that the people were in danger 'of breaking out into dreadful deeds of sedition' and exhorted them 'to console, to guide and to sustain them'.[1]

This period towards the end of the famine was characterised by cruel evictions and the violence that often followed them, and by the inadequate working of the Poor Law and the beginnings of the mass movement of emigration.

John MacHale and the Irish bishops, weary with the prospect of more years of famine and despair, on 21 October 1847 presented a memorial to the Lord Lieutenant, the Earl of Clarendon, in an attempt to put before the Government the causes of distress. In the memorial the bishops state that they are 'filled with grief and alarm' at the prospect of the continuation of the famine in certain areas of Ireland. They then speak about the distress that is widespread owing to the want of sufficient employment. They say that it would be useful

> with a view of promoting vigorous and effective remedies, to refer to the causes from which have sprung the evils of our present condition.
>
> These causes are found in the unjust and penal enactments which, in other days, deprived the great bulk of the people of

the rights of property, thus discouraging industry by debarring them of its fruits. . . . It is to the violation of the principles of justice and of Christian morality from which these enactments had sprung, and not to any innate indolence of the people, that we may trace their depressed social condition, which, sinking gradually into still greater misery, terminated last year, by the failure of the potato crop, in the famine so tremendous in its havoc, and of which the present season threatens the appalling recurrence. . . .

If the labourer is worthy of his hire, an axiom of Natural, as well as Revealed Religion; and, if doing to others as we should be done by be the golden standard of Christian morality, it would be a violation of those sacred maxims to appropriate the entire crop of the husbandman without compensating him for the seed or the labour expended in the cultivation of the soil.

Yet laws sanctioning such unnatural injustice, and, therefore, injurious to society, not only exist, but are extensively enforced with reckless and unrelenting rigour while the sacred and indefeasible rights of life are forgotten, amid the incessant reclamation of the subordinate rights of property!

The legitimate rights of property, so necessary for the maintenance of society, we have ever felt it our duty to recognize and inculcate. The outbreaks of violence and revenge which sometimes, unfortunately, disgrace the country, we deplore and reprobate; but in justice to their general character and habits, we feel it our duty to declare our conviction that there is not on earth a people who exhibit more respect for law and order, under such unheard-of privations, than the people of Ireland.[2]

The bishops say that in such a terrible crisis which threatens such destruction of human life they are 'anxious to preserve the souls of their flocks from crime, and society from the danger of disorganization'. The bishops state that they do not want just 'gratuitous relief' but employment of a productive and remunerative kind. They ask for measures calculated to prevent a 'recurrence of famine and promote the prosperity of the country'. For this the bishops ask for 'an equitable arrangement of the relations between landlords and tenants, founded on Commutative Justice'. They say that without this they

> despair of seeing the poor sufficiently employed and protected, the land sufficiently cultivated, or the peace and prosperity of the country placed on a secure foundation. Large tracts of land capable of cultivation are now lying waste; the coasts abound in fish which would give a large supply of food: encouragement to work these and other mines of wealth with which the country is teeming would be well worthy of the solicitude of Her Majesty's Government.
>
> The poor are patient and long-enduring, though suffering grievously; they are looking with hope and confidence to Her Majesty's Government for relief; a prompt and humane attention to their wants will save the lives and secure the lasting gratitude of Her Majesty's most faithful people.[3]

The sentiments expressed in this letter are echoed in a letter written about the same time from James Tuke, a member of the Quakers who was touring the west of Ireland at this time and reporting back to the Central Relief Committee of the Society of Friends in Dublin. He refers to the letter of the bishops and is very hopeful on reading Lord Clarendon's reply. Clarendon appears to be very sympathetic:

> In common with your Lordships I deeply commiserate the distress of the people, and fear that in many localities the means indispensable for the maintenance of the destitute are lamentably deficient.[4]

Clarendon agrees that they should learn the lessons of the past and try to remedy the underlying causes of the present evils:

> The eternal principles of justice and Christian morality can never be violated with impunity; and the unrighteous

legislation of by-gone times has left traces which must be long and severely felt. By penal enactments, doubtless, industry was discouraged, property was unequally distributed; the growth of a middle class was retarded; the people were demoralized, and the whole fabric of society was [made] hollow and insecure.

Lord Clarendon goes on to say that if the entire crops of the husbandman are appropriated without compensating him for his labour the sacred maxim of 'do as you would be done by' is violated.

But on the other hand, if the owner of the soil, who is as much dependent upon it as the occupier, be deprived of his fair and reasonable share of its produce; if he can neither obtain rent nor the surrender of his land, and is in fact dispossessed of his property by a non-fulfilment of the conditions upon which he shared his rights with another, then beyond doubt a similar infringement of the maxim occurs.

Lord Clarendon then says what the Government will do:

No general claim to assistance can be established. Legislature has placed a large sum, under favourable conditions, at the disposal of the landowners, and I know that this will afford much employment to the poor in work really productive, and I trust that Parliament will see fit to sanction a measure which, while strictly guarding the rights of property, shall at the same time place the relations between landlord and tenant upon a footing more sound and satisfactory than at present.[5]

During this period there was much discussion in Parliament and in the British press of the breakdown of law and order in Ireland. The Irish had always been presented to the English as disorderly and in constant need of coercion acts. This criticism of the Irish character is disputed strongly by the Quaker, James Tuke. He says, 'It is doubtful whether any other people would have endured their late terrible privations with equal patience and submission to the laws.'[6]

After the evictions, the Irish towns were filled with starving peasants with nowhere to go. As the winter of 1847 arrived, the situation became worse and the feelings of anger towards the landlords and the bailiffs increased. Incidents of murder and lawlessness were reported in the press and discussed in Parliament. It was claimed by some that the Catholic priests were inciting their flocks to murder and issuing such instructions from the pulpit. Archbishop MacHale wrote to Lord John Russell refuting these allegations. The letter was printed in the *Freeman's Journal*. He received a reply from Lord Clarendon, the Viceroy. In it Clarendon praised MacHale's 'eloquent and just' defence of the clergy. He says, 'no clergy in Europe can be compared with the Irish for zealous, self-sacrificing, faithful performance of most arduous duties.' After praising them some more he goes on to say

> But among a class so numerous, it is not to be expected that all should be equally good, that some should not be more passionate and less prudent than others; and thus, although perhaps unintentionally and without reflection on its consequences, that they should misuse the influence that they possess.[7]

Clarendon says that because the 'admonition or punishment with which those reverend persons meet with at the hands of their ecclesiastical superiors' is secret, 'the exercise of spiritual authority is doubted; and the Press asserts, and the public believes, that the Catholic clergy of Ireland are the irresponsible promoters of disaffection and disorder'.

Clarendon suggests two courses of action: that the clergy should publish their exhortations to their flocks 'inciting them to order, and industry, and goodwill' and that the heads of the Church should publicly 'encourage and approve the clergy who walk in the path of duty, and publicly warn or punish those who, although faithful in the performance of their religious duties, may be heedless of their obligation to society. . . . I address myself to your Grace, knowing that if your Grace should see fit to lead the way, others would not be slow to follow.'

Archbishop MacHale answered the letter promptly. He pointed out that the means of relief for the people of the west of Ireland was utterly inadequate and

> as long as they are in such destitution, without any sure prospect of the mitigation of their sufferings, the peace and order of society will be exposed to imminent danger. And though the clergy should be unceasing, as they have hitherto been, in their exhortations to patience, it is to be feared that their exhortations will often lose their effect on men urged on by the impulses of hunger and despair.
>
> No matter; the clergy will continue their pious and peaceful exhortations, knowing that they have a conscientious duty to perform. . . . without any reference but to Him Who will reward the good works done for His glory and in His name.[8]

MacHale points out that it was for this purpose 'of preventing by seasonable measures of relief the threatened derangement of society, that the episcopal deputation waited upon your excellency'. The Archbishop stresses the dangers resulting from the situation where 'our town swarms with crowds of paupers ejected by some of the neighbouring gentry from their holdings; and the struggling people are burdened with the support of these outcasts from their homes'. MacHale once again asks for relief and deplores the prospect of yet another coercion act:

> It is not yet, I trust, too late. Without such relieving measures on a larger scale than that already before the public, coercive measures will irritate rather than heal, and the evils of our social system are likely to become more inveterate.[9]

Some of the most hurtful attacks on the Irish priests and bishops made in the English press were made by the Catholic English aristocracy. One of the most notable of these attacks came from Lord Clifford, who believed that the name of Catholics had been injured by the actions of the Irish priests and, in particular, by Archbishop MacHale. Clifford had been active in 1834 in helping the

Government in their efforts to prevent the promotion of John MacHale to the position of Archbishop of Tuam. He had described MacHale to Gregory XIV as a political agitator and a firebrand and had supported the idea of the appointment of an English ambassador in Rome to control the Irish bishops. Clifford was connected by marriage to Cardinal Weld, who resided in Rome in the early 1840s, and he was able to wield some influence, but on the death of Weld and the appointment of Cardinal Acton, his influence waned. Clifford, who was described by D'Alton in his history of the Archbishops of Tuam as one of those 'pestilent intriguers who have so often skulked within the shadow of the Vatican', represented MacHale to Propaganda in the latter years of the famine as 'not averse to civil commotion'. MacHale then wrote to Propaganda to proclaim his unswerving principles against revolution. There did not appear to be much notice taken of Clifford's accusations in Rome and eventually Clifford apologised to Archbishop MacHale for his attacks. MacHale then described Lord Clifford as 'a benevolent and charitable nobleman'. However, the attacks on the Irish priests continued. In 1847 a Major Mahon of Stokestown, Roscommon, was shot dead. There followed a crusade against the Irish and particularly against the clergy. On 6 December Lord Farnham in the House of Lords accused the parish priest of Stokestown, Fr McDermott, of having instigated the murder by denouncing Mahon. Fr McDermott denied the charges, but *The Times* denounced him and other newspapers followed.

Archbishop MacHale received a letter from the Catholic Lord Arundel and Surrey asking him if the allegations were true. He wanted to know if the priests were denouncing men from the pulpit in order that they might be murdered. MacHale wrote at length to Lord John Russell and replied to Arundel and Surrey's letter. He told them that these charges against the clergy were calumnies and if clergy were abetting crimes they would be suspended from the duties of their office. He said that vague charges could not be deemed proper accusations. 'Your Lordships will not, I trust, imagine that I am now vindicating or excusing intemperate language, which I deplore.' He would always admonish intemperate language, but priests did have the right to denounce oppression and injustice and very often these priests, who were in the last stages of sickness and exhaustion, were men of blameless and laborious life, and however intemperate the language might be, it was usually accompanied by the reprobation of crime. Lord Arundel, who later became the Duke of Norfolk, continued in his correspondence with MacHale and became one of his most sincere supporters.

In his letter to Lord John Russell, MacHale's tone was not so conciliatory. He was filled with anger against those who would accuse his priests:

> Such sacred duties, punctually, perseveringly, and disinterestedly discharged, should, one would imagine, if not entitle them to the gratitude of those who are entrusted with the well-being of society, at least have shielded them against their censure.[10]

Many priests died during the famine, many 'carried the victims of pestilence, which others had shunned from the dread of contagion, and deposited them in their graves'. The Archbishop accused the Government of encouraging the calumnies as a justification for their lack of help for the starving. Frederick Lucas in the *Tablet* said, 'The stories of priestly instigations to murder are a collection of the grossest, foulest and most unfounded falsehoods.'

Archbishop MacHale also attacked the English press and their

> atrocious calumnies, concocted by some of the habitual defamers of our creed and country, issued from some latent source, without a name, without a date, without a defined locality. . . . They first appear in one journal. Then without delay, they are seen in another. The reflections of the odious monster are thus multiplied through the manifold mirrors of the public press. . . . The assassin's arm is assumed to have been raised on account of the priest's reprehension of some great public delinquency. Whereas in reality such reprehension seldom reaches the perpetrators of murder, who resort to other places rather than the house of God.

MacHale once again repeats the assurances that the Church would punish any priest guilty of instigating murder or any other crime: 'Were any clergyman found so to abuse his ministry as to excite any of his flock to any crime whatever, he would most surely be suspended from his sacred functions, and visited with the heaviest censures of the Church.'

MacHale suggests that 'amid the confiding and reverent mass of worshippers' there can occasionally be found 'some discreet persons of the Pharasaical school' who regret the introduction into a sermon of the Epistle of St James and 'the apostle's fiery denunciation of the rich oppressor of the poor, who "defrauds them of their wages; and their cries ascend to heaven" '. He says these men are often 'official personages as well as secret emissaries,– sent thither for the purpose of taking note of the public instructions'.

The Archbishop pours scorn on those people who read these calumnies in the press. He refers to the 'sensitive delicacy' of the educated classes and of 'the moral tone which pervades them' and of the 'refinement of the age' in which such productions 'are relished by your fashionable public'.[11]

John MacHale himself, together with Dr O'Higgins, the Bishop of Ardagh, was publicly attacked by the Catholic Earl of Shrewsbury, who sought to help the Whigs by joining in the accusations of Lord Farnham and Lord Roden, the Grand Master of the Orange Lodge.

However, many English Catholics were anxious that the Irish clergy should not think that they also thought like Lord Shrewsbury. One such Catholic was a young priest, Robert Whitty, who writes to Archbishop MacHale from the Convent of the Good Shepherd in Hammersmith in March 1848:

> I am anxious to put your Grace in possession of the true state of the case as regards the feelings of the recent Oxford converts towards the Irish church and Ireland in general. It would be very natural in Ireland to suppose them to be mixed up with Lord Shrewsbury and such English Catholics on the subject. Still I can assure your Grace, from a very intimate acquaintance with the chief of them, that such an idea would be very erroneous. . . . I spent the whole of last week with Mr

Newman and his Oratorian community at Maryvale, near Birmingham; and I can assure your Grace that though some of them may and do object to the severity and strength of language used in the late controversy; and though as a body, they would deprecate entering into a contest which is beyond the sphere of their duty, they, including Mr Newman himself, from whose lips I have it, strongly disapprove of Lord Shrewsbury's letter; and if occasion offered it would not shrink from expressing this.

Perhaps, my Lord, I may tell you that with no old Catholic priest or bishop in England is Mr Newman as well as his immediate friends more intimate than with myself. . . . The truth, then, is, some of them, such as Oakeley and Ward, go quite as far as Lucas, and agree with him thoroughly on Irish matters; most of them agree with Lucas's principles, and are anything but hostile to Ireland or Irishmen as such.

I write thus openly to your Grace merely for myself, and, of course, in confidence, that you may understand the facts. . . . Don't be led astray by their supposed connection with any bishops or noblemen in England; it may not be so very close as a person might infer from hearsay. Most of them, too, were Tories at Oxford; but this is no reason why, in altered circumstances, they may not have radical principles now.[12]

The letter of Lord Shrewsbury to which Whitty refers was an open letter addressed to the Archbishop of Tuam and the Bishop of Ardagh in which Shrewsbury accuses them of meddling in political agitation while neglecting the spiritual concerns of their flocks. Dr MacHale replied to these charges:

From the execrable calumnies of the English journals which your Lordship re-echoes with such emphatic fidelity, the public would be apt to infer that this diocese abounded in the murders and atrocities that have excited such general horror. How do the facts, however, stand?

Of all the murders and outrages on account of which commissions have been issued and the ordinary course of law has been suspended, not a single one has taken place within this diocese, though of all the dioceses in Ireland containing at once the most numerous and destitute population.[13]

MacHale admits that there have been 'an abundance of convictions' for such crimes as the seizures of 'cabbage and turnips by starving creatures'. The Archbishop says that he does not use this fact by way of an 'invidious contrast with other dioceses' that are disturbed 'notwithstanding the incessant zeal and preaching of their pastors' but to show the frame of mind of the conspirators who have represented Tuam as a place of incessant murder and violence.

The Earl of Shrewsbury also accused the Irish of being ungrateful for the help given to them in the famine. This charge particularly angered MacHale, as he had been most meticulous in his care to thank every donor, however small the donation.

In his personal attack on MacHale, Shrewsbury accused him of being unwilling to act with the Government or to accept Government help for the Church when it was offered. Shrewsbury said that MacHale's vast diocese was 'destitute' of places of worship. MacHale replied to this by saying that owing to the zeal and sacrifices of a generous people and clergy, they had recently erected between ninety and a hundred slated chapels 'with a view to capaciousness and convenience rather than beauty'. MacHale said the Irish people would not be bribed by 'a few churches and mended roofs'. Shrewsbury also accused the Irish as lacking the virtue of temperance and of 'popular subserviency'. MacHale replied that the priests had always encouraged the 'sacred virtue' of temperance and, with regard to Government support, the clergy did not want 'coils of ministerial patronage gently and successively drawn around the Church, until she should perish in the deadly embrace'.

Despite Archbishop MacHale's vigorous response to the Earl of Shrewsbury, in which he accused Shrewsbury of 'grossly insulting' the Catholic hierarchy of Ireland, Shrewsbury's accusations reached Rome and the Irish bishops were required to answer the complaints that their chapels were used for political purposes and they had incited the people to murder. Cardinal Fransoni wrote to the bishops saying that he did not believe the stories that were reaching Rome, but he asked for information. Archbishop Slattery wrote to the Cardinal explaining the situation and the difficulties faced by the Irish clergy.

In 1847 and 1848 there was a movement to restore diplomatic relations between the Court of Rome and the Court of St James. For this purpose the British Ambassador, Lord Minto, was sent to Italy. On 12 December 1847 Lord Lansdowne made a speech in Parliament, saying:

> There is no court in Europe in which it will be more useful than in Rome for the British government to explain the nature of our transactions, to lay open to that court, their nature and condition, or to induce that court to use its peculiar sources of influence in certain parts of her Majesty's dominions.[14]

It was thought by some that the Earl of Shrewsbury wanted his Italian son-in-law to become the Papal Nuncio in London. One of the positive outcomes for John MacHale of the attack on the Irish clergy in the English press was a lasting friendship that he formed with an Englishman, Charles Waterton. Waterton, as well as being a member of the House of Lords, was a distinguished naturalist. In January 1848 he was writing to a member of the Ursuline Community of Waterford:

> I see by today's paper that the Archbishop of Tuam has done me the high honour to notice me in his splendid letter to Lord John Russell. I have not the happiness to know his Grace personally, and I cannot bring myself to write to him to acknowledge the compliment. . . . I would rather have one single word of praise from the present Archbishop of Tuam than a whole chapter of encomiums from English royalty itself. . . .
>
> I see with sorrow, in a London paper of today, that the good and charitable but soft-brained Lord Shrewsbury has joined the ravenous pack of English blood-hounds to run down and worry Archbishop MacHale. I do hope that his Grace will

make this weak and foolish peer pay for his intolerable impertinence. He deserves a bastinado most richly.[15]

Shortly after this, Waterton began a correspondence with the Archbishop, which was to develop into a warm friendship. In February 1848 he once again refers to the Earl of Shrewsbury:

The Earl of Alton is again laid low . . . I suspect, by an observation in your Grace's reply, that my Lord has had his eye on his Italian son-in-law for the Papal Nuncio in London. If so, I can at once account for what has taken place. Our hungry Minister has, no doubt, a vehement longing for the last remaining Catholic chestnuts in Ireland; and he has cajoled the 'pious fool' to lend his paws. If so let us rejoice that the precious fruit is still safe, and laugh at the simpleton who has been base enough to help the rogue. . . .

Reverting to Ireland, I took my tomahawk so soon as the infamous attack had been made in the House of Lords against her holy hierarchy, and continued to use it when he of Alton Towers joined the impious crusade. But when I heard the cannon roar from Tuam's impregnable fortress, I laid it down again as it was not wanted; and I have only to add, with every deference and respect, that should in future my feeble service be of use to Ireland, I will take it up again, and do my best to show myself her friend.

In the meantime, begging a remembrance in your Grace's prayers, I have the honour to be, my dear Lord archbishop, your Grace's ever faithful friend and servant.

Charles Waterton[16]

In February 1848 Lord Lansdowne moved the second reading of the Diplomatic Relations Bill, which attempted to restore diplomatic relations between Britain and Rome. Lansdowne maintained that it was desirable to heal the long-standing breach between the two governments and the bill would put an end to the 'irregular methods' of communication used by past governments. Lord Stanley replied to Lansdowne by saying:

You know that the Pope has influence over your Catholic subjects, and you seek to obtain an influence over the Pope, in order to prevent his interference with your Roman Catholic subjects being carried on in a mode offensive to you. Now, that is, in plain English, the object of the Bill.[17]

The bill was supported by Lord Shrewsbury and also by Dr Wiseman, who was then the Vicar-apostolic of the London District. However, it was looked on with suspicion by the Irish hierarchy and also by Frederick Lucas, the editor of the *Tablet*. In an article in the *Tablet* the false accusations against the Irish priests were discussed:

Falsehood upon falsehood streamed through the Orange press. Conspiracies – not even founded in fact – were hatched daily. Landlords were made to receive threatening letters on whom their poor neighbours had never bestowed anything but blessings. Peers were made to fly the country who never so much dreamed of danger. Men were foully murdered who yet live and laugh at these diabolical inventions of Orange mendacity.

The *Tablet* accused the English Government of being accomplices

in these villainies. Ministers have an end to serve by the general belief in these frauds, both here and in Rome. The Marquis of Lansdowne made no secret of their intentions. He frankly avowed that the government was bent upon renewing diplomatic intercourse with Rome, in order to use Roman influence for the management of the Church in Ireland. To accomplish this end, it was expedient not merely to use friendly expressions in the Holy City, but to have it believed there, and throughout Europe, that Ireland was an Aceldama, and the priests instigators to bloodshed and that the only safety of the Church in Ireland consisted in taking counsel with St James's as to the spiritual well-being of that ill-fated land.[18]

For the purpose of uniting Catholic opinion against the bill, Frederick Lucas founded the Society of St Thomas of Canterbury. He initially encouraged the Earl of Shrewsbury to take on the presidency of the Society, thinking that influential names would be helpful, but after Shrewsbury's attacks on the Irish clergy and the *Morning Chronicle's* declaration that 'the British Protestant public are deeply indebted to the Earl of Shrewsbury', the Earl resigned his position.

In March 1848 the Society of St Thomas of Canterbury met in London to protest against the Diplomatic Relations Bill and to denounce the Whigs' attacks on the Irish Catholic clergy. Lucas made a rousing speech:

> The authors and promoters of the Bill desire, not benevolently to repeal a penal law; not to wipe away a reproach from England; not to abolish a legislative insult upon Rome; but by the aid of English fleets and armies to coerce the Holy See into becoming an instrument of party warfare within these realms . . . with a double perfidy, they labour perpetually to interpose the Holy See between Ireland and their iniquities. . . .
>
> If these wretched Whig traders in politics cannot govern Ireland through Justice, they cannot govern it through Rome'.[19]

In February 1848 Paul Cullen wrote to Archbishop MacHale with some urgency:

> Your Grace would do well to write frequently upon our Irish affairs to the Propaganda. I think our British friends and the ambassador [Lord Minto] are working heaven and earth against us: calumnies are not spared. Minto wanted the Pope to write to the bishops and complain of the murders. The Pope refused.
>
> I explained matters to the Pope and showed him how the priests were calumniated, and that oppression was the only source of the murders. . . .
>
> Here we are very quiet. The Pope is not frightened either by the radicals, who would drive things on to a revolution, or by

the fears of old, cautious fellows, who look upon every reform as a revolution. However there is a vile infidel party throughout Italy ready to pounce upon the Pope. . . . This party is supported by Minto and the English. . . . Your letter to the Propaganda has done a great deal of good.[20]

Notes

1   Bernard O'Reilly, *The Life and Times of John MacHale* (1890), II, pp. 9–11.
2   Ibid., pp. 24–5.
3   Ibid., pp. 26–7.
4   James Tuke, *A Visit to Connaught* (A Letter to the Central Relief Committee of the Society of Friends, 20 November 1847).
5   Clarendon quoted in O'Reilly, op. cit., pp. 28–30.
6   Tuke, op. cit.
7   MacHale MSS, O'Reilly, op. cit., p. 32.
8   Ibid., p. 34.
9   Ibid., p. 35.
10   Ibid., p. 64.
11   Ibid., pp. 64–5.
12   Ibid., pp. 70–71.
13   Ibid., p. 77.
14   Ibid., p. 105.
15   Ibid., pp. 91–2.
16   Ibid., pp. 92–3.
17   Ibid., p. 106.
18   Edward Lucas, *The Life of Frederick Lucas* (1886), p. 94.
19   Ibid., pp. 300–301.
20   O'Reilly, op. cit., II, p. 109.

12

TUMULT IN EUROPE

'It is beneath the Imperial dignity to refuse anyone the liberty of speaking out; it is unworthy of God's priest not to give utterance to his convictions.' (St Ambrose)

IN 1848 EUROPE was in turmoil. The Orleanist King of the French, Louis Philippe, was overthrown in March and a French Republic proclaimed, with Louis Napoleon as President for four years. There was a rising in Vienna, which resulted in the flight of Metternich. There were nationalist risings in Bohemia and Hungary, and in Switzerland the Swiss Federal Constitution was established. In Germany the Frankfurt Parliament was attempting to unite Germany on liberal principles and in Italy the nationalist movement under Garibaldi was gaining ground.

The Government of Great Britain, although having some concerns about Chartism, the situation in Ireland and other possible revolutionary movements at home, did not discourage the continental revolutionary movements and in some situations actively encouraged them. Palmerston, the British Foreign Secretary, sent Lord Minto to Italy to give 'moral support' and advice to the Italian Liberals. British encouragement was enough to start open revolution in Sicily in January 1848. At the time, Lord Minto was encouraging Italian revolution, a situation presaging danger for the Papal States, and he was also trying to court the Pope to re-open diplomatic relations with Britain.

The accession of Pius IX in 1846 had been greeted with joy by his temporal subjects in the Papal States and by his spiritual followers throughout the Church, as he was known to be a Liberal and an advocate of enlightened progress. One of his first acts was to proclaim an amnesty for all those imprisoned in the Papal States for political crimes and an invitation for those who had fled abroad to

155

return. The Italians were ecstatic in their praise of 'Pio Nono' and thronged the streets of Rome in their enthusiasm for him. He tried to carry out practical reforms for Rome by the improvement of street lighting and the railways. He encouraged scientific and agricultural societies and tried to carry out his liberal ideas by granting freedom of the press and beginning a consultative assembly where laymen would take part. Pius IX also made attempts to separate the spiritual and temporal powers of the Pope.

Many conservative European leaders did not favour Pius's liberalism, and there were many Italians who saw in him a certain naivety, knowing that Mazzini and Count Camillo Benso di Cavour, a politician who founded the newspaper *Il Risorgimento*, which reflected Italian National aspirations, were not to be thrown off course by a reforming Pope.

The British Government was encouraged in its attempts to restore diplomatic relations with Rome by some prominent English Catholics – the Earl of Shrewsbury, who had ambitions for his son-in-law, Prince Doria, and more surprisingly by Dr Nicholas Wiseman, a leader of English Catholics who in 1840 was named Coadjutor Vicar-apostolic. In his *Memoirs*, Charles Greville, a political diarist, writes in December 1847:

> A few days ago I met Dr Wiseman, and had much talk with him about Rome and the Pope's recent rescript about the colleges in Ireland. He said it was all owing to there being no English ambassador at Rome, and no representative of the moderate Irish clergy; Irish ecclesiastical affairs were managed through MacHale through Fransoni, head of propaganda, and Fr Ventura, who has the Pope's ear; and he strongly advised that Murray and his party should send an agent to Rome, and that Lord Minto should communicate with Fr Ventura, who is an able and good man, deeply interested in Irish affairs and anxious for a British connection. He talked a good deal about the Pope, who, he said, had not time to enquire about these matters himself, and took his inspirations from the above-named personages; that he is of unbending firmness in all that relates to religion, but liberal and anxious to conciliate England.[1]

The Irish hierarchy were, for the most part, very concerned about the discussions taking place in Rome. They thought their situation would be misrepresented and felt very threatened by any alliance of the British Government and the Pope. Dr Cullen wrote repeatedly to MacHale encouraging him to come to Rome. In February 1848 he wrote:

> It would be well to have some one here to watch the progress of events. . . . The Pope is in such difficulties that it would be the fittest moment [for the government] to get him to do something. If your Grace could get a meeting of the bishops to depute two prelates to act in their name, their representations would be the more efficacious. Or even if you had a provincial meeting, and passed resolutions, and sent an address to his Holiness by one or two prelates, the effect would be very good.[2]

The Archbishop did not want to go at that time because of the famine, but he agreed that after he had completed his visitation of the archdiocese in 1848, he would go to Rome. He arrived there in the late spring of 1848, accompanied by Dr Higgins of Ardagh. They took with them a memorial, dated 27 March 1848 and signed by seventeen out of the twenty-six Irish bishops, to be presented to the Pope. They found on their arrival that they had been preceded by two members of the Irish clergy who had come to speak on behalf of the British Government. These were Dr Ennis, deputed by Dr Murray of Dublin, to speak for the Queen's colleges and Dr Nicholson, a coadjutor from Corfu, chosen by Lord Clarendon as his special agent in Rome. Ennis and Nicholson had arrived some weeks before the Irish bishops and already laid before Propaganda the documents prepared in Dublin. Lord Clarendon had written a letter to Murray in which he had put forward the amended statutes of the Queen's Colleges. This letter was calculated to create a favourable impression on the Pope. His anxiety for the cause of religion in English higher education contrasted well with the situation in the German, Spanish and French universities.

In the memorial presented by Archbishop MacHale and Bishop O'Higgins to the Pope, they first of all referred to the attacks on the Irish priests and bishops:

A tempest of calumny has assailed the Church in Ireland. Our modern Pharisees, truly a generation of vipers, with their lips steeped in the poison of asps, are hissing their slanders not only against our innocent priests, whom they accuse of profaning their churches to sacrilegious uses, and of inciting their flocks to commit murder, but against ourselves as well, as if we tolerated these criminal acts which we beheld with our own eyes.

This whirlwind of falsehood . . . has . . . reached the capital of the Catholic world: so that, when the private letter of his eminence Cardinal Fransoni, sent to ask information on this matter, was lately made public (which was a piece of supreme indiscretion), our priests and our people were filled with the greatest alarm, lest this calumny should carry away the Romans themselves. . . .

We know to a certainty, and affirm it to your Holiness, that these reports about the profanation of the house of God, and the instigation to murder, are pure and detestable falsehoods, as well as our imputed connivance at these criminal deeds, — falsehoods set afloat for the most wicked purposes.[3]

The bishops went on to say that after the publication of Cardinal Fransoni's letter, they were very relieved to know that it had been answered by Michael Slattery, the Archbishop of Cashel.

But no sooner has one peril ceased, than a greater peril looms up. While famine and pestilence are desolating Ireland; while our people are losing all heart, and their bishops are divided amongst themselves; while the revolutions which disturb not only Italy but the whole of Europe, fill people's minds with alternate hope and dread; at this critical juncture, when the fatherly heart of your Holiness is naturally oppressed with increasing cares, the British Government deem the present moment a favourable one to use their most powerful exertions to extort from your Holiness, *per fas et nefas*,[4] certain concessions, the direct tendency of which would be not only to seriously impair the freedom of our ancient Church, but to utterly destroy its independence.

The bishops also claim that the Government agents are at work to try to persuade the Pope to recall his rescript against the Government colleges. The bishops say that not only are some of the Government agents Catholics and even priests, but they have amongst their number an archbishop. This archbishop was the coadjutor of Corfu, Dr Nicholson. The Irish bishops were very frank in their contempt for Dr Nicholson:

> Pardon us, we beseech you, Holy Father, if we make bold here to inquire who and what is this Dr Nicholson, who mixes himself up so officiously with the business of our Church, not, assuredly, for the purpose of advancing the cause of religion, but of helping the government to usurp the rights of religion?
>
> Is Dr Nicholson distinguished for that learning and prudence which fit a man for weighty negotiations? Not at all. With the exception of a certain artfulness, that might help rather in little matters than those of importance, there is nothing in the man to lift him above mediocrity.
>
> Does he enjoy any influence among us?
>
> None whatever, so far as we know. . . . Having no business of his own to attend to, he only minds other people's business, and sows trouble everywhere. . . .
>
> If his zeal, indiscreet though it be, were of a nature to advance the cause of religion, we would not mention his name. But inasmuch as he forsakes that part of the Master's field entrusted to his care, to put his sickle in our harvest, not for the purpose of helping to gather it in, but to ruin it; inasmuch as this shepherd without a flock comes among us to seduce and destroy our flocks, we therefore presume, with all due reverence, to say to your Holiness, – let him go to Corfu, and allow your Holiness and us to care for the spiritual interests of Ireland.[5]

The bishops state that they have learnt that the Government has drawn up new statutes for the Queen's Colleges and has given a copy of them to Dr Nicholson. They wonder why he should conceal these plans from the 'bishops as a body'. The bishops restate their reasons for their opposition to the Queen's Colleges and regret the divisions that have become entrenched among the Irish bishops.

> There is, indeed, between the members of our hierarchy an outward union on all questions relating to Church discipline; but there is no longer any internal union of minds and counsels. And so the question has now come to this: whether henceforward our Irish Church is to be governed by your Holiness through the body of our bishops, or by the British Government through the agency of a few bishops devoted to their interests.[6]

During the summer of 1848 the Cardinals examined the voluminous papers sent in concerning the Queen's Colleges and decided to abide by the former rescript. The decision was sanctioned by the Pope on 11 October.

> After maturely considering all things, the Sacred Congregation could not be induced, in view of the serious and intrinsic dangers of these Colleges, to mitigate the judgement pronounced on them with the approbation of our most Holy Father, and laid before the four Irish metropolitans on October the 9th of last year.[7]

The Cardinals said that they hoped for the creation of a Catholic university 'for giving Catholics a higher education, while securing their faith from all danger'. The Cardinals then stressed the need for 'priestly concord' and expressed the desire that the differences amongst the bishops should be resolved.

The Irish bishops then decided it was time to leave Rome. Ulick Bourke tells the story of how Archbishop MacHale, in company with Dr Higgins of Ardagh and Dr Cantwell of Meath, left Rome in a hired carriage. They were stopped by Garibaldi's volunteers, who had been instructed not to allow any ecclesiastics to leave Rome. The bishops were not dressed in ecclesiastical clothes but in 'bourgeois apparel', as was the custom for Catholic priests in England and Ireland at that time. Bourke says that one of the bishops spoke to the soldiers with 'an air of authority', not disclosing the fact that they were clerics, and the soldiers let them go.[8] This was fortunate, as the very next day the Pope's Prime Minister, Count Rossi, was murdered in broad daylight as he alighted from his carriage to enter the chamber of deputies. Shortly after this, the Quirinal palace was besieged and the Pope had to escape as an exile to Gaeta, where he remained for seventeen months as a guest of the King of Naples.

Archbishop MacHale arrived back in Tuam in December to a tumultuous reception. Thousands of people surrounded his carriage, unharnessed his horses and dragged it into the city. The mission of the bishops to Rome was seen as successful in informing the Pope of the Irish situation and preventing him from being deceived by the Government. The local Catholic gentry invited Dr MacHale to a public banquet to celebrate his return. He replied that he was reluctant 'to accept the honour at such a time', but later gave a speech in which he set out what he had tried to do. He said that repeal of the Union did not seem very near at that time but he said that they should ask for legal pledges of a tenure for tenants and compensation for their outlay in improving their land.

The Government was aware of the tenants' problems and in December 1847 Russell had written to Lansdowne:

> The war between landlord and tenant has been carried on for eighty years. It is evident that this relation, which ought to be one of mutual confidence, is one of mutual hostility; nor do I see that they can be left to fight out the battle with any prospect of better result.[9]

A tenant-right bill was introduced in 1848. It was read a second time and referred to a committee, but that was the end of it. Parliament seemed to be satisfied with a different remedy. During the famine and in the years following it, many landlords had become bankrupt. They could neither meet their obligations under the Poor Law, nor improve their lands. The Government decided to disregard vested rights and to allow the sale of an encumbered estate on the petition of a landlord or a creditor, with the hope that a secure title would attract English investors with capital for developing the land. The Encumbered Estates Act came into operation in 1849. Many people welcomed it but its effect on the smaller tenants was unfortunate. English investors were not attracted and the tenants exchanged one set of landlords for another, who were often harsher in evicting smallholders.

The Whigs also had to deal with the threat of rebellion in Ireland, albeit rather an effete one. The European revolutions had excited John Mitchell and some of his friends of the 'Young Ireland' movement. They were joined by Smith O'Brien, a member of Parliament. After they had vainly sought help from Lamartine in France, they were prosecuted. The jury failed to agree, but eventually Mitchell was found guilty and sentenced to deportation for fourteen years. O'Brien collected round him a handful of peasants, made a wild attack on a police station in Tipperary and was arrested five days later. O'Brien and the other leaders were transported to Australia. The Irish had not supported O'Brien's call to arms. It was condemned by Gavan Duffy and deplored by a saddened Archbishop MacHale on his return to Ireland.

The year 1849 did not look as though it was going to be an improvement on the two previous years. The people of the west of Ireland were still starving and the evictions were continuing relentlessly. Archbishop MacHale had pleaded with the Viceroy and the Prime Minister. He saw his priests struggling to help their dying flocks and did not know where to turn next. He decided to appeal to the Queen. MacHale maintained throughout his life an unswerving loyalty to the Monarch. He believed in a separate Parliament for the Irish but always with the Queen as the Head of State. He saw the loyalty to the Crown as a religious principle, associating republicanism with atheism and anti-clericalism.

MacHale's letter to the Queen was dated the Eve of Pentecost 1849. He begins with a quotation from St Ambrose to the Emperor Theodosius: *Neque Imperiale est libertatum dicendi denegare, neque sacerdotale quod sentiat non dicere* (It is beneath the Imperial dignity to refuse anyone the liberty of speaking out; it is unworthy of God's priest not to give utterance to his convictions). MacHale says that he has been reluctant so far to contact the Queen about the famine:

> The long and strange omission of an appeal to the Sovereign on behalf of her dying subjects can only be accounted for on the ground that your majesty's power is not at all commensurate with the well-known benevolence of your feelings.[10]

The Archbishop then describes some of the sufferings of the people of Ireland and especially those of his own diocese:

> The sun is said never to set on your majesty's dominions. Yet, while its light is gladdening another hemisphere subjected to your sceptre, it goes down, in the immediate vicinity of your throne, on scenes of destitution and death as terrible and heart-rending as it has ever witnessed since it first rose upon mankind.
>
> Your commerce penetrates every region, however remote; and the produce of every clime is wafted in abundance to the favoured shores of England, and yet along the safer and more capacious harbours of the West of Ireland, the people are seen dying in numbers, destitute of the coarsest, nay, the most loathsome food that mortal ever ventured to snatch in the agonies of hunger. They endeavour, all in vain, to protract their lives by eating the poisonous vegetables of the field, or the no less poisonous sea-weeds along the shore.
>
> These are not vague rumours, promiscuously poured on the public ear. . . . I neither write nor speak from vague hearsay. . . . The melancholy facts, with which, however, I shall not now fatigue the royal ear, were the result of my own observation . . . among the poor of Connemara. The dismantled cabins of whole villages which one meets on approaching that sequestered country could not be more unsightly or desolate, had they been ravaged by an invading army. . . . Here is a tale of filial piety, already descanted on by a benevolent Protestant

clergyman of Ballinrobe, and which occurred a day or two before my return . . . .

A young girl, anxious to procure for her aged mother, just dead of cholera, the rites of Christian burial, sought in vain for anyone who might help her. But a few days before her bereavement the good young priest, who was wont to be ever at hand with his ministrations, fell a victim to his priestly charity towards his flock. . . . In the midst of the wilderness surrounding her cabin, the young girl, to whom her filial piety gave preternatural strength, carried the corpse of her parent for more than a mile, and buried it in a grave; a day later she was herself laid by the side of her mother, a victim to the fearful malady, or rather to her own heroic daughterly love.[11]

Dr MacHale then proceeds to indict Russell's Government for their neglect of the Irish people:

There are sins of omission as well as commission; and the former are those for which persons in high and public station are most frequently responsible.

In an answer made by your Majesty's Viceroy to the memorial address to him in October 1847, praying the seasonable intervention of the Government to snatch, by timely aid, the people from famine, it was admitted that to save the lives of the people was the first and paramount duty of the Government. The strongest hopes were held out that this duty would be faithfully performed. . . .

Your ministers parade the laws for providing for the poor, as a proof of the government's solicitude to protect the lives of the people.

But the amount of relief allowed, even if regularly applied, could not sustain life for any length of time. Again, so many impediments are thrown in the way of relief, that numbers perish ere they can obtain it. And finally, those who, at vast sacrifices and by denying themselves the necessaries of life, make some tillage, are precluded from all relief unless they make a surrender of their land![12]

The Archbishop explains his appeal to the Queen by comparing the situation to Flavian appealing to the Emperor Theodosius for the people of Antioch:

> Would it not be an everlasting reproach that a pastor of the Catholic Church should not attempt, even though he should not succeed, in behalf of the doomed but innocent people of a province, what Flavian achieved for the guilty people of Antioch? The people of Ireland have not insulted your Majesty; they have not broken your statutes; they are guiltless of any crime, and yet they are enduring the most excruciating of all deaths, starvation with a patience that transcends all belief.
>
> The efforts of individuals in their behalf are beyond all praise. The instances of heroic charity shown by subscribers from England as well as from Ireland and, in short, from the continent of Europe as well as America, which have come within my knowledge, are no less surprising than the silent and resigned endurance of the victims whom they are desirous of rescuing from death.
>
> But private benevolence, how heroic soever, is not adequate to cope with the vastness of the calamity. . . . It requires Imperial aid on such a scale and administered in such a manner that, while it saves the lives of the people, it may enable them by profitable labour to draw out the unexplored riches of their fertile but neglected country.
>
> To all our applications for such aid one unvaried answer has been given by your majesty's servants, the inadequacy of the means at their disposal and the reluctance of the legislature to increase their amount.
>
> Were an enemy to invade the shores of England, and to threaten the lives or the liberties of its inhabitants, all the available resources of the Empire would instantly be placed at the disposal of the Minister to repel the hostile aggression. Let but the glory of the British arms suffer a temporary eclipse in far-distant India, millions are voted at the beck of the Minister,

armies and navies are transported as if with a magic celerity, to repair the national disaster.

Yet now, when the lives of thousands of your faithful subjects in Ireland are sacrificed to an enemy that could be arrested by a far less expenditure, your ministers tell the world that they have at their disposal no means to save your people's lives!

This unfeeling indifference is a bad requital for the valour and fidelity with which Irishmen are pouring out their blood in defence of your Majesty's distant dominions, while their nearest relatives at home are perishing by starvation in the midst of plenty![13]

MacHale then asks the Queen to call to her councils 'able men, such as fear God, in whom there is truth, and hate avarice'.

In the meantime, Queen Victoria had resolved with her consort, Prince Albert, to pay a visit to Ireland. They did not want too much ostentation as it would seem unfitting because of the famine. Nevertheless, there was much discussion in Dublin as to how the visit was to be arranged and who should visit her and so on. Archbishop Murray wrote to Archbishop MacHale on 20 July 1849:

It is, I believe the wish of our bishops, as it is also mine, to attend her Majesty's levee on the occasion of her first visit to Ireland. Would it be your Grace's wish to offer her, on that occasion a similar mark of respect?[14]

MacHale replied to Murray that he thought it would be a good opportunity in an address to the Queen to talk about the sufferings of the people of Ireland. Murray replied in a hurried note on 25 July that the time was too short for general deliberation, but he asked for MacHale's signature on an address that contained no reference to the famine. MacHale replied on the 30th of the month, declining to affix his signature to any form of address that did not contain reference to the sufferings on which 'Christian bishops should not be silent'. MacHale enclosed with his letter a suggestion of an address which he said had been approved by several of the bishops. After welcoming the Queen and offering 'profound homage' and 'dutiful fealty' MacHale says:

> It is to us a source of affliction that the joy inspired by your Majesty's coming among us is clouded by the thought that poverty and destitution unexampled in any other country of the civilised world, and aggravated by four successive years of famine, have so prostrated the people of Ireland as to make them unable suitably to indulge the gladness of their kindly disposition, or to invest the welcome of their generous hearts in the suitable outward expressions and enthusiastic manifestations with which they would not have failed, in less adverse circumstances, to greet the advent of a well-beloved sovereign.[15]

MacHale then went on to talk about the unjust laws, especially the latest coercion act 'stripping the people of their constitutional rights'. Murray replied immediately, saying that he could not use MacHale's address but had altered his own somewhat to mention the famine:

> On an occasion so truly cheering as the present, we will not place before your Majesty a detail of the many woes of our suffering poor, the thought of which has, we know, pressed already so severely on your majesty's parental heart.[16]

Murray also paid tribute to Prince Albert. He said he was aware of his many titles, but for him the most important one was 'it is that the happiness of your Royal Highness is closely bound up with the happiness of our beloved Queen'.

Archbishop MacHale did not sign the address and neither did he attend the Queen's levee.

Notes

1 Charles Greville, *The Greville Memoirs,* III, p. 107.
2 Bernard O'Reilly, *The Life and Times of John MacHale* (1890), II, p. 117.
3 Ibid., pp. 122–3.

4   'By good or evil.'
5   O'Reilly, op. cit., II, pp. 124–6.
6   Ibid., p. 131.
7   Ibid., p. 147.
8   Ulick Bourke, *Life and Times of the Most Reverend John MacHale* (1883), pp. 152–4.
9   Sir Spencer Walpole, *Life of Lord John Russell,* I (1891), p. 466.
10 O'Reilly, op. cit., II, p. 179.
11 Ibid., pp. 179–80.
12 Ibid., pp. 181–2.
13 Ibid., pp. 183–4.
14 Daniel Murray, *Correspondence between Dr Murray and Dr MacHale* (1885), p. 7.
15 Ibid., p. 14.
16 Ibid., p. 15.

13

New Confidence for the Church in Ireland and England

'parturiunt montes, nascetur ridiculus mus!'
(Horace, quoted by Benjamin Disraeli)

IN THE SPRING of 1849 the Archbishop of Armagh, Dr William Crolly, died. Armagh was the seat of St Patrick and, traditionally for both Catholics and Protestants, the seat of the Primates of all Ireland. The election of a successor to Crolly was watched with great interest in England and Ireland. Archbishop Crolly had been a supporter of Dr Murray in his acceptance of the National Education scheme and in his general amenability to the English Government.

Three candidates were suggested, John O'Hanlon and Joseph Dixon who were professors at Maynooth, and Michael Kieran, a parish priest. Dixon and Kieran were favoured by Dr Murray and the British Government and Dr O'Hanlon by MacHale and the majority of the Irish bishops. The Pope remained an exile in Gaeta, but there were still the usual machinations of various parties to encourage him to favour their chosen candidate. In the north of Ireland, Dr MacNally, the Bishop of Clogher, said that there were fears expressed by some important local Protestants, who inquired whether there was 'any danger' of MacHale becoming Primate. In July 1849, William O'Higgins, Bishop of Armagh, wrote to Dr MacHale asking him to write to Rome about the situation and encouraging him to go to Paris where Meyler and Ennis and Cooper were 'perpetrating calumnies' against O'Hanlon and MacHale. In August, Archbishops Cantwell and MacHale went to Paris together with Bishop Denvir. MacHale also wrote to Cardinal Fransoni in Rome. In his letter he says that Dixon has 'all the gifts of industry and talent necessary toward faithfully teaching the younger students at Maynooth'. He

169

describes Kieran as 'a good parish priest'. He says of O'Hanlon 'the Rev. John O'Hanlon merits by his talents, his learning, and the varied maturity of his gifts, as well as by the fruitful result of his labours in every position he has filled, to be preferred far above the two others on the list'. He says that the times are difficult and that perils 'threaten our holy faith. . . . Our bishops at present are surrounded on every side by artful and designing wickedness, and tempted by all manner of seduction.' In normal times Dixon or Kieran could be placed at the head of a 'suffragen diocese', but would be 'quite unfit to face the higher and more weighty duties of the primatial office'.

At the end of the letter Archbishop MacHale makes another suggestion:

> Wherefore, inasmuch as I only find one of the three candidates designated whom I judge to be worthy, I should most earnestly recommend, in case the Rev. Mr O'Hanlon is not chosen, the Very Rev. Paul Cullen, President of the Irish College in Rome, a man not only admirably qualified for such a dignity, as is well known to your Eminence and to the Fathers of the Sacred Congregation, but who would be most acceptable to the entire body of bishops and to the Irish clergy.
>
> Under him or Dr O'Hanlon there would be security for the Catholic faith and the authority of the Holy See.[1]

The Holy See appeared to take Dr MacHale's advice and appointed Dr Cullen as Archbishop of Armagh and Primate of Ireland. At first Dr Cullen refused the appointment. Dr Kirby, the Rector of the Irish College in Rome, in a letter to MacHale, tells of Cullen's reaction to the appointment:

> The news has come upon him like a clap of thunder. He repeatedly refused, within the last two months, and sustained his refusal by what appeared to him the most cogent reasons.[2]

Eventually Dr Cullen was persuaded by Cardinal Fransoni to accept. The position of Rector of the Irish College in Rome was then given to Dr Kirby. In December, when the secretary of Propaganda wrote to Archbishop Slattery of Cashel to announce the appointment of Dr Cullen, the letter stated that the appointment was 'mainly to cherish and strengthen episcopal unity' in Ireland.

It was hoped that Dr Cullen would come to Ireland early in 1850, but he was still in Rome in March 1850. He wrote to MacHale on 24 March:

> I am sorry to inform your Grace that I am still in Rome. I went last week . . . to see his Holiness who is quite well and preparing to return. He expects to be here on 10 April.[3]

However, although Cullen was still in Rome, he was busy organising a national Irish synod, which he hoped would take place shortly after he was enthroned in Armagh. In his letter to MacHale he mentions various questions that will call for treatment at the synod: education, matters affecting the faith and liberty of the Church, the condition of the poor, regulations for the clergy, secular and regular, and the removal of abuses. He asks for MacHale's advice on what the synod will discuss. While in Rome he was investigating canon law and drawing up 'regulations for the clergy'. He was also considering the setting up of a Catholic university. In a postscript to his letter to MacHale he mentions the Catholic university:

> P.S. – I forgot to say a word about the university. I shall do everything possible to promote the project. I fear however that the committee now acting will do no good. Mr Battersby and Father Spratt are not well fitted to commence the work. Perhaps it may be discredited unless some of the first men in Ireland, lay and clerical, be induced to give their names to the committee. It would be better to delay a few weeks in order to get a regular committee appointed. I wrote to Rev. Mr Cooper and begged of him to explain how matters stand. Above all things we are to avoid dissensions on the question; otherwise we cannot succeed. – P.C.[4]

Father Peadar MacSuibhne, who has published the letters of Paul Cullen, finds this postscript of some significance in trying to answer the question that became important later, as to whether Cullen, who had lived forty years in Rome, was ignorant of Irish conditions or whether, as the agent of the Irish bishops to Propaganda, he had a thorough knowledge of Irish affairs. Fr MacSuibhne describes Battersby, dismissed by Cullen as not 'well-fitted', as being a well-informed and scholarly historian.

The town of Thurles was chosen as the venue for the national synod as a favour to Dr Slattery, whose health was not very good. The synod was to be in two sessions, the first beginning on 22 August, the second on 29 August. It ended on 9 September 1850.

The importance of the Synod of Thurles lies not so much in its enactments and decisions, important as these were, but in the fact of its taking place. It was seen both inside and outside of the Catholic Church as the sign of the emergence of the Catholic Church in Ireland after the age of persecution. It was now clear to the people of Britain and Ireland that Ireland was to remain a largely Catholic country. The appointment of Paul Cullen as Apostolic Delegate as well as Archbishop of Armagh reinforced the loyalty of the Irish Church to Rome. The synod was opened amid great ceremony and spectacle. It took place in the theological college at Thurles and in the cathedral. Charles Bianconi, a prominent man in Ireland, had lent beautiful paintings from his art collection to decorate the walls of the college and the cathedral. The scene was colourful and picturesque, the priests and bishops dressed in their robes and members of religious orders in their distinctive habits. The ceremony began with the chanting of the *Veni Creator* in the college chapel and then a procession from the chapel to the cathedral, where the priests and prelates were awaited by the people. The scene is described in the *Illustrated News:*

> The bell from the Cathedral tower tolled solemnly, and the Litany was chanted in true Gregorian cadence, while the procession passed along in splendid array, until it was lost sight of under the arched portal of the Cathedral.[5]

For the people of Ireland who had recently passed through the horrors of the famine, the ceremony with its colour, solemnity, incense and sacred music was moving and entrancing. It filled them with hope and thanksgiving in the midst of their mourning and desolation.

Archbishop MacHale was selected to preach at the second public session of the Council on 29 September. He chose for his subject, 'The Church, Christ's Kingdom upon Earth'. He used the opportunity to talk about the role of the Church in education, a subject that was hotly debated at the synod. One of the primary objects of the synod was to reaffirm the right of the Church to superintend and direct the public education of Christian youth, and to affirm the supreme authority of the Holy See in deciding all questions pertaining to doctrine and morals in the matter of education. MacHale spoke about the dignity and importance of the Synod of Thurles, 'this episcopal senate, assembled under the auspices and control of the successor of St Patrick, clothed with the delegated dignity of the Holy See'. He said that:

> It is through the medium of its congregated councils, through acts that embody the wisdom and authority of its bishops under its venerable Head, that the majesty of this kingdom is particularly displayed.

MacHale went on to speak about the authority of the Pope:

> The Pope is everywhere. His voice is heard, his influence is felt, and his authority is owned, not only in the august oecumenical assemblies, . . . but wherever the faith is endangered, or its intrepid champions exposed to peril, or the holy discipline of the church attempted to be changed or trampled on. . . . From the same centre issued the impulse to which Europe was indebted for the erection and support of its schools and colleges, which sprung up with amazing rapidity and success, encouraged and sustained everywhere by episcopal synods and councils.[6]

Archbishop MacHale then spoke of the schisms, revolutions and upheavals through the centuries that had deprived the Church of her authority:

> From the close of the Council of Trent to the present period, the Church has been in fetters throughout almost all Europe, and incapable of that free and harmonious action which, through its canonical councils, always regulated by the Popes, it exercised in the preceding ages.
>
> With the authority of the bishops thus shackled, the charitable and educational establishments, which they were wont to foster and guide, fell almost exclusively under the control of secular agencies.

MacHale speaks about 'The step-dame influence of secular power' which enfeebled the Church and brought about the 'partition of her functions'.

> Between Virtue and Knowledge, between Morality and Science, an unnatural divorce was attempted, as if they had not flourished in all their vigour when wedded together under the tutelage of the Catholic Church.
>
> Of the shoots of the Tree of Knowledge, bitter experience has taught the fruit to be the knowledge of evil as well as of good; whereas, it is only when engrafted on the stem of Faith, and watered with the dews from heaven, it becomes so rich and fragrant as to give a foretaste of eternal life.
>
> Science itself is subjected to minute analysis for the purpose of resolving it into independent sources, as if all knowledge could not be traced to its own heavenly origin, or as if the various colours and names it assumes from the refracting mediums through which it passes were not, like the variegated rays of the solar spectrum, all derived from the great original and eternal light of the word, 'which enlighteneth every man that cometh into this world'
>
> It would seem as if one distinct domain, and that sufficiently limited, had been assigned to the Church, whilst a

larger one, of indefinite extent, is claimed for secular science, over which, it is contended she should exercise no control.

But holding her high and sacred position, as the noblest emanation of God's infinite knowledge in this world, she has not ceased, and never will cease, to exercise her reasonable dominion over all the subordinate sciences, allowing the human mind the fullest scope in their cultivation and development, provided they come not in collision with those sacred truths that are entrusted to her custody. . . . For more than fifteen centuries the entire dominion of the civililized world belonged to her, . . . its sciences, its arts, its civilization, its history, its laws, and its institutions for promoting the welfare of mankind. And am I to be told that the treasures of her wisdom, and the trophies of her authority . . . are to be rifled and given over to some of her disobedient children against that very Church by which they were created?[7]

The Synod of Thurles subsequently went on to vote against the secular university colleges proposed by the Government and to recommend the setting up of a Catholic university in Ireland. This idea had been recommended by the Pope, who envisaged a university similar to that of Louvain in Belgium. The idea was taken up enthusiastically by Cullen, who was supported by Archbishops MacHale and Slattery, but not by Archbishop Murray, who persisted in his support for the Government colleges. MacHale had been ordained and consecrated bishop by Daniel Murray and was conscious of his virtues, but he disagreed strongly with him on matters of education and on his relationship with the Government. Cullen at the beginning of each session had asked that the discussions should take place in a spirit of 'charity and mildness' and all the bishops were anxious that there should be harmony amongst the hierarchy, even if there was not complete agreement.

The synod ended as it had begun with solemn ceremonies and joyful festivities. In his closing address on 9 September, Dr Cullen once again referred to the new era of liberty for the Catholic Church in Ireland. He said that the assembled bishops and congregation were to be congratulated on 'the happy termination of this most important assemblage, this new and solemn proof and attestation of the renovated youth and strengthened fidelity of the Catholic Church in Ireland'. However, he stressed that the struggles of the Church were not at an end. This theme is re-echoed in the address of the bishops at the close of the synod:

> The synod has been the most important assembly held in the Church in Ireland since the time of St Patrick. Its chief object was to decide on the measures necessary for preserving in spite of surrounding perils the faith handed down to us by our persecuted forefathers.[8]

The bishops once again condemn 'the propagation of error through godless systems of education' and warn parents to safeguard their children from 'the dangers which prevail'. The bishops also refer to the proselytism practised by some groups in Ireland:

> The spirit of proselytism which followed in the wake of the famine is still in existence; yet the people still prefer to suffer starvation rather than renounce their faith. To the credit of the respectable and enlightened portion of our Protestant brethren it can be said that they indignantly reprobate the scandalous system of proselytism.

The bishops encourage the priests to redouble their efforts to increase the number of schools and to be assiduous in visiting and inspecting them. They are asked to 'organise and direct those pious associations for the diffusing of catechetical knowledge and the caring of the poor'. The bishops say that they would be guilty of criminal neglect if they did not raise their voices to defend the poor against injustice:

> We behold our poor not only crushed and overwhelmed by the awful visitations of heaven but frequently the victims of the most ruthless oppression that ever disgraced humanity. . . . We see them treated with a cruelty which would cause the heart to ache if inflicted on the beasts of the field and for which it

would be difficult to find a parallel save in the atrocities of savage life. The desolating track of the exterminator is to be traced in too many parts of the country, in the levelled cottages and roofless abodes whence so many virtuous and industrious families have been torn by brute force without distinction of age or sex, sickness or health and flung upon the highway to perish in the extremity of want.[9]

The bishops warn the oppressors of the poor of the penalties threatened by the Gospels for those who perpetrate such cruelties, but ask the poor themselves to bear their trials with patience and avoid secret societies and illegal combinations, which the Church condemns. The address was unanimously adopted by the synod.

The end of the synod also marked an address by the Catholic University Committee to the people of Ireland. The committee had been appointed by the national synod to carry out 'this great national undertaking'. In the address the bishops explain that their intention to establish a Catholic university is in accordance with the wishes not only of Pope Pius IX but of his two predecessors. They speak about happier times when Ireland was famed throughout Europe for her learning and scholarship. They talk about the dangers of education devoid of religion and how the horrors of revolutions in Europe and especially in France bear witness to the evils that result when religion is separated from public education.

The bishops go on to explain why there are particularly weighty reasons for providing a Catholic education for the youth of Ireland. It will provide an antidote to the poison being diffused through evil literature and strengthen them in their contacts with persons of strong anti-Catholic opinions. It will impart a higher tone to the Catholic body, creating a greater interest in the welfare of the Catholic religion, and encourage a taste for Catholic art and literature and diffuse the living principle of faith through the whole Catholic body. The bishops say that many Catholics think that the project is not possible, but they believe that with general co-operation it will succeed.

The address was signed by the four archbishops and by Drs Cantwell, Haly, Foran, Derry and Leahy. Thus the synod closed amid an atmosphere of optimism. The bishops felt that 1850 was to be a turning point in the fortunes of the Catholic Church in Ireland. Archbishop MacHale was encouraged by the emphasis placed on the importance of education and particularly by the strengthening of the link between secular and religious education.

While the Catholic Church in Ireland was feeling encouraged and strengthened by the Synod of Thurles, the Catholic Church in England was given new life and invigoration by the papal bull of Pius IX to abolish the long-standing regime of apostolic vicariates in England and to re-establish a regular diocesan hierarchy. The outcry that greeted this decree came as a surprise to the English Catholics. Rumours of the restoration of the hierarchy had reached England some years before and it seemed likely that Lord Minto, the British envoy in Rome, knew of the plan and that he had informed Lord John Russell. The outcry was on two accounts: it was claimed by many, including most of the Anglican bishops, that by creating new dioceses, the Catholic Church was ignoring the authority of the Crown, and by using the existing titles, it was taking no notice of the Anglican episcopate. In England the latter criticism did not apply, as the new sees were named from places not used by the Anglicans, and in Ireland the Catholics and Anglicans had used the same titles for centuries.

The Irish titles, however, had produced a certain amount of contention. Thackeray, a seemingly tolerant man with a great affection for the Irish, on his tour of Ireland in 1842, was quite affronted on seeing on the wall of a monastery that it was founded with the approbation of 'His Grace, the most Reverend the Lord Archbishop of Tuam'. Thackeray's comment was:

> The most Reverend Dr MacHale is a clergyman of great learning, talents and honesty, but His Grace the Lord Archbishop of Tuam strikes me as being no better than a mountebank; and some day I hope even his own party will laugh this humbug down. It is bad enough to be awed by big titles at all, but to respect sham ones! O stars and garters! We shall have his Grace the Lord Chief-Rabbi next, or his Lordship the Arch-Imaum.[10]

Nicholas Wiseman, who was to be the new Cardinal-Archbishop of Westminster, heightened the tension by proclaiming the restoration of England 'to its orbit in the ecclesiastical firmament'. Wiseman was well known in England and Woodward states that no one familiar with Wiseman's rather pompous and flowery style would have paid much attention to his words, but the English Protestants gave them a sinister and aggressive meaning.[11]

In November 1850 Cardinal Wiseman took up his duties as Archbishop of Westminster. Russell, in the same month, wrote an open letter to the Bishop of Durham in which he complained about papal aggression and the 'insolent and insidious step' in establishing a Catholic hierarchy in England. Russell's letter produced yet more strong feelings and the *Examiner* demanded a new penal law to punish papal interference in the temporal affairs of Great Britain, such as the actions of the bishops assembled at Thurles. In February 1851 Russell introduced a bill prohibiting the use of ecclesiastical titles already taken by the Church of England. The first clause of the bill inflicted a penalty of £100 on any bishop every time he used his title. The bill also authorised the confiscation for the State of all property bequeathed to them under those titles. In the preamble of the bill it declared that 'the attempt to establish, under colour of the authority of the See of Rome, sees, provinces or dioceses' not bearing the names of sees already in existence was illegal.

The bill was not without its opponents. It was opposed by Gladstone and the Peelites and ridiculed by the rising star of the Tories, Benjamin Disraeli. During the debate in which Russell tried to justify his action, one that did not sit easily on a Liberal Prime Minister, Disraeli said, 'I find the noble Lord seeking as the basis of his bill, not the visit of Dr Wiseman to England, but the Synod of Thurles.' He compared the bill to a mouse begotten of the mountain of agitation – '*parturiunt montes, nascetur ridiculus mus!*'[12]

John MacHale's reaction to the bill was to write a public letter to the Prime Minister, which he signed with his full title. He once again professed his loyalty to the Crown but accused the Government of being afraid of the projected Catholic university and wishing to seize the money that had been collected for it. MacHale accused them of trying once again to destroy the Catholic religion:

It openly and avowedly contemplates the destruction of their priesthood, embracing all the orders of the hierarchy, without which no Catholic people could survive.

It renders void every deed or writing made, signed, or executed, after the passing of the bill, by or under any name, style, or title, which same person is, by the recited Act, prohibited from assuming; and for every offence of the assumption of the name, style, or title of archbishop, bishop, or dean of city, town, or district of the United Kingdom, . . . every prelate not belonging to that favoured establishment, which you admire so much for its toleration, shall pay an hundred pounds.

Why! there is scarcely a day of his life in which a Catholic bishop has not to perform such deeds and sign such documents . . . – not all California itself would liquidate the pecuniary forfeits which he would incur during a moderate term of episcopacy.[13]

The Irish members of Parliament were relatively united on this occasion and able to use their powers initially to defeat the bill and force Russell from office, but he was able to return without much delay and the bill was eventually passed in August with a large majority in both houses. The vociferous opponents of the bill in Parliament were dubbed 'The Irish Brigade' and by those less favourable 'The Pope's Brass Band'.

The Government had succeeded in passing a measure that was impossible to implement but that had caused enormous offence to Catholics and served to stir up sectarian hatred. This was demonstrated the following year, in the sectarian Stockport riots. Like MacHale, John Henry Newman protested about Russell and felt that he should be 'brought to account for calling the religion of one third of the British Empire a superstition and a mummery'. Newman was able to rejoice at Russell's discomfiture over the unfortunate bill:

Lord John has struck his foot against a rock and has fallen. A sunken rock, for they did not believe so insignificant a thing as

British Catholicism would harm them – but it has shivered them . . . they have gone down in a smooth sea and under a smiling heaven. They are in again, to their own disgrace; like slaves, obliged to finish their own set work, and drink their own brewing.[14]

Notes

1   Bernard O'Reilly, *The Life and Times of John MacHale* (1890), II, p. 220.
2   Ibid., II, p. 221.
3   Peadar MacSuibhne, *Paul Cullen and his Contemporaries,* I, p. 335.
4   Ibid., II, p. 45.
5   Quoted in O'Reilly, op. cit., p. 234.
6   MacHale, *Sermons and Discourses* (1883), pp. 409–13.
7   Ibid., pp. 414–17.
8   Peadar MacSuibhne, op. cit., II, pp. 56–7.
9   Ibid., pp. 57–8.
10   W. M. Thackeray, *The Irish Sketchbook* (1842), pp. 220–21.
11   Llewellyn Woodward, *The Age of Reform* (1938), p. 522.
12   Horace, 'The mountains are in labour, they will bring forth a ridiculous mouse!'
13   Bernard O'Reilly, op. cit., II, p. 252.
14   John Henry Newman, *Letters, Diaries and Notebooks,* pp. xiv, 232.

14

TENANT RIGHT

'There is one great question, one paramount grievance which is calculated to annihilate our unfortunate divisions and restore the spirit of union among Irishmen; and that is the Land question.' (John MacHale)

IN 1847, IN THE AFTERMATH of the famine, Archbishop MacHale and his fellow bishops had written to Lord Clarendon asking for changes in tenant law that might bring about an improvement in the living conditions of the majority of the Irish people. Clarendon's reply, although dwelling on the outbreaks of violence in Ireland, did seem to contain some seeds of hope. He recognised the need for a more secure relationship between the landlord and the tenant-farmer. The Royal Commission appointed during Peel's ministry had said that the labouring classes of Ireland endured greater suffering than anywhere else in Europe. The Devon Commission heard 146 witnesses who recommended that tenants should receive compensation for improvements on their land. Nevertheless, the situation did not change except in the increase of emigrants leaving the shores of Ireland year by year. Bills for compensation for tenants were introduced in 1845, 1846, 1848 and 1850, but they were not strongly pressed and did not go beyond the committee stage. The British Government continued to be preoccupied with other concerns. In 1847 after his visit to Connaught, the Quaker, James Tuke, remarked:

Few things have struck me more since I have become personally acquainted with Ireland, than the very inadequate knowledge which prevails among my countrymen generally, of the great variety in the circumstances and conditions of the people which is found throughout that country.[1]

182

In 1849, in the *Westminster and Foreign Quarterly Review,* the MP G. Poulett Scrope writes with some energy that it is not in England's interests to do nothing about the 'frightful state of things' in Ireland. He says there is a need to redress grievances of a political and religious character but at the moment the need is for some action on behalf of the

> physical misery of her unemployed millions, the moral and industrial paralysis of the bulk of her population and the deplorable waste and mismanagement of her vast natural resources.[2]

Many people in England at this time believed that Ireland was overpopulated and that mass emigration was the only solution. Lord Monteagle presided over a committee of peers to inquire into a large scheme of colonisation from Ireland. They maintained that there was not enough land in Ireland for the population and the subsequent unemployment was a danger to public peace. Poulett Scrope denies that this is the case in any area of Ireland:

> It could by judicial management of the natural capabilities of its soil alone (without speaking of fisheries, minerals, water-power, commerce, and other extra-ordinary resources) be made to support its existing population (and more) in comfort, and that by means not inconsistent with 'social order, or the profitable existence of property' and without any of that 'danger to the public peace' which is so awfully paraded before our eyes in almost every one of the resolutions.[3]

Like MacHale, Poulett Scrope says that the public peace is only threatened by 'despair' and the 'barbarous systems of tenure'. He marvels at the lack of drainage in 'that moist climate', saying that vast tracts of land are not cultivated at all, especially in the west: 'one entire moiety of the province of Connaught is yet unredeemed from a state of nature'. He says that at one time it was thought that Norfolk and the Lincolnshire wolds were only fit for rabbits but now they produce luxuriant crops providing not only employment but large profits for their owners. He has reason to believe the qualities of the soil in the west of Ireland to be superior:

> Everyone knows this but they have somehow persuaded themselves that this is only to be done by the introduction of large farms and large capitalists; and that, in order to put the land in their hands, it must first be taken out of those of its present occupiers, which can only be done by removing them; that is, in their notion, by taking them altogether out of the country.

Poulett Scrope says that the capitalists are afraid of agrarian outrages, yet these have been relatively few, there being some in Tipperary and a few other districts:

> All the world knows with what patience and lamb-like resignation the poor inhabitants of Mayo and Galway, of Limerick and Kerry, and of the Western extremity of Cork and generally of Connaught, have borne their unexampled sufferings of the last three years.

Scrope maintains that every one knows the problem, every writer on Ireland, every witness before the Devon Commission have declared the cause. Parliament has been amply informed of it:

> The land is in the hands of nominal and embarrassed proprietors, who either cannot, or will not, themselves improve their estates, nor allow such terms of tenure as will induce others to improve them, and carry on a spirited system of cultivation . . . laws that maintain the proprietor in a false position, when he is utterly unable or unwilling to dispense his duties; maintain him as a great public nuisance; a sort of dog in the manger, making no good use of the land himself, yet preventing others from using it; locking up that great heaven-provided store-house of wealth – the soil– and hindering it from becoming available for the support of starving multitudes.[4]

Scrope says that it is not surprising that Irish agriculture is in a state of paralysis. Commerce would be paralysed by a system that 'forcibly maintained bankrupt merchants of manufacturers in positions with exclusive monopoly of all commercial transactions'. The remedy he advocates is not to send people to Canada and Australia, but to get the land into the hands of improvers, or to encourage existing tenants to lay out capital in improved cultivation, by the 'concession of some durable tenure, or a right to compensation for the value of their permanent improvements'. He says that three measures are needed immediately to:

1. Stimulate improvement on the part of landlords.
2. Stimulate enterprise, industry and expenditure of capital by occupiers of land.
3. Provide productive employment by authorities.[5]

Scrope disagrees with the idea held by many English people that 'nothing can be done for the Celts'. He believes rather condescendingly that although they 'may be deficient in some of the faculties that so highly distinguish and elevate the Anglo-Saxon all over the globe' they are excelled by nobody in 'hard work of a simple kind'. Scrope may not have echoed MacHale in his opinion of the Celt but his remedies are the same and he certainly echoes MacHale's letter to the Queen when he states the principle that land is originally invested in the Crown or the State in trust for the people, who have a right to reclaim it, which in turn gives them a title to a permanent property. This, he says, has been the custom of all nations.

The failure of Russell's Cabinet to pass any measure of relief for Irish tenants produced a new agitation. In the diocese of Ossory, the Earl of Desart had evicted 442 people from his estate. In October 1849 two local Catholic curates, Fr O'Shea and Fr O'Keefe, founded a protection society in Callan on Desart's estates. The society tried to obtain rents fixed by a valuer independent of the landlord and members pledged not to take the land of any evicted tenant who had paid rent at this value. This was similar to a practice followed in the north of Ireland, known as the 'Ulster custom'. The collective opinion of tenants on matters of rent and eviction was used to put some kind of constraint on the landlords. In the north a payment was made by the incoming tenant to the outgoing tenant, usually between £10 and £20 an acre. This gave the farmers some incentive to improve their land, but this custom was only backed by public opinion, not by law. In 1847 Sharman Crawford MP tried to legalise this 'Tenant right' but he failed. The cause was taken up by the Presbyterians and the Presbyterian General Assembly petitioned Parliament for tenant right. The Callan Protection Society inspired similar groups all over Ireland.

In April 1850, Frederick Lucas, an English convert to Catholicism who founded the *Tablet* and also became an MP, wrote to Archbishop MacHale asking for his support at the approaching conference for tenant right:

> The hope among those with whom I have spoken is universal that your Grace would use your influence to have the West well represented in the conference.[6]

Lucas says that they would like MacHale himself to come, but failing that, to send his representative. He wrote again on 27 April, saying that he was making use of MacHale's name, and then again in May:

> I venture most respectfully to suggest that there should be amongst us some Western voice to push us on if we lag behind the necessities of the West, and to put on the drag chain if we go too far.[7]

Lucas is full of enthusiasm for the league. When writing, he is taking legal advice on the possibility of getting land valued and thus compelling landlords to accept a fair rent. He believes that they might have a test case in Kilkenny, which may in turn become 'a new Clare, and secure emancipation for the tenant, as Clare secured it for the upper and middle classes of society'.

Archbishop MacHale supported the Tenant League as vigorously and as passionately as he had supported the repeal of the Union. In May 1850 he wrote to John O'Connell, Daniel O'Connell's son, who wanted to revive the Repeal Association and recommended to him the land question.

> There is one great question, one paramount grievance which is calculated to annihilate our unfortunate divisions and restore the spirit of union among Irishmen; and that is the Land question, or the assertion of primitive right of man, sacred in every Christian country, to enjoy in security and peace the fruit of his industry and labour.[8]

MacHale says he rejoices at the 'amalgamation of interests and of opinions which the assertion of the Poor man's right is about to create'. John O'Connell was only a shadow of his father but, because of the almost legendary nature of his father's reputation, the name still commanded the loyalty of the people, and when John O'Connell joined with Duffy, Lucas, Gray and the Lord Mayor of Dublin, together with Greer and Dr M'Knight from the north, to extend an invitation to all for a conference on tenant right, the joining of these disparate groups gave weight to the invitation.

These groups held a conference in Dublin in August 1850. Clergy, Catholic and Presbyterian, and lay people met in the common cause. They joined together and became known as 'The Irish Tenant League'. The aims of the Tenant League were the three 'Fs' – fair rent, fixity of tenure and free sale. The newly formed Tenant League, which contained members from the north and south of Ireland, wanted to achieve its aims by seeking parliamentary support for changes in the land law. Many newspapers provided support, leadership and direction, notably Gavan Duffy and the *Nation*, John Gray of the *Freeman's Journal*, Frederick Lucas of the *Tablet*, James Knight and the *Banner of Ulster*, and John Maguire and the *Cork Examiner*.

At the conference in Dublin two hundred delegates met from all religious denominations. They felt that their unanimity was complete and they now had a firm basis to go to the House of Commons. The motives of Frederick Lucas and his companions were common justice and humanity and the knowledge that a suffering population was unable to help itself. Lucas declared:

that our efforts will be ineffectual unless we have as representatives men of known honesty, who will withhold support from any cabinet that will not advance these principles . . . that an equitable valuation of land for rent should divide between the landlord and the tenant the net profits of cultivation, in the same way that profits would be divided between partners in any other business where one of them is the dominant partner and the other the working capitalist, who takes upon him the whole risk.[9]

The Times denounced the Tenant League, saying that it meant 'Tenant Right and Landlord Wrong', and many politicians said that its principles would lead to communism. The League produced fears about property rights, particularly among landlords. The Callan association had wanted industrial employment for the 'labouring classes'. Everywhere there were charges of 'socialism' and 'communism'. Many feared a revolution such as those that had taken place all over Europe in 1848. The Tory press denounced the League as a 'monstrous coalition between the Romish priesthood and the communism of other creeds'. Frederick Lucas tried to answer the criticisms both by letters to *The Times* and in his own paper, the *Tablet:*

The friends and advocates of Tenant Right had no hope of success except through persuasion; as they believed that, by adoption of their principles, all classes would be benefited, and none injured; and as they were persuaded that the arrangement contemplated would give riches and security to the Irish landlord and a wider field to English commerce, they were determined to do their best to remove the unfounded prejudice, and to make it known that their ranks were not composed of 'ranting enthusiasts' but of men of sense and reason, from whom the calamities of the time might now and then extort a rash phrase or a vehement illustration, but who desired nothing, and would be content with nothing, but practical remedies for an intolerable abuse.[10]

In his arguments against *The Times,* Lucas repeats the sentiments of Archbishop MacHale, who constantly argued that the practices of Irish landlords and English landlords were fundamentally different:

> As a class the English landlords look on both sides of the bargain, consult for the interests of the tenant, expend their own capital on the farm, carefully make it their own interest that the tenants shall thrive and prosper, and would hold it at once disreputable and foolish to hold up their lands to private auction, and to lease them to the highest bidder. . . . The necessity for interference in Ireland arises mainly from the long-continued, permanent and hopeless refusal of the Irish landlords to follow the example of their English brethren.[11]

The newly constituted League met for the first time on 9 August and it was at this meeting that Duffy's ideal of a parliamentary party emerged. Because of his associations with the 'Young Ireland' movement and its subsequent attempt at revolution, Duffy was still regarded by many as rather wild, but Archbishop MacHale held him in high regard as an honest and single-minded man, one who was not self-seeking and who had the interests of the poor of Ireland at heart. Duffy also numbered amongst his friends Thomas Carlyle, J. S. Mill and the future Cardinal Newman.

In the autumn of 1850 there was a series of outdoor demonstrations in support of the Tenant League, and a few sitting MPs came forward to endorse the League's programme. At the same time in England the restoration of the Catholic hierarchy was causing uproar and early in the following year the Irish MPs acted together as the so-called Irish Brigade to defeat the first reading of Lord John Russell's Ecclesiastical Titles Bill. Events were moving towards the foundation of a parliamentary party. This was further facilitated by the representation of the People's Act of 1850, which applied to Ireland. This greatly expanded the franchise in the Irish counties by giving the vote to tenants of holdings valued at £12 or more, even when they had no beneficial interest in the property. This was the first instance in the United Kingdom of valuation without reference to ownership.

The Ecclesiastical Titles Act and the activities of the Irish Brigade led to the foundation of 'The Catholic Defence Association of Great Britain and Ireland'. On 14 August 1851 Archbishop Cullen wrote to Archbishop MacHale telling him of the meeting that was to take place for the purpose of forming this Association:

> On next Tuesday the aggregate meeting of Catholics, so long spoken of, is to take place. I have agreed to take the chair. Dr Slattery and some other bishops will attend. I hope your Grace will be with us. It is important to show at the present moment that we are strong and united.[12]

The meeting took place in the Rotunda in Dublin on 19 August 1851. On the morning of that day the streets leading to the Rotunda were crowded from an early hour. Besides Dr Cullen and Dr MacHale there were nine other bishops present, five hundred priests and four thousand laymen, with about fifty thousand outside. The purpose of the Catholic Defence Association was to obtain redress of Catholic grievances by parliamentary action. In the opening speech Dr Cullen was at pains to point out that he was not interfering in politics:

> In thus coming forward today, I do not consider that I am intruding into the domain of politics, or travelling beyond the sphere of ecclesiastical duty. The present does not appear to be in any way a political movement. It is, rather, a great manifestation of Catholic feeling in favour of the liberty of our holy Church.[13]

The next speaker was Archbishop MacHale. The *Freeman's Journal* reports that:

> He was received with the most enthusiastic demonstrations of applause, which were again and again repeated, amid waving of hats and handkerchiefs, the entire meeting standing and exhibiting every mark of veneration and respect.

Dr MacHale did not give a long speech, but expressed his distaste for the bigotry of the British Government in their reintroduction of penal laws:

> The Catholic bishops might be allowed to express astonishment at the strange manner in which their disinterested services to the commonwealth have been recently requited.
>
> We had just passed through as severe a crisis as ever tested the patience and fidelity of the pastors of the Catholic Church. We had witnessed the diminution of our flocks and the desolation of our country. We had beheld scenes of suffering which few bishops were ever fated to contemplate, and but few flocks to endure. We had exhorted our devoted people to respect property to such an extent that a conscientious casuist might well question if this respect did not interfere with the first principle of self-preservation. And seeing our precepts practically carried out by a patience so prodigious that no Spartan virtue ever approached it, – nay, such as the heroic acts of the martyrs never surpassed, – who could imagine that the prelates, who were instrumental in soothing the public discontent and preserving the public tranquillity amid these awful trials, were to be singled out by our rulers as the first victims of a bigoted proscription? . . .
>
> But I must have done. This is not a meeting of one district, or province, or even of Ireland alone. It is made up of Catholics from the Three Kingdoms. Here we have the learned Bishop of Edinburgh, who is restoring the fallen temples of his own country, and kindling with the heat of his own eloquence the sacred fire, which, in times of persecution, was concealed by his predecessors, and lay since then so long hidden among the valleys of Scotland. . . .
>
> You must, therefore, be anxious to hear those champions of our country's rights and religion who have recently filled such a space in the public eye. On their wrestling with tyranny, in the great Parliamentary circus, the grateful admiration of Ireland was fixed. . . . On their ears, fatigued and torn with

continued abuse and blasphemy, the music of their country's applause must now fall with peculiar sweetness.[14]

The 'champions' that MacHale is referring to were the Irish members of Parliament. He had long wanted an independent Irish party that was committed to neither Whig nor Tory and felt that Russell's unfortunate bill might have the effect of uniting the Catholic members of Parliament and, in particular, the Irish members. Dr Cullen had also expressed this view in a letter to MacHale earlier in the year:

> P.S. – I suppose the penal laws will pass. I think it well that they should be opposed. But at the same time I think the law cannot injure us very much. Perhaps it may have the effect of making us all unite as we ought.[15]

MacHale's speech was succeeded by that of William Keogh, MP, a well-known lawyer whose eloquent resistance to the Ecclesiastical Titles Bill had won him much popularity amongst the Irish. In his speech he declared:

> We will have no terms with any minister, no matter who he may be, until he repeals that Act of Parliament and every other which places the Roman Catholic on a lower platform than his Protestant fellow-subject.[16]

Other prominent MPs at the meeting were George Henry Moore, a wealthy landlord, and John Sadleir, a businessman, who, it has been suggested, was later immortalised by Dickens as Mr Merdle in *Little Dorrit*.[17]

After the August meeting an agreement was reached between the Catholic Defence Association and the Tenant League. The MP for Rochdale, William Sharman Crawford, who owned 6,000 acres in County Down, was a long-standing advocate of tenant right. He was approached by Lucas and Duffy, who were anxious that the two associations should not work at cross-purposes. Duffy distrusted the

Catholic Association but Lucas persuaded him that their aims were similar. Crawford was on friendly terms with the Irish Brigade and brought along leading Brigadiers to the meeting with Lucas and Duffy. Crawford drafted a bill that was accepted by both groups. The bill was a watered-down version of tenant demands, incorporating fair rents and free sale but without fixity of tenure. The League proposed to build up an Irish Parliamentary party, independent of all other parties, which would oppose each Government until one formed that would remedy Irish grievances. There seemed to be some genuine hope of success because at this time Parliament was deeply divided. The Tories had been split into Conservatives and Peelites, while the Whigs, already divided between Liberals and Radicals, had been discredited by the Ecclesiastical Titles Bill and were further divided by Russell's quarrel with Viscount Palmerston, the Foreign Secretary.

In November 1851 Archbishop MacHale took part in a great banquet for the Irish representatives at Ballina. This was intended to give further impetus to tenant right. On that occasion he said that it was 'not without feelings of reluctance' that he shared in the festivity. He spoke about the poverty and suffering that was widespread in the area, which had had to contend with first the famine and then the evictions. He quoted passages from Goldsmith's poem *The Deserted Village,* speaking about the sad and empty areas where previously there had been 'bustle and cheerful life'. MacHale then gave a prophetic warning to those who were to represent the Irish people: 'It is not by a small dribbling of patronage that the interests of our country are to be advanced'. He then denounced the man who 'barters with the government to get a small share of patronage'.

Russell's Government finally fell on a Militia Bill. It was replaced by a minority Tory Government under Lord Derby. The *Nation* commented:

> The most villainous administration that ever marred Irish affairs is hopelessly foundered. We thank God very heartily for their downfall. Old and bitter enemies fill their places. But if it were Satan himself, instead of Scorpion Stanley, who became

Premier of England, the change would be a welcome one to the Irish people.[18]

The Tory Government struggled to hang on to office in the early months of 1852. It soon became clear that Derby had no intention of considering Sharman Crawford's bill. The Government made itself more unpopular in Catholic eyes in June 1852 when it issued a Royal Proclamation in the London *Gazette,* reminding Catholics that it was against the law to exercise ceremonies of their religion in public and to wear religious habits. A procession of Catholic schoolchildren went ahead without incident, but fighting began the following day and then riots broke out. Ardent English Protestants sacked Catholic churches and houses in Stockport.

At the General Election in 1852 MacHale and Cantwell and many of the Irish clergy were extremely active in campaigning for tenant right. MacHale worked closely with Frederick Lucas throughout this period and was daily denounced in the English press as a dangerous agitator. The Irish Independent Party made sweeping gains in the south and was reinforced by many new members committed to the Tenant League. Nearly fifty MPs, including Frederick Lucas who was elected for Meath, were committed to tenant right and independent opposition. Results in the north were disappointing for the League, as they failed to gain a single seat. Some of the Presbyterians from the north had conflicting feelings about tenant right. They also feared the growing power of the Catholics. Sharman Crawford, who had put up for County Down, lost his seat in Parliament.

In September 1852 a conference was held in Dublin attended by forty MPs who passed a resolution calling on its members to remain 'independent of' and 'in opposition to' all governments that did not make part of their policy to give to the tenantry of Ireland a measure fully embodying Sharman Crawford's Bill.

On 28 October there was a smaller conference on the religious question. This was not called by the Catholic Defence Association, which was undergoing some internal problems, but by a new group known as the Friends of Religious Freedom and Equality. At this meeting twenty-six MPs pledged to demand the repeal of the

Ecclesiastical Titles Act and the removal of all remaining Catholic disabilities. The Tenant League now had the balance of power in the minority Tory Government and the idea of an independent Irish party seemed quite feasible. Sharman Crawford's Bill was taken up by Sergeant Shee, MP for Kilkenny. In December 1852, when the Tories had failed to hang on to the Government and Lord Aberdeen formed a coalition ministry, the prospects for the independent Irish opposition looked very promising.

Notes

1   James Tuke, *A Visit to Connaught* (1847), p. 4.
2   Poulett Scrope, from 'The Irish difficulty and How it must be met', in *The Westminster and Foreign Quarterly Review* (January 1849), p. 3.
3   Ibid., p. 7.
4   Ibid., pp.11–12.
5   Ibid., p. 15.
6   Bernard O'Reilly, *The Life and Times of John MacHale* (1890), II, p. 288.
7   Ibid., 15 May 1850, p. 290.
8   Ibid., pp. 282–3.
9   Ibid., pp. 292–3.
10 Edward Lucas, *The Life of Frederick Lucas MP* (1886), p. 392.
11 Ibid. pp. 393–4.
12 Peadar MacSuibhne, *Paul Cullen and his Contemporaries,* II, p. 85.
13 Ibid., p.91.
14 *Freeman's Journal,* cited in O'Reilly, op. cit., pp. 267–8.
15 Peadar MacSuibhne, op. cit., II, p. 78.
16 Quoted in O'Reilly, op. cit., 23 August 1851, II, p. 271.
17 Humphrey House, *The Dickens World* (1941), p. 29.
18 *Nation*, February 1852.

15

THE CATHOLIC UNIVERSITY

'It will be the Catholic University of the English tongue for the whole world'. (John Henry Newman)

IN 1847 AND AGAIN in 1848 it was recommended by the Pope that a Catholic university should be founded in Ireland. This suggestion was in answer to the fears of the majority of the Catholic bishops about the Government's founding of the Queen's Colleges, dubbed the 'godless colleges' by an English MP. The university was to be modelled on that of Louvain, which had been restored in 1834. Archbishop MacHale seems to have been enthusiastic about this venture, and indeed it would be surprising if he had not been, considering his opposition to the Queen's Colleges and his interest in Catholic education. The first definite resolution in favour of the Catholic university emanated from Tuam on 26 January 1848, and at the provincial Synod of Tuam in January 1849 the bishops expressed 'full concurrence in the recommendation of His Holiness to found a Catholic University' and offered 'cheerful co-operation towards its establishment'.[1] They promised subscriptions and commissioned Dr Derry of Clonfert, the secretary of episcopal meetings, to enter into correspondence with those who might assist the project. In a letter to Pius XI, MacHale wrote:

> Already measures are in progress for carrying out your Holiness's instructions as to founding a University; and she [Ireland] will best evince her gratitude to your Holiness and the nations who succoured her by erecting Catholic Colleges which, as in former times, will afford gratuitous education to the English as well as the Irish, and from which missionaries will go forth to bear the faith of Rome over all the regions of the earth.[2]

196

This was before Cullen came to Ireland, but once he became Archbishop of Armagh, Apostolic Delegate and Primate of Ireland, he was charged with the establishment of the university and became the driving force behind the venture. The subject of Irish education was frequently discussed in the English press. *The Times* of 22 January 1850 took exception to MacHale's recent pastoral letter condemning the Queen's Colleges. They called it a 'side-winded defence of the blessings of ignorance' and quoted at length 'a few gems'. MacHale says:

> In the long succession of errors that have darkened the face of Christianity there has not been one that did not strive to recommend itself by superior progress, and that had not knowledge or enlightenment in broad characters, legible to its deluded followers, and there has not been a pastor in the church who raised his voice or issued his warnings against those selfish or corrupt impostors who make a merchandise of human souls, that was not stigmatized in his day as the patron of ignorance and the foe of enlightenment.

Two days later, MacHale's pastoral letter is again discussed:

> Man is naturally a preserving animal. . . . The naturalist . . . mourns over his lost dodo: in America, where they have nearly shot down the Red Indians, they are now vainly endeavouring to keep up the race; and in Ireland . . . Dr M'Hale and many of his brethren are bent on preserving ignorance. . . . Their real opposition is not to any *theory* of education. No one can trace in their writings and conduct any real resemblance to those among ourselves who object on producible and defensible grounds to these new colleges, as the intended nuclei of a system which is to separate religion from education. Dr M'Hale knows indeed the value of this plea, and does not neglect it. But it is not really his own. His position is much further away from right reason. . . . He is afraid, not of any *theory* but of the *fact* of education.
>
> Ireland is certainly, a country of bogs. Metaphorically, it is

occupied, for the most part, by one thick, interwoven, noxious, swampy forest. There has been a little clearance towards the north; . . . Ignorance, prejudice, idleness, misery, grow side by side in great profusion, and draw each other up to a marvellous height. All manner of unclean beasts alternately slumber and raven in their shade. We can hear their cries at this distance, – Rebellion roaring from its cave; Mistrust spitting at all who approach it whether friend or foe; conspiracies of most gregarious instinct, and insane hatred howling for blood. Here Dr M'Hale is at home . . . on one point he has no doubt. None have any right to meddle with them but himself and his brethren. . . . Such is the mistake of the great majority of the Romish hierarchy in Ireland . . . and they must be taught that it is so. . . . Ireland, as well as England, is under the territorial jurisdiction of the QUEEN and the control of her government. . . . We cannot change the race or the climate . . . but we can educate. . . .

'But why not leave us to educate?' say Dr M'Hale and his friends. For two reasons, each of which is sufficient in itself – you cannot, and you will not. The Romish priesthood cannot educate. They have, as a body, neither the moral nor the physical means – the minds, the learning nor the money. . . . Something might be done by English wealth towards bringing a better class into the priesthood. . . . But are we to leave the giant unassailed, till . . . we are freed from every Irish priest of the species M'Hale? . . . They know that their power over their flocks depends mainly on their resemblance to them and sympathy with them. Will they consent to be altered, and so destroy their influence?[3]

Despite the cynicism of *The Times* there was great enthusiasm for the projected Catholic university. A committee was formed and in March 1850 appealed for funds. At the Synod of Thurles the Irish bishops once again expressed their determination to follow the advice of the Pope and found a Catholic university and the committee was reconstituted and now included bishops, priests and laymen.

In April 1851 Dr Cullen wrote to Fr John Henry Newman:

> My dear Dr Newman,
> For the last few months several of the Irish bishops have been engaged in collecting funds for the purpose of establishing a Catholic university in Ireland. The collection has been very successful and little doubt can now be entertained of the success of our undertaking; at least it appears evident that the people are willing to supply means to support such an institution.
>
> Having hitherto attended merely to pecuniary matters we must now proceed a step further. . . . In this matter your advice would be of great importance. . . . Should you have any intention of coming to Ireland this season your presence at the meeting of our committee in Dublin would be most useful. Indeed if you could spare time to give us a few lectures on education you would be rendering good service to religion in Ireland.[4]

Newman's initial response to Cullen's overtures was non-committal, although he did think that some use might be made of the English married clerical converts. He had been concerned about the Catholic Church's failure to make use of them. After some consideration, Newman's imagination became fired with the idea of the Catholic university: 'It will be the Catholic University of the English tongue for the whole world.'[5] Cullen visited Newman twice in July 1851 and on the second visit proposed that Newman should be the first Rector. Newman was reticent at first, as he did not want his involvement with the university to interfere with his responsibilities to the Birmingham Oratory, but his fellow Oratorians encouraged him to play an important role in the university: 'What I should desire is, to do as much work for the university as possible with as little absence as possible from this place.'[6] For the time being he was just a member of a subcommittee, but in September he wrote to Cullen saying that he would agree to do the lectures. He asked for Cullen's advice:

I consider I ought to know better than I do the state of public opinion and knowledge in Ireland on the subject of education, and your own ideas what Lectures ought to be about, in order to be useful.[7]

Cullen's reply is of some interest: 'What we want in Ireland is to persuade people that education should be religious. . . . There is one fine subject which should not be omitted: the services rendered by the Catholic Church and its Pontiffs to literature'.[8]

In September Newman made his first visit to Ireland and on 12 November Newman was offered the presidency of the university. It would seem to have been on Cullen's own initiative that the presidency of the university was offered to Newman. Indeed, it showed some vision and courage on the part of Cullen. Newman was respected and renowned for his academic and religious achievements. He also had experience of university life, but on the other hand he was a recent convert and an Englishman. There does not seem to have been any objections on the part of the Irish bishops to Newman's appointment. When the Catholic University Committee met on 12 November 1851, they unanimously passed a resolution to invite Newman to be President of the university and the motion was said to have had 'Dr MacHale's strong support'.[9] When Dr Cooper wrote to Newman formally to offer him the position he said the proposal 'was spoken to in terms of warmest approbation by Dr MacHale'.[10] Cullen also wrote to Newman two days later to inform him of the decision. In his letter he says 'the *summum imperium* should be in the bishops, but that the president should have the entire acting discretion'. Newman joked in his letters: 'I mean to be Chancellor, Rector, Provost, Professor, Tutor all at once, and no one else anything!'[11]

Three years were to elapse before the university opened, but Cullen favoured delay on account of the distinct lack of support from Archbishop Murray for the scheme. Newman was also much engaged at this time with a lawsuit in England and also in preparing his lectures. Nevertheless, he was still very enthusiastic for the project:

It is a most daring attempt but first it is a religious one, next it has the Pope's blessing on it. Curious it will be if Oxford is imported into Ireland, not in its members only but in its principles, methods, ways, and arguments. The battle there will be what it was in Oxford twenty years ago. . . . I am renewing the struggle in Dublin with the Catholic Church to support me. It is very wonderful – Keble, Pusey, Maurice, Sewell, etc., who have been able to do so little against Liberalism in Oxford, will be renewing the fight, alas, not in their persons, in Ireland.[12]

Much has been made of MacHale's later opposition to Newman as Rector of the Catholic university. However, he did vote for Newman's appointment as President initially. MacHale was also known to have great admiration for Newman, both for his scholarship and for his courage. A factor that may have caused problems with the university negotiations at this time was the relationship between MacHale and Cullen, which seems to have been deteriorating. In December 1851 Cullen wrote to MacHale:

I have just received a letter from Cardinal Fransoni on the position of your affairs, in which he insists on the necessity of having efficient men at the head of each diocese. . . . The Cardinal desires me to write to your Grace about the state of some of your suffragens. . . . It has been stated at Rome that Dr Ffrench has not been able to visit his diocese for years and that Dr O'Donnell since his consecration never visited the famous parish of Oughterard. . . . In the letter from Cardinal Fransoni and in another from His Holiness, great anxiety is expressed about providing for the wants of any diocese that may appear neglected, inasmuch as our present circumstances require great energy and activity *in iis qui praesunt.*[13]

Bernard O'Reilly states that MacHale had written 'a most curious letter' on the top of this missive.

There also seems to have been some disagreement between Cullen and MacHale on the amount of involvement of the bishops in the running of the university. On 16 and 17 February 1852 Cullen wrote to MacHale advising that the Holy Father should be petitioned to send a brief authorising the erection of the university – 'If your Grace approves of the petition you will have the kindness to sign it and to get it signed by Dr Derry'. On 18 February 1852 Dr MacHale replied to Dr Cullen:

It is desirable to have the Brief for the erection of the University in accordance with the rescripts for that object, and the petition will have my full concurrence.

Your Grace is already aware that the bishops feel that they, and they alone, have the right to found and govern the Catholic University, and that any other body or committee associated with them was only provisionally established and for preparatory arrangements.

I can now further state that the bishops of this province . . . declared that they looked on the Committee only in a mere provisional and subordinate light and they never meant, nor would they consent to delegate their own rights to any body whatever in which a majority of laymen and clergymen could overrule the bishops.

The occasion of obtaining the Brief may be the most seasonable for putting the erection and future government of the University on a proper footing. It may not be amiss to consult all the bishops on the form of the petition and the nature of the Brief. If not, as we should endeavour to secure their co-operation, our petition, I think, should fully recognize their rights, so far that, in drawing up the code of laws by which the University is to be governed, as well as in making the appointments and disbursing the funds, the bishops alone are to have the entire authority.[14]

MacHale refused to sign the petition as he thought it should be signed by all the bishops. On 20 February he again wrote to Cullen:

My Dear Lord,
Any petition to the Holy Father on the subject of the

> University, should I think, have the signatures of all the bishops. . . . Confining it to the archbishops and the suffragens who are of the Committee would appear to encourage the notion of some members of the Committee, that they are a permanent body, to which bishops had transferred or delegated their trust. . . . I feel I cannot be a party to interfere with the rights of the other bishops. . . . I decline signing the petition in its present form.[15]

While this correspondence was taking place, Dr Murray, Archbishop of Dublin, died. Dr Murray had not been a supporter of the Catholic university and after his death things became a little easier. Cullen wrote to Newman 'very probably his successor will be well disposed to take an active part in establishing the new University'.[16] As it turned out Cullen himself very quickly succeeded Murray as Archbishop of Dublin, which made it possible for him to play an even more dominant role in the university affairs. Joseph Dixon became Archbishop of Armagh.

Meanwhile, at the request of Cullen, Newman was preparing to come to Ireland to give some lectures. These lectures seem to have given Newman great problems – 'The truth is, I have the utmost difficulty of writing to people I do not know'.[17] This of course was Newman's great difficulty with the university. Until September 1851 he had never set foot in Ireland and was totally unacquainted with the Irish bishops, the clergy and the people. For the lectures, he had decided to begin with Oxford, as he thought it was important to argue not just 'on the assumption of Catholicism, but in the way of reasoning, and as men of all religions may do'. However, he did not want to say too much about Oxford for fear of antagonising the Irish Nationalist Party. Newman seems to have agonised over these lectures. He wrote that they 'try me more than any thing I ever did' and that they 'have oppressed me more than any thing else of the kind in my life'.[18] Newman, while having great sympathy with the Irish, had little knowledge or experience of the country or its people and so seems to have felt constantly ill at ease. The lectures were held in May and June and were well attended and successful. Newman later produced a book, *Discourses on the Scope and Nature of University Education*, which contained these and subsequent lectures, and they later formed the first half of his classic, *The Idea of a University*.

Newman's opening discourse reveals his difficulties and his skills in coping with them. He had to satisfy Dr Cullen and his insistence on a strictly Catholic university. He had to appease the Irish nationalists who wanted the university to be thoroughly Irish and he had to speak to those of the mind of Dr Murray who thought the foundation of a Catholic university both unnecessary and impracticable. Newman talked about his experiences in England and in Oxford, to demonstrate his neutrality in Irish affairs and to appeal to the potentially anti-clerical lay element in his audience. He invoked the history of the Catholic Church to show that the controversy surrounding mixed education does not involve 'immutable truth' but merely 'practice and expedience'. He then reminded his listeners that in this case the Pope 'has spoken and has a claim on us to trust him'.[19]

On 20 May 1852 the papal bulls arrived appointing Dr Cullen to Dublin and on 29 June he was installed in the Pro-Cathedral with great ceremony as Archbishop of Dublin. This appointment made it easier for Dr Cullen to be increasingly involved in the affairs of the university and to act on his own initiative without consulting the other bishops or indeed Newman himself. On 4 July 1852 Newman wrote to Cullen to ask that, for the present, a vice-rector should not be appointed. He regarded this appointment as very important, as whoever held the position should not only have the requisite abilities but he must 'see things from the same point of view as I do'.[20] Newman felt that he was not in a position at that time to know enough suitable people. Newman did not receive a reply to his letter but in October 1852 Cullen wrote to Newman:

> There is a most excellent clergyman here at present who would I think, be admirably suited to aid in establishing the University . . . . He is known almost everywhere in Ireland and is beloved by all. He is of most kind and gentlemanly manners, very humble and at the same time a most highly-instructed ecclesiastic. His name is Dr Taylor. He would accept the office of vice-president. No one would co-operate more fully with you than this gentleman.[21]

In January 1853 Dr MacHale received a letter from Dr O'Hanlon of Maynooth describing for him the events of the latest University Committee meeting:

> The chair had been scarcely taken by his Grace of Dublin, when Dr Haly of Kildare proposed that Dr Taylor should be appointed vice-rector of the university. This motion was seconded by the Archbishop of Armagh and warmly supported by Dr Cullen. . . . It was resisted by Bianconi and a few others. . . .[22]

O'Hanlon says that Dr Taylor was a worthy priest but describes his talents as 'mediocre', but 'In truth, all opposition was fruitless, as the whole business was manifestly pre-concerted, and the measures had been taken to ensure its success'. In the event Dr Taylor was appointed secretary to the University Committee. Newman later noted that he was in reality Cullen's secretary 'to save him the trouble of writing to me'.[23]

In January and February 1853 Newman wrote to press Cullen for instructions regarding the university but received no reply. Newman was already experiencing difficulties in his relationship with Cullen. Newman realised that Cullen had his problems. Cullen was a stranger in Ireland, having spent most of his adult life in Rome, and the Irish bishops 'looked on his coming from Rome with the same jealousy and apprehension as the English bishops had looked on Dr Wiseman'. Cullen did not seem capable of confiding in or consulting Newman, who says that Cullen did what he had learnt to do at Rome: 'to act, not to speak – to be peremptory in act, but to keep his counsel; not to commit himself on paper; to treat me, not as an equal, but as one of his subjects.'

For much of 1853 Newman waited for instructions from Cullen. Autumn 1854 had been the intended opening date and Newman feared that the venture would fail if preparations did not start soon. Early in the new year Newman heard from Rome, where Wiseman had intervened with the Pope, who had agreed to issue a formal Brief as a way of starting the university. Newman offered to go to Rome but Cullen advised him against it. Cullen learnt that Wiseman had suggested that Newman be made a titular bishop to give him more authority, but in February 1854 Cullen wrote to Monsignor Barnabó, Secretary of Propaganda, to advise against it:

> While I would have the greatest pleasure in seeing a man so learned and saintly as Mr Newman raised to the highest dignities, nevertheless I thought that perhaps it would be better to wait a little until things are in better shape.[24]

In February 1854 Newman set out once again for Dublin. He was about to set up the university at last. He intended first making a tour of Ireland to visit the bishops, to inquire about the state of schools and colleges and to advertise the new university to potential teachers and students. Unfortunately Ireland was experiencing its worst winter since 1814 and it was snowing hard for much of Newman's journeys. Things were made worse by his contracting a bad cold. During his stay at Waterford, Newman made a disastrous visit to a convent school. He thought he had made rather a good speech to the girls, but 'the Mother Schoolmistress did not know he had made it, or even begun it, and still asked for a speech . . . to make it up, he asked for a holiday for the girls', which the Mother Schoolmistress 'flatly refused'. Newman nevertheless drank her 'raspberry's vinegar which much resembles a nun's anger, being a sweet acid'.[25] Newman's cold had got worse, and faced with the prospect of his next destination, Tuam, the see of 'The Lion of the West', Newman's heart sank and he decided to cut short his tour and return to Dublin.

On 18 May 1854 the bishops met at last to approve the university's status and formally recognise Newman as Rector. Not long afterwards Newman met Archbishop MacHale, who, Newman says, shook hands with him 'with so violent a cordiality, when I kissed his ring, as to punish my nose!'[26]

Despite this cordiality and MacHale's evident respect for Newman, the relationship between the two men did not go well. It reflected to some extent the worsening relationships between Newman and Cullen and between MacHale and Cullen. During this period MacHale and Cullen began to disagree strongly in matters political. Cullen seems to have been a reserved man with few close friends. He was suspicious of anyone whom he felt was sympathetic to revolutionary ideas. One of these men was Frederick Lucas, who was not only a political ally of MacHale but a good friend of Newman. Newman did not agree with all of Lucas's politics but thought him 'an honest good man'. Newman said later:

> Lucas was the only friend of the Archbishop [MacHale] I knew. He it was, I suppose, who had persuaded Dr MacHale to take part in my nomination; and had I put myself forward, instead of Dr Cullen being in the front (whom Lucas could not stomach), I think Lucas would have mediated between Dr MacHale and me, and would have overcome for me many difficulties – but this is speculation.[27]

Archbishop Cullen did not approve of Newman's friendship with Lucas, and Newman described Cullen's conduct towards Lucas as 'too painful to talk of'.[28]

On 4 June Newman officially took up his post as Rector and proposed to open the Classical and Mathematical Schools on Friday, 3 November, and schools of Medicine, Civil Engineering and other physical and material sciences as 'soon after as possible'. The university began with twenty students, one of whom was the young Daniel O'Connell, the grandson of 'the Liberator'. Newman began the publication of the *University Gazette,* which came out weekly and contained announcements and essays, mostly by Newman himself. At the end of 1854 it was taken over by Robert Ornsby and became a monthly periodical. Newman's main task, however, was to engage suitable professors. Cullen was very nervous about Newman's appointments and was constantly fearful that first of all Newman would appoint too many Englishmen, and then later that Newman would appoint 'Young Irelanders'.

As MacHale's relationship with Cullen worsened, he became less and less co-operative in the university affairs. His letters to Newman are curt and unhelpful. After Newman wrote to MacHale asking for his approval of some property he had acquired and the appointment of teachers for the university MacHale replied:

From this it appears that to consult the archbishops on the purchase of schools or the fitness of professors is a matter of mere courtesy. On the subject of the list forwarded (to me) I have only to remark that, with the exception of a very few, I know nothing of the individuals it contains, and could not venture to express approval or disapprobation of them, even if I considered it the appropriate occasion.

I purpose to express my opinions when the opportunity shall offer of meeting, assembled and acting together, the prelates to whom the provisional appointment of the professors is intrusted.

It is likely that he felt that Cullen and Newman were running the university together without consulting the other bishops. In fact, Newman's relationship with Cullen was equally difficult. Cullen had a tendency to procrastinate, which Newman found difficult to work with. Sometimes situations arose that required immediate action and Newman was forced to act on his own initiative. One such occasion was the purchase of a medical school which became vacant in Cecilia Street, Dublin. It came on the market at a reasonable price and was fully equipped. In all the Dublin hospitals, only three had any Catholic practitioners and so it was a very useful acquisition. Newman frequently wrote to ask MacHale for his co-operation and on this occasion MacHale wrote that decisions should be taken with the consent of all the bishops. Newman's reply to Dr MacHale was respectful yet spirited. The bishops had gone to Rome for the definition of the Doctrine of the Immaculate Conception, so Newman sent his correspondence with MacHale to Cullen in Rome.

The Lion solus has roared at me, and I have roared again, and the roarings are done up in a letter, and sent to Dr Cullen at Rome.[29]

In 1854 Frederick Lucas was also in Rome, complaining to the Pope about Archbishop Cullen's political sympathies. Archbishop MacHale, while he initially thought it unwise of Lucas to go to Rome, was very sympathetic to his cause. Cullen in turn wrote to Newman, complaining about Lucas and possible Young Irelanders.

He wrote in January 1855: 'I hope you will make every exertion to keep the University free from all Young Irelandism, of which the spirit is so evident in the *Nation*'.[30] In Newman's reply, he speaks of those who are 'admirable persons now', meaning those who used to be Young Irelanders. Cullen also disapproved of the activities of many of the students who went to plays and went hunting in pink.

In 1854 and 1855 the situation for the education of Catholics in Britain and Ireland was changed considerably by the abolition of the religious tests for matriculation and for the receiving of a university degree. This meant that it was now possible for Catholics to go to Oxford and Cambridge. Newman found this situation particularly difficult. On the one hand, he did not want the Catholic bishops to allow young Catholics to go to Oxford as he felt that Oxford was a dangerous place for Catholics, and on the other hand he said that he would rather 'do good to English Catholics in Oxford than in Dublin'.[31] One of the problems of the Catholic university in Dublin had been the numbers of English Catholics who studied there, and Newman was not happy at the thought that their education was being paid for by the Irish poor. His relationship with the Archbishops of Tuam and Dublin was still not good. MacHale did not cause him further trouble, as after he acquiesced in the synodal decrees of 1854 he disappeared from the scene. In a meeting of the bishops in June 1856, Newman described himself as waiting for the 'lion' to attack, but he did not, and he described MacHale's friend, Dr Derry of Clonfert, as always kind and courteous. Relationships with Dr Cullen, however, grew worse and in April 1856 Newman wrote to a friend:

> Poor Dr C! I should not wonder if he is quite dragged down with anxiety. The great fault I find with him is, that he makes no-one his friend, because he will confide in nobody, and be considerate to nobody. Everybody feels that he is emphatically close, and while this repels friends, it fills enemies with nameless suspicions. . . . He is as vehement against the Young Irelanders as against the MacHaleites, against the MacHaleites as against the English.[32]

On another occasion Newman said of Cullen that it was a wonder he did not 'cook his own dinners' he was so distrustful of everyone.[33]

By this time Newman was getting tired. He had agreed to be Rector for a limited number of years and intended to resign in 1857. This he found difficult to do as there was still so much unfinished business. He set out for Ireland for the last time on 26 October 1858. He gave various lectures and finally left Ireland on the fourth of November. On the twelfth he sent his formal resignation of the rectorship to the archbishops. The university still did not have a charter and repeated efforts to gain one from the Government failed. In 1865 the O'Donaghue moved in Parliament for a charter for the university. In January 1866 the bishops petitioned the Home Secretary, Grey, and submitted a draft of a charter. Palmerston's Government proposed to issue a supplemental charter empowering the Queen's University to grant degrees to the students of the Catholic university. This was bitterly opposed by the Queen's Colleges and was invalidated by the court of chancery on a technicality. Trinity College could have come to the rescue by extending its own charter to include the Catholic University, but it preferred to keep its monopoly. Gladstone put forward a bill in 1873 that received strong opposition from the Nonconformists. Four years later Isaac Butt's bill was also rejected and in 1879 the attempt by the O'Conor Don also failed. In 1882, University House in St Stephen's Green officially became University College. This continued for another twenty-three years. The Medical School, however, was successful in gaining a charter and continued to thrive.

Various reasons have been put forward for the failure of the Catholic university; MacHale and Cullen have both been blamed. Newman himself, though commanding enormous respect intellectually and spiritually, was possibly not a good administrator. However, many commentators do not see the venture as a failure. While it lasted, many students received a good education and many recalled with pleasure the easy-going, relaxed and friendly atmosphere of the university. Monsignor Martin Brennan in his review of Fergal McGrath's book *Newman's University: Idea and Reality*, which was published in 1951, puts the blame squarely on the Government for not allowing the university to confer degrees. He does not spare Newman himself in his criticism:

> Had the government not been so intransigent in this matter, the University would have been an immediate and lasting success and posterity might have been spared the peevish despondencies and sensitive petulancies of Newman in the face of real or imaginary grievances. As proof of this contention, witness the immediate and continuous influence of the Catholic Medical School.[34]

Brenan, who was president of St Patrick's College, Carlow, in the early 1950s, goes on to say of Newman:

> One other point: it is undeniable that Newman was what would nowadays be called a snob, that he considered the ordinary student body should come from the leisured or 'gentleman' class.[35]

He says that Newman complained that the Irish clergy were

> ever looking about for poor scholars, cheap lodging houses and schools for affiliation. I am coming then to feel strongly that whatever the kindness of bishops and priests to me personally, they can never be supporters of the University unless the age of poor scholars revived.

If it did nothing else the Catholic university filled the gap in Irish education, which was left until the foundation of the National University in 1908. Archbishop MacHale and the Irish bishops generally have often been criticised for their attitude to Trinity College and later on for their lack of support for the Queen's Colleges. In a paper written by Robert Donavon, secretary to the Commissioners of the National University of Ireland, in 1909 he says:

> Their [the bishops'] policy has been represented as a policy of obscurantism . . . as an opposition not to a proselytising

ascendancy and a monopoly of privilege, but to the spread of real knowledge and the growth of genuine culture.[36]

Donavon says that the bishops were fighting a campaign for equal rights and in struggling for the liberty of religious education they fought a national as well as a religious campaign. Trinity College commanded revenues of £90,000 a year and, according to Donavon, until the date of the royal commission in 1907, had 'not spent one sixpence on the scientific study of agriculture in a country absolutely dependent on that industry for its existence'. Trinity College had also left the field of Gaelic literature 'unexplored' and 'had left its own great store of Irish MSS. uncatalogued'. On religious grounds Trinity College remained for many years a purely Protestant institution, despite the fact that in 1873 religious tests were abolished for all those except in the faculty of Divinity.

The criticisms raised against the bishops for their rejection of the Queen's Colleges would seem to have been more reasonable, and the colleges won the support of many Irish nationalists and Catholics, including Dr Murray, but as Donavon maintains, they were the first institutions established anywhere in the world that excluded Religion and Theology and they were not self-governing. The State was to be, and to remain in control. Donavon maintains that far from being a failure, the Catholic university was to achieve final victory in the National University founded in 1908:

> Is it failure to have set up at whatever sacrifice a noble ideal that has never been lost sight of and comes slowly to be realized? There is no interruption of continuity between the Catholic University opened by the bishops of Ireland in 1854 and the two principal institutions out of which the leading constituent college of the National University of 1908 is to be built.[37]

When the National University was founded, no fraction of the State endowment could be used for religious purposes, but it was allowed to have a chair of Theology. Added to this, the National

University was self-governing, a privilege not allotted to the Queen's Colleges. Donavon says of Newman: 'He trusted to the future and on the whole his trust was justified. In due season the fruit of the good seed that he sowed in many fields is being gathered.'

Notes

1 Fergus McGrath, *Newman's University* (1951), p. 90.
2 Bernard O'Reilly, *The Life and Times of John MacHale*, II, p. 491.
3 *The Times*, 24 January 1850.
4 Peadar MacSuibhne, *Paul Cullen and his Contemporaries*, II, p. 76.
5 Ian Ker, *John Henry Newman* (1988), LD xiv 257, p. 376.
6 Ibid., LD xiv 316, pp. 376–7.
7 Ibid., LD xiv 357-8, p. 377.
8 Peadar MacSuibhne, op. cit., II, p. 98.
9 McGrath, op. cit. p. 122.
10 Ibid.
11 Ian Ker, op. cit., LD xiv 394, p. 377.
12 Ibid., LD xiv 389–90, 377–78.
13 Bernard O'Reilly, op. cit., II, pp. 492–3.
14 Ibid., pp. 497–8.
15 Ibid., pp. 494–5.
16 Peadar MacSuibhne, op. cit., II, p. 123.
17 Ian Ker, op. cit., LD xv 66, p. 378.
18 Ibid., LD xv 98-9, p. 380.
19 Ibid., p. 383.
20 Ibid., p. 397.
21 Peadar MacSuibhne, op. cit., II, p. 139.
22 Bernard O'Reilly, op. cit., II, p. 499.
23 Ian Ker, op. cit., p. 401 (Newman, *Autobiographical Writings*, p. 295).
24 Peadar MacSuibhne, op. cit., II, p. 155.
25 Ian Ker, op. cit., LD xvi 53, p. 407.
26 Ibid., LD xvi 172, p. 409.
27 McGrath, op. cit., p. 127.
28 Ibid., p. 127.
29 Ibid., p. 327.
30 Ibid., p. 349.
31 Ibid., p. 380.
32 Ibid., p. 390.
33 Ian Ker, op. cit., LD xix 379, p. 461.
34 Quoted in Appendix to McGrath, op. cit.

35 Ibid.
36 Ibid.
37 Ibid.

16

DISCORD BETWEEN MACHALE AND CULLEN

'Under Dr Cullen's rule a reign of terror prevails in Ireland.'
(Frederick Lucas)

IN DECEMBER 1852 Archbishop MacHale had great hopes for the Independent Irish Party. He himself did not want to owe allegiance to Whig, Tory, Liberal or Peelite and had always advocated independence for the Irish members of Parliament. Aberdeen had formed a coalition ministry of Liberals and Peelites and, with fifty members, the Irish Independents looked set to wield some power and influence. They had promised to support no government that did not take as part of its policy, Irish demands for tenant right. They also had among their numbers, many talented members. Frederick Lucas was a rising young orator and journalist. Charles Gavan Duffy was well known for his political theories and the part he had played in the Young Ireland movement. William Keogh, a talented lawyer, was a likeable, charismatic figure with great charm and John Sadleir seemed to be an astute businessman. All appeared to be committed to the cause of tenant right and had supported the pledge to remain independent of any government that did not adopt their demands.

It was therefore a great blow to Irish hopes when on the advent of the Aberdeen Coalition, Keogh accepted the post of Solicitor General for Ireland and Sadleir became Lord of the Treasury. Another member of the Independent Irish Party, Edmund O'Flaherty, also accepted a Government position as Commissioner for income tax. They were immediately denounced by the Tenant League and the Friends of Religious Freedom and Equality. George Henry Moore, their old colleague and former friend, immediately denounced them as pledge-breakers and wrote to Archbishop MacHale asking him for his opinion and support.

215

This, MacHale was very ready to give. He wrote an open letter to Moore in which he condemned the pledge-breakers for violation of public morality:

> On the strict and religious obligation of fidelity to such covenants there can be no controversy – an obligation the more sacred and binding in proportion to the numbers committed to such engagement, and to the magnitude and sacredness of the interests which they involve. Dissolve the binding power of such contracts, and you loosen the firmest bonds by which society is kept together.[1]

MacHale was supported in his denunciation by the bishops of Meath, Cloyne, Killala and Killaloe and it was expected that the other bishops would follow suit. Keogh and Sadleir had now to seek re-election and the public indignation was such that most people assumed that they would not be successful. The Tenant League opposed them vehemently, but bribery, poverty and despair made people congratulate them on their new positions in the hope that they too might profit by their success. They hoped particularly to gain patronage for their sons. To a young man born into the lower middle class in an Irish country town, the civil service was seen as a 'golden ladder' to success.[2] Keogh also had the support of the Bishop of Elphin, Dr Browne. The Bishop of Kildare, Dr Haly, also gave open support to both Keogh and Sadleir. This enabled the people to salve their consciences, thinking that the local bishops must be acting rightly. The action or lack of action that most angered the Tenant League and Archbishop MacHale was the silence of Dr Cullen. He had previously been a supporter of the Catholic Association and of the Tenant League. It was felt that, as a bishop, he would disapprove of pledge-breakers, and as an Irish patriot, he would see the damage done by their actions to the movement for tenant right. It was expected that, like MacHale, he would denounce those members who had accepted office. Instead he remained silent. Cullen made no attempt to explain his position. However, it soon became evident that he was becoming very wary of clergy involvement in politics. He supported legislation from Rome that was against such involvement and in the next few years a number of incidents occurred in which priests active in the Tenant League were punished for alleged infringement of ecclesiastical discipline. It is likely that, although Cullen was willing to join battle against the Government on an issue such as the Ecclesiastical Titles Bill, which was in direct opposition to a decree of the Pope and the Catholic Church in Britain, such issues as 'Tenant right' were those of secular politics, which he probably felt were not the concern of the Catholic priest. He was also never easy as a colleague of such men as Charles Gavan Duffy. He continued to think of the Young Ireland movement as revolutionary, in the same mould as Mazzini's Young Italy, a movement that he hated profoundly and with reason, for he had been in Rome during Mazzini's occupation and had witnessed and felt the terror of revolution. His long sojourn in Rome had also made it difficult for him to understand constitutional government. For him opposition always smacked of revolution. He did not understand that for democracy to work, there needs to be opposing views, legitimate differences of opinion, both in the Church and in the country at large. For John MacHale, during his years as a bishop, his religious duties did not seem to be separate from his concerns for the poor and his political interests. In the west of Ireland he had seen the people dying around him, and their cries for help had moved and stimulated him in his determination to better their lot in every way, economic, religious and educational. Cullen's apparent abandonment of the Tenant League and the Independent Irish opposition seemed inexplicable to MacHale and their relationship never recovered; in fact, it grew worse and worse as the years went on. This was disappointing for MacHale, as he had suggested Cullen as the next Archbishop of Armagh and he had assumed that he would have an ally in his fight for Irish interests. MacHale had had a difficult relationship with Murray, who had been given the title 'castle bishop' by many, on account of his unwillingness to cause trouble or appear to disturb the peace, but Murray was of a different generation, and while MacHale had found him frustrating, and had opposed him on many accounts, he was still able to respect the saintly old man who had ordained him.

Cullen seemed to feel that Aberdeen's Government, although it had no intentions of doing anything about the demands of the Tenant League, was more sympathetic towards Catholics. Aberdeen himself had not voted for the Ecclesiastical Titles Bill and did listen to some Catholic grievances. He later sanctioned the appointment of Catholic chaplains in prisons and the armed services, putting them on virtually the same footing as their Anglican counterparts.

In 1854, in a letter to Propaganda, Cullen says that bishops 'should be allied neither with the government nor with the popular party, but should be men who occupy themselves with their proper duties as good bishops'.[3] In a letter two years later he writes in reference to the Keogh-Sadleir affair:

> I took no part whatever in this controversy because I saw that, if on the one hand Mr Keogh were to be blamed for having violated his promise, on the other hand it could be claimed in his favour, that the promise was rash, and injurious, and therefore not binding. . . . I should say however that it seems to me an incalculable advantage to have Catholics in positions concerned with the administration of law in Ireland.[4]

Popular indignation at the defection of Sadleir and Keogh was so great that despite the selfish interests of certain sections of the Irish people it seemed impossible for them to be re-elected, but the charming Mr Keogh was sponsored by Dr Browne and was re-elected accordingly. When asked years later about his actions, Dr Browne said, 'Sure the sweet words of him would coax the birds off the trees.'[5] Sadleir did not get re-elected to Carlow but, with the help of the Rev. James Maher, an uncle of Dr Cullen's, he was finally elected for Sligo. The subsequent careers of the pledge-breakers were not auspicious. O'Flaherty eventually fled the country with debts of £15,000. Sadleir, a banker and financier, had to resign as Lord of the Treasury in January 1854, accused of bribery and corruption, and in February 1856 he killed himself dramatically on Hampstead Heath to escape his financial difficulties. It is in the manner of his failure and death that Sadleir has been compared to Dickens's Mr Merdle in *Little Dorrit*. In his preface to the book, which was published in 1857,

Dickens says: 'If I might make so bold as to defend that extravagant conception, Mr Merdle, I would hint that it originated after the rail-road share epoch, in the times of a certain Irish bank, and of one or two equally laudable enterprises.'[6] Humphrey House in his book on Dickens says that Dickens privately told his friend, Forster, that he had 'shaped Mr Merdle himself out of that precious rascality'.[7] However, Keogh continued quite successfully in his career, becoming Attorney-General in Palmerston's Government, and the initial defections made it so much easier for other Irish members of Parliament to accept office. There remained a solid core of Irish opposition for some time but it began to dwindle.

In January 1854 MacHale tried to breathe new life into the remnants of the Independent Opposition by holding a great meeting in Tuam. Moore, Gray, Lucas and Duffy all spoke at a huge banquet presided over by the Archbishop. The meeting was not successful in saving the party but it did have one beneficial side-effect. At the banquet a Mr Christopher Kelly spoke at some length on the system of bribery and jobbery in buying Irish votes. Dr Gray of the *Freeman's Journal* also spoke. He described the situation in 1847 when the Irish members of Parliament had promised to support Lord George Bentink's bill to grant £16 million for railways. The MPs were sent for by Russell, who told them that if they supported Lord George they would cease to have a claim on Whig patronage. As a result of these speeches, questions were asked in the House of Commons and it was revealed that there were 16,000 salaried posts at the disposal of the Government. *The Times* declared that it was high time that competitive examinations were held for these positions and so a blow was struck against open political corruption.

Towards the end of 1854 there was more disruption in the Independent Opposition Party. Serjeant Shee, who had formerly been in charge of the Tenant League Bill, introduced a Land Act which the members of the League believed would make matters worse for the tenants. Fr Matthew O'Keefe, one of the priests of Callan who had been instrumental in setting up the Tenant League, wrote an open letter denouncing the bill. The Bishop of Ossory forbade the young priest to attend any more League meetings and to play any further part in politics. This action of the bishop's caused great consternation among clergy and laity alike, especially as it was felt that the Bishop of Ossory had the backing of Archbishop Cullen. It was becoming increasingly clear that Cullen's sympathies were moving away from the Tenant League. He supported legislation against clergy involvement in politics and a number of incidents occurred in which priests active in the Tenant League were punished for their activities. The supporters of the Tenant League and of the Independent Opposition were alarmed by Cullen's seemingly changed position. Frederick Lucas, in particular, realised that without clergy support, political movements, parliamentary elections and bills had little chance of success. The middle class in Ireland was weak and the clergy were the natural leaders of the people. When Fr O'Shea was silenced as well, Lucas said that 'these were not isolated incidents but part of a systematic concerted plan to introduce an entirely new state of things into the relations between the priests and the people of Ireland' and that

> on the success or failure of the plan, not the mere discipline of the church alone but the dearest rights and interests of the people of Ireland, of the Catholics of England and Scotland, and of the Catholics throughout the Colonies are concerned.[8]

Lucas was sure that if the Pope were to hear of the true condition of things in Ireland, he would understand the necessity for the political involvement of the clergy. He did not believe that the 'final decision of ecclesiastical authority would be to silence the mouths of honest men'.[9]

Convinced of the rightness of his case, Lucas prepared to set out for Rome to complain about the activities of Archbishop Cullen. Lucas's mission would seem to have been doomed from the start. Paul Cullen was well respected in Rome. Having lived in Rome for so long, he had many friends there. Constitutional government was not familiar to most Italians and was viewed as dangerous by many. It was not likely that Italian cardinals would understand the situation in the British Isles any better than Cullen. Added to this, Dr Cullen was the Apostolic Delegate – the voice of the Pope in Ireland. Lucas's visit to Rome coincided with that of the bishops, all of whom assembled there in early December 1854 for the promulgation of the doctrine of the Immaculate Conception. Before he went, Lucas obtained testimonials from various reputable people. Cardinal Wiseman paid tribute to him as a politician, as did the bishops of Beverley and Nottingham. He was encouraged by a letter to the *Tablet* from his friend Canon Oakley. He was also encouraged by members of the religious orders and, in particular, by the Jesuits. Lord Arundel and various members of the aristocracy also gave him testimonials. Lucas arrived in Rome on 6 December just in time for the definition of the Immaculate Conception. Knowing the problems that faced Lucas, Archbishop MacHale was wary of encouraging Lucas in this unprecedented step, but Lucas was an intelligent and honest man and had prepared his case thoroughly. On 15 December he wrote home:

> I have had conversations with Dr MacHale. Dr MacHale did not – nor did anyone else – understand the whole scope of the business at first, and he said he had written home . . . to dissuade me from coming to Rome, and to carry on the fight with vigour in Ireland. On giving him a further explanation, and showing him the extent of the move we were making, he completely came round to our view, and expressed great satisfaction, and spoke repeatedly with the greatest confidence of the result.[10]

MacHale was completely in sympathy with Lucas and, admiring his courage, he eventually gave him his support. Lucas was organising a memorial that was to be numerously signed by the clergy and forwarded to Rome. MacHale pressed Lucas to hurry with this venture and also to secure the signatures of MPs.

At first, despite problems with his health, Lucas felt that things were going well. Everyone spoke with great reverence and affection about the Pope, Pius IX. Lucas had an interview with Cardinal Wiseman. Lucas reports:

> He did not wish to feel himself in direct opposition to Dr Cullen. It seemed to imply that he felt himself in opposition as

regarded opinion and policy, but that he wished still not to make it a complete break.[11]

All the professors of the Irish College in Rome were against Lucas. While in Rome, Cullen tried to secure for himself the appointment of all the professors in the Irish College in Paris, but opposed by MacHale and Dr Derry, he was overruled. On meeting MacHale after this affair, Lucas wrote 'Dr MacHale is in great spirits' and that he treated the Irish College as the 'stronghold of corruption and will have no terms with it'.[12] However, MacHale's good spirits were not to last long. On 7 January 1855 Lucas wrote that he had met Monsignor Barnabo, the cleric who replaced Cardinal Fransoni as head of Propaganda, and he 'seemed very much displeased with something Dr MacHale had said, and repeated that such a course (whatever it was) made the church a democracy not a monarchy'.[13]

On 9 January Lucas had an audience with the Pope. During the conversation the Pope mentioned the differences between Cullen and MacHale. He told Lucas that he was concerned about this and asked him to sow the seeds of peace and good understanding. The Pope also told Lucas that he was always getting complaints about Archbishop MacHale from England, but although he had not taken any notice, he acknowledged that MacHale was 'a bit strong'. Lucas explained to the Pope about the tenant question and how both MacHale and Cullen had supported the Tenant League. Lucas left the Pope feeling that the interview had gone well and with the promise of another audience. On 21 January Lucas had a meeting with Cullen. He had promised the Pope that he would be amicable and felt that he had tried hard, but on 26 January he wrote, 'Dr Cullen did not give one indication of a desire for any amicable settlement'.

on the contrary he wanted to get rid of Lucas, break up the party, discourage opposition to the government and 'put down public opinion in Ireland'. Cullen also gave a great tirade against Lucas's friend and colleague, Duffy, calling him a 'wicked man' and when Lucas tried to defend him, he became quite violent. Lucas felt at the time that Cullen's anger arose from the fact that he had his 'back to the wall'.[14]

Lucas was disappointed by MacHale's return to his diocese on 5 February, as he had hoped for his further support. In his next audience with the Pope the Pope told Lucas to write everything down and give it to Monsignor Talbot who would have it translated into Italian. This Lucas did in a very lengthy document called the 'Statement'. During this time Lucas' health was continuing to deteriorate. On 29 January he travelled to Naples with Fr Kyne and John Stuart Mill and spent the next few months working on the 'Statement'. In it he set out at length the situation in Ireland and attacked Dr Cullen vehemently – 'under Dr Cullen's rule a reign of terror prevails in Ireland'.[15] Lucas came back at the end of May with his 'Statement' still not complete, but his health forced him to return to England, where he died in October aged forty-four. His death was mourned by many and was felt to be a great loss to the Catholic community both in England and Ireland. He was acknowledged to have been a man of great talent and integrity, whose passionate desire for social justice sometimes led him to extremes in his speeches and writings. He numbered among his friends many illustrious men, bishops, politicians and writers. It was a puzzle to many, including Newman, that Cullen should have distrusted honest men such as Lucas and Duffy, yet had given his support to swindlers and cheats like Sadleir and O'Flaherty. Lucas was buried at Brompton cemetery, and on the day of his funeral Archbishop MacHale celebrated a Requiem Mass for him in the cathedral at Tuam.

Lucas had described MacHale, in the early part of his visit to Rome, as being in 'great spirits'. Indeed the visit of the bishops was not meant to be an occasion for controversy but a celebration of the definition of the Immaculate Conception of Our Lady. Archbishop MacHale composed a poem in Gaelic to mark the occasion, which he declaimed in front of the assembled cardinals and bishops. Pius IX encouraged MacHale to translate it into English, as there were many English-speaking bishops, particularly from the 'new world'.

A pilgrim from the sainted Isle
On which amid the darkest storm,
The Ocean's Star ne'er ceased to smile,
 And guard its ancient faith from harm,
'Twould ill become no voice to raise
To sound the stainless virgin's praise.

Hail, thou, to whom God's angel bright
  Brought down the tidings from the skies,
That, full of grace and heavenly light,
  Thou wert all lovely in his eyes.
Hail thou, of all God made the best,
His Virgin-Mother ever Bless'd!

When in this darksome veil of tears
  Our weary pilgrim days are run;
When death's approach awakes our fears,
  Do thou, Sweet Mother, with thy Son,
Plead and show forth thy gracious power,
And light our passage at that hour.[16]

MacHale's enjoyment of his stay in Rome was short-lived. The difficulty was brought about by the illness of Cardinal Fransoni, with whom MacHale had enjoyed a good relationship. His position was taken by Monsignor Barnabó, who on one occasion took it upon himself to deliver a lecture to Dr MacHale. MacHale could not put up with this and proclaimed that 'it was the privilege and duty of the Pope alone to lecture bishops'.[17] Barnabó was very offended and his subsequent appointment as Cardinal Prefect of Propaganda, on the death of Fransoni, meant that while Cullen had a firm ally in Rome, MacHale had an enemy.

    MacHale intended to leave Rome in early February and obtained the Pope's permission to do so. He did not want to spend any more time away from his diocese and he did not want to embroil himself any further in arguments with Cullen or Barnabó. However, on 3 February, MacHale was handed a letter by Monsignor Talbot. It was a copy of a letter given to the Pope by Dr Cullen. In it Cullen professes his wish that there should be 'peace and concord' between the bishops and priests in Ireland. He states that this has not happened:

> When the Irish Prelates met under the Right Reverend the Secretary of the Congregation of Propaganda, to take counsel about their own affairs, the Archbishop of Tuam without the slightest provocation, made many complaints and accusations, and among many other things reproached me with violating ecclesiastical discipline, and with invading the rights of my brother-bishops. I asked him to put these accusations in writing, which he has not done, so that these complaints remain unanswered.
>
> While these occurrences so unfavourable to peace were happening in Rome, I received letters from the bishop of Ossory, my suffragen, informing me that some priests and laymen had joined hands for the purpose of lowering the episcopal authority; that a memorial had been drawn up against me, which had been sent for signatures to the priests of several dioceses, so that, thus signed, it might be laid before the Holy See. A priest of the Province of Tuam writes that great efforts were made to obtain signatures for this document in the diocese of Tuam. . . .
>
> While they were thus in obscure corners getting up this memorial, a layman, Charles (Gavan) Duffy by name, published in his journal the *Nation*, several articles full of falsehood and abuse of me, and endeavoured to disseminate the charges which the aforesaid priests were secretly hawking about . . . . In the *Nation* of 20 January appeared a letter from three priests belonging to the diocese or Province of Tuam, inviting Mr Duffy to a public meeting and banquet (just as he was last year invited to a public dinner in Tuam, the Archbishop himself being present); and the authors of the letter praise this gentleman's labours in defence of the ecclesiastical and civil rights of Ireland, – although they know perfectly well that in 1848 he had excited the people to rebel, and that his journal now contains many things which favour revolution and

popular sedition, besides the bold attacks recently directed by
him against the bishops. . . . There is one thing, however,
which I think might greatly conduce to concord, – namely,
clearly to establish who is the author of dissension.

From what I have stated, it is evident that the Archbishop
of Tuam considers me to be responsible for it. . . . I think,
however, that the complaints of his Grace are devoid of all
foundation in fact.[18]

Cullen then goes on to say that he wants MacHale to put his
complaints in writing and have them 'duly examined'. He says that if
he is found to be at fault he will 'submit to the penalty' but 'if they
are unfounded, it is high time that the Archbishop of Tuam should
understand it to be so'.

MacHale was determined that unless he was expressly
commanded otherwise by the Pope, he would leave for Ireland as
planned on 5 February. He knew that a general eviction campaign
had begun throughout Ireland and that the clergy, demoralised by
the new rules against involvement in politics, were afraid to counsel
the people. He wrote an immediate answer to Cullen's letter. At the
head of the original draft, he wrote 'A reply to the Holy Father against
Dr Cullen's insolent calumnies of Feb 2, who strove to prevent me
from returning with the Bishops of Clonfert and Clogher'.[19]

MacHale begins his letter with a query about the timing of
Cullen's letter to the Pope. As both he and Dr Cullen had been in
Rome six weeks since the last meeting of the Irish bishops and the
secretary to Propaganda, it seemed odd that Dr Cullen had chosen
the time just before MacHale's departure to give his letter of
complaint to the Pope. MacHale says that this proceeding is not
conducive to 'peace and concord'. MacHale goes through Cullen's
letter, trying to answer each point. He says:

It is clear, therefore, that there may exist a temporary difference
of opinion among us, without its following, as a consequence,
that he who differs from others is necessarily opposed to
brotherly concord.[20]

MacHale refers to Cullen's accusation that MacHale said he was 'usurper of the rights of other bishops'. He says it was an 'inaccurate rendering' of what he said. MacHale explains that the bishops assembling in Dublin for their yearly meeting had enacted that the Catholic University of Ireland should be governed by the whole assembly of bishops. At the meeting of the bishops in Rome they discovered that Propaganda had changed the situation and that the university was to be run by the four Archbishops, with a casting vote given to the Apostolic Delegate (Dr Cullen):

> This most important change in the University Statutes I learned all of a sudden, and being persuaded in my conscience that the change would be most injurious to the University, I freely expressed my opinion thereupon. . . . All this explanation I made in order to show that in fact the entire government of the University would be in the hands of the Archbishop of Dublin. . . . After this exposition, however, I added that, if it please the Holy See to have the University so governed and administered, that I would most certainly submit to the will of the Holy Father.[21]

MacHale says that two other prelates expressed the same view. In a subsequent letter, written some weeks later from Tuam, MacHale speaks of the complaints about Mr Duffy and the Tuam banquet:

> The motive . . . which dictated the invitation proffered to Mr Duffy to be present at a meeting and a public dinner was not his tendency towards revolutionary principles, – but his fidelity in keeping to the solemn and honour-binding pledges which he and others had solemnly taken, and who stood by these pledges in the British Parliament.

MacHale explained in this letter the situation in Ireland:

> Truth and justice require that I should submit to your Holiness that a large number of priests and bishops living in Ireland have been of late years placed in such very peculiar

circumstances, or in such relations towards their faithful people, that these relations, in view of any rule of conduct in political matters, should be most seriously examined.

He also explained about how the pledge-breakers had been supported by bishops:

In one word, so long as the members of the Catholic body content themselves with advancing their own private interests, there is no thought of remedying a single one of the evils of which we complain.

In his letter MacHale once again says that disagreements between clerics do not constitute quarrels and discord:

It is one thing to create, without reason and of express purpose, discord in the Church of God; but it is quite another thing to express one's opinion about matters relating to the church and the welfare of the faithful, with all due deference to the judgement of the Holy See, and with all care to respect those laws of charity which we are to observe towards all. Differences of opinion there must be even on the most important matters, on every side of a debate among bishops and priests: this is a matter of course.[22]

Notes

1   Nuala Costello, *John MacHale* (1939), pp. 114–15.
2   Bernard O'Reilly, *The Life and Times of John MacHale* (1890), II, p. 345.
3   Quoted in Patrick Corish, *A History of Irish Catholicism* (1967), p. 20.
4   Ibid., p. 24.
5   Nuala Costello, op. cit., p. 116.
6   Charles Dickens, *Little Dorrit* (1857), Preface.
7   Humphrey House, *The Dickens World* (1941), p. 29.
8   Edward Lucas, *The Life of Frederick Lucas MP* (1886), II, p. 100.
9   Ibid., p. 98.
10 Ibid., 15 December, p. 109.
11 Ibid., p. 110.

12   Ibid., p. 111.
13   Ibid., p. 114.
14   Ibid., 26 January, pp. 123–5.
15   Ibid., p. 242.
16   Bernard O'Reilly, op. cit., II, pp. 362–3.
17   Ibid., p. 365.
18   Ibid., p. 368.
19   Ibid., p. 373.
20   Ibid., p. 375.
21   Ibid., pp. 375–7.
22   Ibid., pp. 379–82.

17

THE PROBLEMS OF THE WEST

'Should they [priests] be silent under the circumstances here described, they must be numbered among those who are called in the Sacred Scriptures, 'blind watchers, . . . silent dogs, that cannot bark.' (Third Council of Tuam)

VISITORS TO IRELAND in the mid 1850s saw a country that had changed significantly in the last ten years. They saw improvements in agriculture, more variegated crops, herds of cattle in the fields, and flocks of sheep on the hills. Cardinal Wiseman, who visited Ireland in 1858, spoke of the growing prosperity of the people and the lack of any 'feeling of subjection'. He marvelled at the building of churches and the phenomenal growth of the Catholic Church. But as he himself remarked, he was aware that there were areas of Ireland where poverty and suffering were endemic.[1]

The west of Ireland was still such a place. The people laboured on difficult land with the constant threat of eviction and their plight was made worse by an increase in the Protestant proselytising activities.

Edward Nangle had been active in Achill for some time and the famine brought further opportunities to encourage 'converts' to Protestantism with the promise of food and clothing. For this reason these converts were known as 'soupers'. After the famine Nangle wrote that it had been a judgement of God for national sins, these being:

1. Unatoned for blood. 2. Idolatry, especially when sanctioned by the rulers of the Country. 3. Profane neglect of the House and Ordinances of God – e.g. travelling and amusement on the Lord's Day. 4. Wafer worship.[2]

230

Nangle continually raged against the beliefs and activities of the Catholics. In a Catholic catechism written in the beginning of the century, it stated that a sin such as a vain word, or an 'officious or jesting lie', was a venial sin, but 'the theft of a pin or an apple, is not weight enough to break charity between man and man, much less between God and man'. Nangle used this quotation extensively to show the Catholic disregard for sin.

In the 1850s the chief centres of Protestant missionary activities moved from Achill to the parish of Clifden and the valley of Castlekirke on the shores of Lough Corrib. An Englishman, the Reverend Alexander Dallas, regarded the Irish as heathens and felt himself called by God to save them. He visited Cork in 1843, and in 1846 wrote a religious tract which he described as 'a voice from heaven to Ireland'.[3] He distributed thousands of copies of his tract and in 1849 founded the Irish Church Mission to Roman Catholics. He watched over the movement from London and Dublin but took a special interest in Connemara. After visiting Castlekirke he realised that the ranks of the Catholic priests had been thinned by the famine and Mass was only said every third week. He built a school at which food was provided. He then extended his operations to Clifden, where he had the co-operation of the local landlord, Mr D'Arcy. D'Arcy's son, Hyacinth, took orders in 1852 and helped him in the movement. Their efforts were appreciated by the Protestant Bishop of Tuam, Lord Plunkett.

The previous Lord Plunkett had bought a shooting lodge at a beautiful spot of Tourmakeady on Lough Mask. He liked it so much that he subsequently bought the surrounding estate. The son who succeeded him became the Protestant Bishop of Tuam and subsequently the treasurer of the Irish Church Missionary Society.

Nangle was also given encouragement by the Church Missionary society and its funds. In 1851 the whole of Achill Island was purchased from Sir Richard O'Donnell, more than half the property belonging to the Church Missionary Society.

In 1852 Lord Plunkett made a visitation to the diocese, where he claimed to have confirmed 1,294 people, 840 of them being converts from the Church of Rome. This information was reported widely in the press and was coupled with disparaging references to Archbishop

MacHale as a 'political agitator'. In October 1852, following a letter written by MacHale to Lord Derby in the *Freeman's Journal*, MacHale received a letter from Pope Pius IX telling him to guard against losing his flock and mentioning the letter to Derby, which the Pope felt lacked moderation – 'not in accordance with the prudence which befits a bishop'.[4] MacHale replied immediately to the Pope to reassure him, particularly about the issue of proselytism. He explained to the Pope how many Catholics had become Protestants in order to be able to feed themselves and their families, but usually returned to the Catholic fold as soon as they were able.

In 1853 Mr S. C. Hall once again visited the Protestant colony on Achill to see for himself what was happening there. He was a loyal Protestant and considered 'every conscientious accession to the Protestant faith as a contribution in aid of the well-being of the state',[5] but despite this he was shocked by Nangle's activities. He describes a boy who was sent away from the orphanage without food or clothes because he was naughty. In reply Nangle stated that he was not deprived of clothes as he was given back the 'rags he came in'. Hall also wrote:

> It was impossible to appreciate the magnanimity of the poor, miserable, utterly destitute, and absolutely starving, inhabitants of Achill, who were at the time of our visit enduring privations at which humanity shudders, – and to know that by walking a couple of miles and professing to change their religion they would instantly have been supplied with food, clothes and lodging. Yet these hungry thousand – for it would scarcely be an exaggeration to say that nine tenths of the population of this island were, in the month of July last, entirely without food – preferred patiently to endure their sufferings rather than submit to what they considered a degradation. Such fortitude we do believe to be parallel in the history of any 'ignorant and unenlightened' people since the creation of the world.[6]

Nangle's activities in the west of Ireland continued to attract criticism from Catholic and Protestant, from both Irish and English people. In

1857 he was attacked by the *Belfast Mercury* and some years later by the *Liverpool Mercury*. He was accused by a young lady of 'appropriating rents for private use'.[7]

At this time a great sum of money, £100,000, had been raised in England to provide a daily ration of food for children of all denominations. In distributing the money, Plunkett and Dallas decided that a scriptural, i.e. Protestant, education should be given with the food ration. Consequently, mission schools were established in many places. Plunkett built a school that Catholic children were obliged to attend. At first there was no protest as the parish priest, Fr Peter Ward, did not know what to do. However, on the appointment of a new curate, Fr Peter Conway, the situation changed and Fr Conway turned the children out. The bishop's daughters were filled with zeal and with the Reverend Mr Townsend visited houses and accosted people on the road. They even brought an ex-Catholic priest to the area to revile the faith he had abandoned. Townsend visited the monastery school, where he was ejected by a militant monk. Evictions followed the failure to attend church and school. Some tenants emigrated, some worked in the monastery or on Fr Ward's farm, and some died in Ballinrobe workhouse. Fr Peter Ward was very anxious in that environment and asked that he should be sent somewhere else. MacHale appointed Fr Patrick Lavelle to the parish. Lavelle already had somewhat of a reputation and had been a brilliant student at Maynooth and a professor at the Irish College in Paris, but had quarrelled with the President. He was not anxious to quarrel with Plunkett but wrote to him saying that he understood that his lordship's tenants were coerced to attend the Protestant schools. He said that he thought the bishop was not fully aware of the situation: 'I trust your Lordship's sense of fair-play to leave the children of your Catholic tenantry to the training of the Catholic teachers provided for them'.[8] The bishop replied that he had in his schools only those whose parents had chosen to send them. Lavelle was pleased and said that the bishop's letter was 'the harbinger of peace and goodwill among all parties in this parish'. The bishop then wrote that he would not bind himself to any course of action and begged to decline any further correspondence.[9] Lavelle appealed again to the bishop, as the bailiffs, Bible readers, teachers and clergymen were harassing the people. In his appeal Lavelle said that he would not want his children brought up in an alien faith and the poor peasants had rights no less that the peer. Lavelle asked the parents to be prepared to face eviction, and the following day no Catholic children attended the Protestant school. Plunkett then fined the tenants and impounded their cattle. They were abused by the teachers and threatened by the Miss Plunketts. The bishop then warned them that 'a notice to quit shall be served on tenants throughout the estate'.[10] In 1860 there were sixty ejections at the Castlebar assizes against the tenants of Tourmakeady. Fr Conway intervened to bring about a compromise. Plunkett agreed that two tenants should be evicted and others must submit to stripping of their lands. Fr Lavelle withdrew his prosecution of a Tourmakeady parson who had threatened to shoot him with a revolver. However, Plunkett disregarded the Castlebar arrangement and in November the work of eviction began, aided by soldiers from the Curragh, the police, the Sheriff and the 'crowbar brigade'. Sixty-eight persons were without shelter, including an old man of eighty and a baby in a cradle. The crimes they had committed were such things as insulting a Bible-reader and lending a cart to Fr Lavelle. Lavelle published details in the press. The *Times* proclaimed it a 'hideous scandal'. Lavelle fought Plunkett in the law courts and in the press. In 1862 Lord Plunkett died, then Miss Plunkett and the Reverend Townsend left. The land was sold to an Englishman, a Mr Mitchell of Bradford, and peace was resumed.

In 1855 Charles Gavan Duffy had decided to leave Ireland for Australia. He had decided that the political life of Ireland was dead and there was no more hope for Ireland than 'a corpse on the dissecting table'.[11] MacHale, though sorry to see him go, furnished him with warm letters of recommendation to bishops and other people of influence in Australia.

In 1857 the cause of tenant right and Independent Opposition received another setback in the Mayo election. There were three candidates, Captain Palmer, Ousely Higgins and George Henry Moore. Higgins and Moore had been in Parliament for some time. Moore was immensely popular and a loyal supporter of tenant right. Higgins, on the other hand, had become a follower of Sadleir and held office for the Government. He held in his possession the appointments to all the government offices in the county, from the highest judicial office to the village policeman and postman.

In 1857 all the bishops of the province assembled in Tuam for the consecration of John MacEvilly as Bishop of Galway. MacHale used the occasion to appeal to the electors to reject Higgins, who had betrayed his pledge. He also issued a pastoral letter in which he condemned bribery and once again warned the people not to trust those who had deceived them. Many priests went much further in their denunciation of Higgins, Fr Luke Ryan saying he would vote for 'the devil himself' rather than Ousely Higgins.[12] Moore and Palmer were elected. Higgins then lodged a petition complaining that there had been intimidation. The affair was tried before a select committee in the House of Commons and MacHale was called to give evidence. Fr Peter Conway and Fr Luke Ryan, both priests under MacHale's jurisdiction, were charged with 'spiritual intimidation'. In the witness box, in reply to a question as to his position in the Catholic Church, MacHale said that he was the Archbishop of Tuam. The committee replied that they were unable to recognise such a title. On being questioned further MacHale said openly that in the previous election he had supported Higgins, but after Higgins had accepted government patronage, he would prefer to support Palmer, even though he was a Conservative. MacHale said that he regarded the selection of those who made the laws of the land, a moral question, and he felt that he had a right to speak. He himself would not put forward a candidate but would try to assure the success of a good one. He regarded this as part of his civil rights. MacHale's questioner asked him whether he thought the priest should have more influence than the landlord. MacHale replied that a man's vote was between himself and his God. After interrogating MacHale further about the difference between a priest giving advice and coercion, the questioner said that it was not distinct. MacHale replied, 'When there is a mist before the eyes it is very difficult to see objects distinctly.'[13]

The Committee sat for ten days and came to the conclusion that there had been 'undue influence and spiritual intimidation' and that Moore's return was void. Moore, in consequence, lost his seat and did not return to Parliament for eleven years. This was a great tragedy for Ireland and Independent Opposition as Moore was an honest and intelligent man who could perhaps have done something to save the tenant right movement.

In August 1854 the second Provincial Council of Tuam was held. The decrees of this Council were approved by Rome in March 1855 and the provision of hospices for priests broken down by age and illness was especially praised.

As the nineteenth century wore on and the modes of transport became more advanced, many people in the Church favoured greater centralisation, both nationally and internationally. Archbishop Cullen as the Apostolic Delegate was anxious that Ireland should be more uniform in its practices and that the country in turn should draw closer to Rome. MacHale in opposing this was regarded as somewhat backward. In 1854 Barnabó had suggested to MacHale that he might be an 'internuncio' between the Irish Catholic Church and Propaganda, sending regular accounts to Rome on the position of the Irish Church. MacHale declined the offer, saying that he had enough to do to govern the church at St Jarlath's and on the last day he would deem it quite enough to give an account of his stewardship of that metropolitan see.[14] In declining the position MacHale probably made Barnabó aware of his continuing view that diplomacy was a kind of chicanery.

In August 1858 MacHale called the third Council of Tuam. At this council the relationship between Church and State was discussed at length. MacHale contrasts the ends of secular and civil society with that of the Divine and Universal Society called the Church. The aim of the civil ruler is to 'provide for the growing wants of a society that is ever changing' and 'a wide latitude is allowed to secular legislators in the enactment of their laws, as well as in the discussion of the principles of public well-being on which such laws may be founded'; in contrast – 'not so ecclesiastics: they have laid before them a model from which they are not permitted to depart.'[15]

While civil society pursues what it calls the necessity of intellectual and material progress,

The Church . . . silently pursues its majestic mission of guarding the treasure of divine truth, which Heaven has entrusted to her keeping, and views the most brilliant discoveries in nature as but so many faint reflections of the Eternal Word, the Uncreated Wisdom. . . .

Our religion then, being a code of laws, and precepts, and counsels, not discovered by reason, but revealed by our Redeemer, its perfection consists in its being transmitted pure as it was received. . . . The duty of transmitting it must be performed by those to whom it has been entrusted.

Hence the practice of councils from the earliest times; several bishops meeting occasionally together to collect the traditions of their respective churches, and to impress the seal of their authority on the sacred treasures of divine doctrine.[16]

MacHale said that these assemblies met in order to protect the faith against error, and subjects to which they often turned their attention were, 'the vindication of discipline against abuses, . . . the decent uniformity of the ceremonies in the administration of the sacraments, the diffusion of a Christian education' and the protection of 'a cloistered monastic life'.

Nor were the occasions rare when the remonstrances of these assemblies were raised against the oppressors of the poor, and the despoilers of God's temple . . . those insidious foes who in every age of the Church, labour to subject its ministers to the influence of a secular policy. . . .

In the eventful annals of the Church there are not found any chapters more interesting than those that record the struggles of its holy and intrepid pastors against the encroachments by which the civil power sought to make the Church its footstool. And as long as the bishops of any country were both able and willing to meet in council, so long were they able to present a wall of brass, within which the sacred interests of faith and morality and mercy to the poor were guarded.[17]

MacHale talks about the changing situation of the Catholic Church in Ireland. The penal days were coming to an end, churches were being built, convents and monasteries set up:

> It is to assist in seconding a change so consoling, and giving it a fresh impulse, that the venerable prelates of this province are assembled. They come to take counsel together, as inmates of the same household, as members of the same mystical body, as witnesses of the faith which they derive from their predecessors . . . in short they come together to help each other to walk more securely in the old ways, resolved not to pass themselves, or suffer others to pass, the ancient bounds, which have been set by our fathers.

MacHale speaks about the different kinds of councils of the Church:

> Faith has no local limits. It is not regulated by the geographical latitude of countries, nor the civil boundaries of kingdoms; and therefore it is fitting that, when obscured or assailed, the different nations of the earth, under the guidance of the Holy Father, should sometimes assemble to illustrate and defend it. This is the purpose of general or oecumenical councils.[18]

MacHale then goes on to speak about national councils of bishops, which meet a little more regularly than general councils, particularly to take counsel together about a common injustice or oppression. He says that provincial councils differ from both of these as it is fitting that they should meet on a regular basis as they are founded on 'two principles dear to the Church, – the regulated freedom of its local authority, and the uniformity of its local discipline'. In later years MacHale was often accused of 'Gallicanism'; his loyalty to the Holy See was never in question, but he did claim a certain independence which in the nineteenth century was beginning to be unpopular. In his address to the Tuam Council, he outlines some of these ideas:

> The manners, customs, and languages of nations being so different that they could not be recast into the same mould,

and being no obstacle to the profession of the same faith, or the acknowledgement of one authority, or the prevalence of essential discipline, the Church has exercised the wisest forbearance in the permission of very subordinate differences of practice, thus strengthening her authority by winning the attachment of widely different peoples.

But that the same people should not be offended or scandalized by a capricious diversity of rites in the midst of them, she has partitioned nations and kingdoms into the smaller divisions of provinces. . . .

Thus we have at once that perfect unity of faith and essential discipline which the supreme authority of One Head is so calculated to secure, and that difference of subordinate practices, arising from a diversity of local circumstances, which the wisdom of the same authority leaves to the experienced discretion of the local pastors.[19]

During the 1850s it was felt by many that the plight of the Irish had improved a great deal, and indeed there were not wholesale deaths of starvation as in the late 1840s, but the evictions continued and so did the emigration. To some extent, as the lot of the people improved even slightly, they were more capable of envisaging a better life overseas and of paying the passage out of Ireland. Emigration, while it seemed the best solution to 'the Irish problem' for many, was a tragic occurrence for the families involved. It was treated to some extent like a death, for there was never any hope that the emigrating person would be seen again. A wake would be held so that friends and neighbours could console the grief-stricken family. As usual, the suffering brought about by the continued emigration was greatest in the west, in the province of Tuam. The third Council of Tuam bore this in mind when making the following declarations:

1. Among the duties of a pastor we must justly rank the care which he is bound to take of the poor and all other unfortunate persons. The priest is God's minister; and to him it is said, 'To thee the poor man hath been given up; to the orphan thou shalt be a helper'; and again, 'He hath

sent me to preach to the poor, to heal the bruised of heart.' The Council of Trent hath, therefore, reason to say 'that by Divine command it is enjoined on all who have charge of souls. . . . to show a fatherly care for the poor and all distressed persons'; and the Roman Pontifical, 'Let widows, orphans and those of tender age rejoice to find in thee a most kind pastor and protector. To such as are oppressed be thou a timely defender. . . . But to the oppressors oppose a firm and efficacious resistance.'

2. Let our priests use the great liberty of speech and action authorized by our civil laws in every subject in the realm for the benefit of the distressed and the poor, whenever they can do so without wounding prudence and charity; let them, as becometh God's ministers stand up as a wall for the House of Israel.

The unheard of sufferings and persecutions borne by our populations . . . . Nor have these fateful and cruel days altogether passed away. They come back again frequently to fill with grief and the sounds of bitter wailing the lowly dwellings of our faithful people. How often are not our flocks reduced to the direst extremities, expelled cruelly from their poor homes. . . .

Let our priests, then, continue to remedy these evils in so far as they can and may becomingly; should they be silent under the circumstances here described, they must be numbered among those who are called in the Sacred Scriptures, 'blind watchers . . . silent dogs, that cannot bark.'

3. Let priests show by their labours and their virtues that they seek not their own interests but those of Christ Jesus. Let pastors, mindful only of the place they hold, and of the sacred character they have the honour to bear, show that they solely love and seek the liberty of the Church and the good of religion, as well as to be the protectors of the poor and wretched; . . .

4. Let priests daily recall to mind that they are called to be a part of the Master's inheritance, that their ordination sets

them apart from the body of the faithful, and obliges them truly to lead a life of integrity and holiness. Hence it is that they ought not to take any part in worldly affairs save only in so far as these can advance the kingdom for God. If they only keep steadily before their eyes both the dignity of the priestly office and the prescriptions of their country's laws, they will certainly promote the spiritual as well as the temporal welfare of their people, in a manner becoming God's priests and the successors of the men who sustained before our days, and with success, the cause of the suffering poor.[20]

Although it may have seemed that the Tuam declarations had fully discussed the question of the part played by priests in politics, Propaganda asked that the 'Dublin rules' agreed by the bishops in 1854 be inserted. These had been passed by national synods in Armagh and Dublin and had sought to limit the activities of clergy in politics. It was thought that Cullen was their instigator. They stated the obligations of priests

to expound . . . the mysteries of faith, the sacraments, the commandments of God . . . . But inasmuch as there is danger that these duties will be neglected, if in the churches they treat of things profane and foreign to religion, we strictly forbid their discussing during the celebration of mass, or within the church in any way, mere secular matters, such as political elections which may easily create dissensions between the pastor and the people, or excite passionate feelings.[21]

The assembly goes on to say that it does not forbid priests from speaking about such things as bribe-taking or the duties of charity and the care for the poor.

Of course this pronouncement could have a wide interpretation, particularly by such characters as MacHale and Cullen, who held very different opinions on what pertained to 'religion'.

Notes

1   N. P. S. Wiseman, *Impressions of a recent visit to Ireland: a lecture delivered in London, 3 November 1858* (1859), pp. 5–6.
2   Henry Seddall, *Edward Nangle* (1884), p. 237.
3   E. A. D'Alton, *History of the Archdiocese of Tuam* (1928), II, p. 52.
4   Bernard O'Reilly, *The Life and Times of John MacHale* (1890), II, p. 434.
5   S. C. Hall, *The Achill Mission* (1844), p. 1.
6   Ibid., p. 3.
7   Henry Seddall, op. cit., p. 212.
8   D'Alton, op. cit., p. 70.
9   P. Lavelle, *The Irish Landlords Since the Revolution* (1870), pp. 515–17.
10   D'Alton, op. cit. p. 71.
11   Nuala Costello, *John MacHale* (1939), p. 127.
12   D'Alton, op. cit., p. 64.
13   Ulick Bourke, *The Life and Times of the Most Reverend John MacHale* (1883), p. 180.
14   Ibid., p. 187.
15   Bernard O'Reilly, op. cit., II, p. 472.
16   Ibid., pp. 472–3.
17   Ibid., p. 473.
18   Ibid., pp. 474–5.
19   Ibid., pp. 475–6.
20   Ibid., pp. 476–9.
21   Quoted by Patrick Corish, *A History of Irish Catholicism* (1967), p. 26.

18

THE RISE OF SECRET SOCIETIES

'It is upon a people, or at least upon upper and middle classes basking in this fool's paradise that Fenianism has burst like a clap of thunder in a clear sky, unlooked for and unintelligible.'
(John Stuart Mill)

AFTER THE DEATH of Lucas, Duffy's emigration to Australia and the debacle of the 1857 Mayo election, in which Moore lost his seat, the situation for Independent Opposition and MacHale's political allies looked bleak. MacHale, however, despite the setbacks made great efforts to salvage the situation and to heal the divisions in the League. The people of the west looked to him for guidance and leadership. In letters written by the Archbishop to Dr Gray of the *Freeman's Journal,* MacHale once again tries to unite the Irish people:

> My Dear Dr. Gray:– Having in my note of last week alluded to the dissensions that have, unhappily, sprung up in the League, I expressed a hope that, for the interest of the tenant class, which you have so much at heart, they would be put an end to, and fresh hope infused into the hearts of the people. . . .
>
> Emancipation never took a more thorough hold of the people than Tenant-Right and the only sure mode of gaining that or any other Right, Independent Opposition.
>
> You are aware of the observations of several friends of the *Freeman* that it has not recently advocated that policy as vigorously as in former times. . . . Now the feelings and interests of the people are so thoroughly engaged in favour of Tenant-Right and Independent Opposition, that I am convinced they will never be reconciled to any other agitation. . . .[1]

There had been attacks by the *Tablet* and the *Nation* against the *Freeman*, which they felt was beginning to be rather lukewarm in the cause that it had previously supported so vigorously. The *Freeman's Journal* had retaliated by attacking George Henry Moore. MacHale again wrote to Dr Gray three weeks later:

The reasons why the difficulties surrounding the Tenant Question appear so great, is the manifest indisposition of some of its friends to work harmoniously together. Unless they resolve on doing so, the same difficulties will continue. As they have the interests of the question at heart, it would not, I think, be hopeless to see them yet exerting themselves in concert to achieve its success. With a common zeal for a great common object, greater personal differences have often been effectually reconciled. . . . The question at present is how the Tenant Question, for which all friends appear especially anxious, can best be promoted. The Tenant League, such as it is, for I am not offering any opinion on its materials or its constitution, is yet the only organized body before the country as a means to further the cause. And the members of Parliament returned on the principle of Independent Opposition are, however few, the recognized Parliamentary party to carry out that principle and through it, the success of the Tenant Question.

Neither of these bodies is as influential as the friends of the Tenant Question would wish to see them. Still by those friends they are recognized as having claims to their support. No doubt there is a large section of Irishmen, including also several of the Catholic body, who look upon them, – all opposition members and League men, – as persons not entitled to much consideration. . . .

In all this there is nothing to preclude a change or improvement in the existing organization, the exercise of a fair and legitimate criticism of the acts of public men, members of Parliament or otherwise.

If the *Freeman* so favourable to tenant Right, and so influential of its assertion of it, should be found hostile to the means adopted by those who are so deeply interested in its success, such a contingency would be embarrassing to them and the question. But not alone the hostility, but the neutrality or indifference of such an organ as the *Freeman* to the popular cause, would cast a damper on the Tenant Right movement.

The first step, I think, toward a proper adjustment should be the cessation of hostilities on both sides. After this people would be in better temper to understand each other; and I have no doubt but all, without any sacrifice of honour from any, would be disposed to merge their personal feelings in a cause of so much importance to the country, and which cannot succeed without a more cordial co-operation among its friends.

I wish I could do anything to bring about so desirable a result. I remain, my dear Dr Gray, yours very faithfully,

John, Archbishop of Tuam.[2]

However, despite MacHale's repeated efforts, the resumption of the powerful days of the Tenant League and Independent Opposition seemed unlikely. Archbishop Cullen was gaining in power. He had the support of Rome, which meant that his voice carried the day in the appointment of new bishops. In previous years Rome had been sympathetic to Irish nationalism and, although never liking the idea of political agitation, the Pope did not want to surrender the control of the Catholic Church in Ireland to the British Government. This was true during the Repeal movement, as despite pressure from the British Government and from Austria, the Pope refused categorically to prohibit the movement.[3] However, the situation changed after 1848. Twelve years later Cullen still recalled the night of the murder of Count Rossi, the Pope's Prime Minister:

It was a night calculated to give some idea of the horrors of the first French Revolution. The perpetrators of that dreadful crime walked in procession through the streets, yelling in their exultation like demons: 'Blessed be the hand that spilt the blood of Rossi.'

Gavan Duffy said that after 1848 'Rome changed its policy in regard to Irish Nationalism'.[4] The papacy grew suspicious of the term 'nationalism'. It became a kind of religion itself, seen as a threat to faith. 'MacHale never saw any threat at all. Cullen saw it everywhere.'[5] Cullen himself said:

> If ever an attempt is made to abridge the liberties of the Catholic Church in Ireland, it will not be by the English government, nor by a 'no popery' cry in England, but by the revolutionary and irreligious nationalists of Ireland.[6]

In his autobiography *My Life in Two Hemispheres*, Duffy sums up the situation of the Tenant League at this time:

> The leaders of the League did not mistake their position. The high tide of success was ebbing fast. They knew they had now opposed to them, three great social forces – the Executive, the bulk of the Catholic bishops, and the entire landed gentry; and with them perhaps only a minority of the people, but a minority which comprised the best priests and the most intelligent farmers and traders in the island. They still came to the Council meetings, aged priests and dauntless curates, who for the sake of the people were facing an hostility which would certainly thwart and might possibly ruin them. They believed that Dr Cullen was more of an Italian than an Irishman, and so wholly immersed in ecclesiastical politics to leave no place for patriotism. They saw with shame that he threw the protection of the Church around some of the worst men in the community, and employed the authority of the Holy See for purposes which it could never have been designed to promote.[7]

Duffy's criticism of Cullen might appear harsh and no doubt Cullen's opinion of Duffy as a revolutionary did not endear him to Duffy, but although Cullen is acknowledged to have done good work in his organisation of the Church in Ireland, in the founding of orphanages and hospitals and in his work for education it is undoubtedly true that for better or worse, his influence brought to an end the involvement of many of the parish priests in efforts to improve the lot of the people, and with that, the demise of the Tenant League.

After the collapse of the Tenant Right movement and the failure of constitutional means of reform, there began the rise of secret societies and movements to support Irish republicanism. The most famous of these was the Fenian Brotherhood, which was founded in the United States in 1858. This was founded by a group of Irish nationalists who had first fled to Paris after the failure of the rising of 1848. They subsequently left Paris for New York, where they were joined by many other disaffected Irishmen. Two of the most influential of these men were James Stephens, an eccentric civil engineer from Kilkenny, and John O'Mahony, a member of an old landowning family from Cork. O'Mahony, a scholar and a linguist, was a believer in social democratic ideals, which he kept to the forefront of the movement. The name 'Fenian' came from the Fianna or ancient mythical warriors and reflected O'Mahony's romantic attachment to Ireland's Gaelic past.

In Ireland the organisation was known as the 'Irish Republican Brotherhood' and came into formal existence in a meeting in Maginess Place in Dublin in 1858. The virtual headquarters of the Brotherhood in Dublin were the upstairs rooms of a Joseph Deniffe, a tailor's cutter. From Deniffe's account, *A Personal Narrative of the Irish Revolutionary Brotherhood*, it is clear that the bulk of the initial membership in Ireland were Dublin artisans, distressed by existing economic conditions. The first members included John Locke, the poet, Heffernon Dunne, the nailor, Garrett O'Shaunessy, an iron manufacturer, and Thomas Clarke Luby, a graduate of Trinity College. At the meeting that took place on St Patrick's day, the assembled members swore the following oath:

> I, A.B. in the presence of Almighty God, do solemnly swear allegiance to the Irish Republic now virtually established, and that I will do my very utmost, at every risk, while life lasts, to defend its independence and integrity; and finally, that I will yield implicit obedience in all things, not contrary to the laws

of God, to the commands of my superior officers. So help me God. Amen.[8]

The nature of the oath demonstrates the optimistic, rather unrealistic nature of the Fenians. The republic that was 'virtually established' often gave the members some problems and at a Fenian trial there was some merriment when a Fenian declared that the republic was 'virtuously' established. However, despite their humble, unsophisticated beginnings, the Fenians were soon capable of raising considerable financial support from America and running their own newspaper, the *Irish People*. After the end of the American civil war they recruited ex-soldiers and by the late sixties created much fear in the minds of the English.

Many people, particularly in England, could not understand why the Irish were so disaffected at this time. John Stuart Mill, writing in 1868, said:

It is upon a people, or at least upon upper and middle classes basking in this fool's paradise that Fenianism has burst like a clap of thunder in a clear sky, unlooked for and unintelligible.[9]

Mill said that the problem for the English was that once again they were ignorant of the affairs of Ireland. A. M. Sullivan in his book *New Ireland* says that potential Irish rebels were unwittingly encouraged by the English press. During the years 1859–60 the English newspapers were wholeheartedly supporting the nationalist movements, particularly in Italy but also in Poland. *The Times* said:

That government should be for the good of the governed, and that whenever rulers wilfully and persistently postpone the good of their subjects, either to the interests of foreign states, or to abstract theories of religion or politics, the people have a right to throw off the yoke, are principles which have been too often admitted and acted upon to be any longer questioned.[10]

And in the *Daily News:*

> Europe has over and over again affirmed that one principle on which the Italian question depends, and to which the inhabitants of Central Italy appeal – the right of a people to choose its own rulers.[11]

In the *Sun:*

> As free Englishmen we assert the right of the Romans and of all nations to have governors of their own choice.[12]

Lord Ellenborough, a Cabinet minister under Lord Derby, stated:

> I will hope that . . . they [the Italians] will rise to vindicate their right to choose their own government, and clutch the arms by which alone it can be secured.[13]

The *Nation,* in a movement that professed to be 'taking England at her word', organised a national petition to the Queen to authorise a public vote in Ireland 'for a native government and legislative independence, or for the existing system of government by the Imperial Parliament'. Half a million adult Irish people signed the petition. It was presented but never answered. Nevertheless the newspapers continued:

> It is quite time that all the struggling nationalities should clearly understand that freemen have no sympathy with men who do nothing but howl and shriek in their fetters. . . . The highest spectacle which the world can offer to a freeman is to see his brother man contending bravely – nay, fighting desperately for his liberty. The lowest sentiment of contempt which a freeman can feel is that by a wretched serf . . . without the manhood to do more than utter piteous lamentations. (*The Times*)[14]

Despite the apparent English approval of revolution, the *Saturday Review* stated in November 1863:

> The Lion of St Jarlath has growled in grievous dudgeon that bucolic tastes are prevailing in Ireland. Archbishop John of Tuam surveys with an anxious eye the Irish exodus, and in a letter to Mr Gladstone he sighs over the departing demons of assassination and murder.

The exodus from Ireland continued despite the apparent growing prosperity. Those leaving Ireland did indeed provide members for the Fenian movement, for many of these felt a hatred for the British Government that was far greater than that of those left behind. They also felt a need to help their families in Ireland, and for many this meant helping them to throw off the English yoke.

In the Archdiocese of Tuam the numbers leaving Ireland were not slowing down. In 1861 the population of the province had fallen to 251,000. Ten years later it had fallen by another fifty thousand to 211,000. The reasons remained the same – poverty, lack of land to rent, and evictions. During this period the Marquis of Sligo and Lord Lucan cleared village after village. Sligo cleared the countryside along Clew Bay so that his brother-in-law, Mr Wilbrahim, could (except for his family and servants) be alone. He gave Captain Houston, a Scot, a tract of land of two hundred square miles at reduced rent. Lord Lucan, after receiving distinction in the Crimean War, returned to Ireland and was reputed to regard his tenants as vermin. The people disappeared so that cattle could take their place. Two hundred families were cleared so that Mr Simpson, a Scottish Presbyterian, could have a farm of 2,000 acres. In later times a racecourse marked the ruins of the populous village of Aughdrinagh. There were numerous other evictors in Mayo. Allan Pollock boasted that he had dispossessed five thousand people. Tenants were fined for such reasons as receiving a tenant's daughter while her husband was away harvesting in England, and for an ass straying on to the road.

Archbishop MacHale and Fr Patrick Lavelle continued to agitate on behalf of the tenants, Fr Lavelle showing a sympathy with the Fenians that was condemned by most members of the Irish hierarchy.

The Church condemned the activities of the Fenians, both because of their violence and because the Church forbade secret societies. In 1826 Leo XII in his encyclical, *Quo Graviora,* had condemned secret societies and this had been supplemented in various other papal documents.

Dr Cullen felt very strongly against the Fenians as he saw them as followers of Mazzini and the continental revolutionaries. He encouraged his bishops and priests to denounce their activities and to refuse them the sacraments. At the end of 1861 in a pastoral letter Cullen warned of the evils of joining secret societies, the Fenians and others. He said that those joining them were excommunicated *ipso facto.* A bishops' meeting in May 1862 considered the matter fully and their resolutions warned 'Catholics against all such combinations' and yet assured the people that the bishops 'cannot be blind to the many injustices they suffer'. At a later meeting in August 1863 the bishops condemned a secret society known as the St Patrick's Brotherhood, as the members swore an oath and had illegal ends. Cullen was very disturbed by a letter from Fr Lavelle to the Tuam *Patriot* in 1864. Cullen sought the advice of Kirby, the President of the Irish College in Rome. He said that Lavelle

> endeavours to show that the Fenians do not come under the Bull of Leo XII. . . . If the *et* in the Leo XII Bull can be taken conjunctively, it would appear there is no censure against societies who endeavour to subvert the Church but respect the throne. Does not that appear absurd? Get us some decision on this point . . . [the Fenians] appear to incur the censure, for by fomenting revolutions, they injure and assail both Church and State.[15]

There was a certain amount of confusion about the different secret societies amongst the bishops. Also writing to Kirby in 1864, Bishop Moriarty says:

> In your last letter you spoke of the danger of secret societies. The difference of opinion amongst ecclesiastics here as to the meaning of the Papal bulls on the subject is causing much

mischief. Dr Cullen and others declare that Fenians and members of the Society of St Patrick incur censures *ipso facto* – and others and some bishops say no, because these societies though against the state are not against the Church. . . . I have made the joining of a secret society a reserved call, and I have commanded the priests not to give Absolution until the society should be renounced *in foro externo*. . . . My dear friend, some of us by our abuse of government drive the people into disaffection and the spirit of rebellion. We can not blame them if they are more logical than canonical in their conclusions.[16]

Alone amongst the clergy, Fr Lavelle was openly and fearlessly preaching the right to rebel on the grounds of Catholic doctrine. Traditionally the right to rebel existed in cases of tyranny. Some theologians agreed with a sixteenth-century Spanish Jesuit who deemed that tyrannicide was justified in certain circumstances. In the nineteenth century it was thought that bad government terminated the divine permission to rule. In a lecture at the Rotunda in Dublin in February 1862, Lavelle argued that Ireland was so misgoverned that she had a right to rebel and should have the sanction of the Church. In an article in the *Tablet* in August 1863, he developed this theme:

1. According to all Catholic divines (Bossuet alone, perhaps, excepted), oppressive rulers may be deposed by their subjects.
2. No subjects in the world are more refinedly oppressed than the Irish people of the present day.
3. Therefore, we have the general and indisputable right to set aside our tyrannical rulers.
4. However at this moment it would be madness or wickedness to make the attempt because resistance would be useless.
5. Still, we have not alone the right, but are bound by the duty, of making all preparations in our power against the day when our oppressor will herself be battling for her existence, and when our efforts will be morally certain of

success. Is this treason? I am then a traitor. Is this disloyal? So am I.[17]

Although the Fenians and the Irish Brotherhood had been officially set up as early as 1854, it was not until the mid-sixties that they became fully active. However, there were various events that brought them to the public gaze and stirred up feelings both in England and Ireland. One of these was what the *Guardian* called 'the ridiculous affair of MacManus' bones'. Terence Bellew MacManus had been convicted in the 1848 rebellion and had escaped to America. He died there in 1861 and it was decided to return his body to Ireland. By regarding MacManus as a national hero it was hoped by the Americans to create sympathy and raise money for the Fenian cause. The body arrived in October and was reinterred at Glasnevin on Sunday, 10 November, the funeral oration being preached by Fr Lavelle. The regular chaplain to the cemetery was unable to take part as Cullen had placed a general prohibition on the whole affair. Cullen did not want the Fenians to profit by the affair and forbade any public ceremonial in any of the churches in his diocese. Cullen's course of action was expressly approved by Cardinal Antonelli in December 1861, as he saw the Fenians in the same, unfavourable light as continental revolutionaries. Antonelli was of the opinion that the Irish clergy would follow Cullen's lead. Most of the clergy did take the lead from Cullen and did not favour revolution and Fenianism, but most were sympathetic to the cause of Fenianism and many did not condemn other organisations such as the St Patrick's Brotherhood. A Requiem Mass was sung by the students at Maynooth for the soul of MacManus.

After the MacManus affair, Cullen appealed to MacHale to suspend Lavelle. This, MacHale refused to do. Lavelle was vice-president of the St Patrick's Brotherhood. He tried to persuade Cullen that the St Patrick's Brotherhood was not a secret society, but this was impossible. He did submit to MacHale in November 1863 on some points, but not enough for Cullen, and in February 1864 Lavelle went to Rome to present his case to Propaganda. Cullen now blamed MacHale equally with Lavelle for support of the Fenians. There was a great deal of correspondence between Cullen and Rome about the Lavelle case. Cullen wrote to Barnabó every week and also regularly to Kirby. In many of these letters he is intensely critical of MacHale.[18] In May 1863 Cullen told Kirby that MacHale was a subscriber to the *Irishman*, a newspaper he describes as 'very wicked for the past' and as the organ of the St Patrick's Brotherhood. In May Cullen wrote to Kirby to let him know that MacHale had had a subscription from O'Mahony of the American Fenians and had acknowledged the gift in the press and sent it to charities in some depressed part of the diocese. He wrote again the following year to say that MacHale had used the words 'benevolent Fenian brotherhood' in the Dublin press. In April MacHale had sent three autographed portraits of himself to be sold at a Chicago Fenian Fair. Dr Duggan, the Bishop of Chicago, had condemned Fenianism. Cullen writes:

> Dr Duggan prohibited the fair – and yet the lion raises his voice in favour of it, even though by doing so he may compromise himself with the powers that be.[19]

In July he wrote:

> Many are beginning to say what is true, that it is a great scandal that the Archbishop does not carry out the Pope's instructions.[20]

Cullen had a powerful ally in Bishop MacEvilly of Galway. He also wrote to Kirby, saying that the Connaught *Patriot* – a 'malicious Garibaldian rag, which is sometimes heretical, sometimes schismatical, and at all times personally offensive to the Head of the Church' – was the avowed organ of Dr MacHale and he had declared it to be 'the true organ of Catholicity in this part of the country'.

Propaganda at last responded by asking Cullen to call a meeting of the bishops to come to some decision about Lavelle. Cullen wrote to Kirby:

> I hope Dr MacHale will after the last letter take some steps against Lavelle. It is too bad to oblige the Holy See to occupy

itself so often with that unhappy priest. One word from Dr MacHale two years ago ordering Lavelle to stay in his parish, and not to act as vice-president of the St Patrick's Brotherhood, would have saved himself and that priest from great evils. I wrote several times to Dr MacHale calling his attention to the conduct of his subject – but all was in vain. His Grace appears to be infatuated about that worthless man. Perhaps also there is another motive, probably Lavelle has letters in his hands which he would publish were he suspended, and their publication might not be agreeable to MacHale. . . .[21]

At the meeting of the bishops that was held in October, Cullen read out the letter from Propaganda and the bishops proceeded to state their opinions. Cullen reported to Kirby that 'Dr MacHale spoke over and over and did all he could to impede progress' and 'We were at the question for about four and a half hours. I made every bishop speak'. Cullen said that the bishops 'lectured' MacHale for his defence of Lavelle but that MacHale remained unmoved. 'I think he will sink or swim by that hero' Cullen told Kirby.

However, the priests of the Tuam diocese rallied to support Lavelle. They presented an address to the Archbishop in December regretting that the Pope had misunderstood the situation and felt compelled to censure 'for undue interference in politics, a clergyman who has certainly done good service in extirpating heresy and proselytism'.

At this time Cullen had much authority over the other bishops. Many of them had virtually been appointed by him, as his influence with Rome remained strong and MacHale's was considerably weakened, especially by his association with Lucas and then with Lavelle. Writing to Rome in October 1864, Dr Dixon, Archbishop of Armagh, writes:

Dr Cullen, as a politician, does not rank as high in Popular favour as Dr MacHale, but what has Dr MacHale ever accomplished?[22]

Dr MacEvilly, the Bishop of Galway, writing to Rome in December 1864, refers to the petition of the clergy for Fr Lavelle in very scathing tones:

> In the diocese of Tuam a memorial has been hawked about from house to house of priests by Rev. Mr Reynolds P.P. Claremorris in favour of Fr Lavelle ostensibly but its real object is to attack Dr Cullen. It also contained a paragraph in favour of Dr MacHale's administration . . . but the latter part was expunged. It is signed by most of the priests thro sheer fear. . . . It is said it is done unknown to Dr MacHale, but everyone knows the contrary to be the fact. Is it not then a sad state of affairs that one or two clerical knaves can frighten mostly an entire diocese to do a thing against their conscience, to lay a memorial before the Vicar of Christ which they know to be untrue. For they know well that at the moment Lavelle is privately celebrating etc. notwithstanding the document served upon him – whether suspension or not I can't say.[23]

It is clear that Dr Cullen and many of the bishops associated MacHale with the views of Lavelle, and Lavelle with the Fenians and revolution. It is difficult to ascertain exactly what MacHale's views were. It is unlikely that he favoured violent revolution for the same reasons that Lavelle did not promote it. In the past he had never supported violence of any kind and in 1843, at the height of the Repeal movement, he supported O'Connell in sending the people home from the meeting at Clontarf rather than indulge in a clash of arms.

Like many people in Ireland, however, he had supported with enthusiasm various movements that he had hoped would better the lot of the people, only to be faced with setbacks and disappointment. This would have given him some sympathy with movements such as the St Patrick's Brotherhood and even the Fenians, though he probably did not support their methods. MacHale knew Lavelle and had supported him in his work against the evicting landlords and the proselytisers. He knew him to be an honest man and a good priest, who had worked tirelessly for the good of the poor. It is likely that his views were reflected in the memorandum of the Tuam clergy, which stated that although they could not justify all that Lavelle had written on politics, it might well be tolerated. It is also interesting to note that MacHale's own nephew, Patrick MacHale, who was to inherit the family home in Tubbernavine, was a Fenian. In notes written by the family it says he saw the police 'coming at Philbin's [the next house down the road] to arrest him. He ran out the hall door and away to America'. It is not known exactly at what date this took place.

In 1862 MacHale received a letter from a priest in America asking for his views on the Fenian Brotherhood. He replied:

> I am much edified by your anxiety 'to get all the information I can give in respect to the *Fenian Brotherhood*, as you wish to encourage it, if good, denounce it, if unlawful and unworthy the confidence of American Irishmen.' I am not able to furnish the information looked for, having no knowledge of its constitution or its rules. However from a recent controversy in Ireland regarding kindred subjects, I have no hesitation in stating that the distinct principles of such associations should be cautiously inquired into and diligently ascertained ere they should be confounded (with such as are unlawful).
>
> To arrive at a safe conclusion regarding them, their respective rules should be examined in the different countries in which they are formed, and thus you may do justice to them and to the public weal, and avoid the danger of rashly committing yourself to an indiscriminate approval or condemnation.
>
> The advocates of St Patrick's Brotherhood in Ireland disown any secret oaths or symbols which its opponents charge it with encouraging. On the existence or absence of such covert and unlawful oaths and covenants among the Fenian Brotherhood you and the American clergy can form your own judgement. . . .[24]

MacHale then says that in the Tuam diocese they do not have the Fenian Brotherhood, as the most effectual association is the link of the faithful with one another and with their bishops and priests. However:

> One erroneous and mischievous notion should be carefully guarded against, which so often confounds a dutiful love of country with treason to the state. The propounders of such a maxim are the worst enemies of government, and have created more ribbonmen and secret societies than ever could spring from an open and vigorous assertion of right and justice. We know from experience, if some have been seduced by wicked and artful leaders into dangerous political courses under the mask of patriotism, others have been made, under self-constituted leaders, unconscious instruments of political corruption, being forbidden to assume the legitimate attitude and speak the language of constitutional freedom in remonstrance against manifold oppression.[25]

Notes

1   Bernard O'Reilly, *The Life and Times of John MacHale* (1890), MacHale MSS. 27 April 1857, II, pp. 528–9.
2   Ibid., May 1857, pp. 529–31.
3   P. Corish, 'Cardinal Cullen and Archbishop MacHale', *Irish Ecclesiastical Record,* (June 1959), p. 397.
4   Charles Gavan Duffy, *League of North and South* (1886), pp. 308–9.
5   Corish, op. cit., p. 399. Charles Gavan Duffy, *My Life in Two Hemispheres.*
6   Edmund Sheridan Purcell, *Life of Cardinal Manning* (Corish, op. cit., p. 399.)
7   Charles Gavan Duffy, op. cit., p. 90.
8   Desmond McGuire, *History of Ireland* (1987), p. 133.
9   J. S. Mill, *England and Ireland* (1868), p. 6.
10 Quoted in A. M. Sullivan, *New Ireland* (1877), p. 96.
11 Ibid., p. 96–7.
12 Ibid., p. 97.
13 Ibid.
14 Ibid., pp. 100–101.
15 Cullen to Kirby, Kirby Papers no. 86, 15 April 1864. Quoted in E. R. Norman, *The Catholic Church and Ireland in the Age of Rebellion,* p. 93.

16 Ibid., p. 93. Moriarty to Kirby no. 93, 1 May 1864.
17 *Tablet*, 8 August 1863.
18 Peadar MacSuibhne, *Paul Cullen and his Contemporaries*, p. 166.
19 Ibid.
20 Ibid., pp. 168–9.
21 Ibid.
22 Pádraic Ó Tuairisg, *Árd-dheoise Thuama agus Cartlann Choláiste na nGael sa Róimh sa naoú haois déag*, unpublished thesis, Tuam archives, K/64/215, 7 November 1864, p. 447.
23 Ibid., K/64/241, 12 December 1864.
24 Bernard O'Reilly, op. cit., MacHale MSS., II, p. 533.
25 Ibid., pp. 533–4.

19

THE NATIONAL ASSOCIATION

'I have nothing to regret, or to retract, or take back.
I can only say – God save Ireland.' (Edward Condon)

IN AUGUST 1864 there were great celebrations in Dublin for the laying of the foundation stone of a National Memorial to O'Connell, which was to be erected in Sackville Street. There was a procession on Monday, 8 August, in which many Church dignitaries took part. The event was celebrated by everybody in Dublin, Catholics and Protestants alike. The day ended with a great banquet in the evening. It was during these events that the idea of a new constitutional political movement was mooted. Many felt that the bishops would not now be averse to a political movement and would not find political gatherings in themselves injurious to the Church. There were a number of speeches at the banquet and Dr Leahy, the Archbishop of Cashel, justified the attendance of the clergy who were there, saying that the clergy had done great service in the cause of Catholic Emancipation. MacSwiney, the Lord Mayor of Dublin, presided at the banquet and there were speeches from Gray, Dillon, Maguire and Kavanagh.

The O'Connell demonstrations in Dublin sparked off a violent reaction in Belfast. An effigy of O'Connell was burnt, the ashes placed in a coffin from which Roman candles were set off. The Catholics retaliated by raiding the Pound District, an Orange stronghold, and hurling stones at Protestant chapels. On 10 August there were fights between mobs of both sides, and these continued on and off during August. The *Manchester Guardian* reported on Wednesday, 17 August:

> Belfast Monday Evening, Five o'clock,– The riots continue
> with increased fury; in fact at the present moment they surpass

in violence anything of the like that has occurred in this unfortunate town for many years. On Saturday night, the Orange party resumed their old work of stone-throwing and house-breaking with renewed zeal. They made a sally on Street Malachy's Church about twelve o'clock and but for the presence of a formidable force of police-men, would inevitably have laid it in ruins. On Sunday evening they wreaked their vengeance on all the Catholics who fell into their hands. During the entire of last night [Sunday] Sandyrow was the scene of constant disturbance. The howling and cheering and reports of firearms were audible all over the entire town. At the first dawn the tumult increased, and the savage scenes which took place on Friday morning were repeated. The mill girls were set upon and beaten. Their clothes were torn from their backs, and many of them were dragged by the hair along the ground. Maddened by these unmanly attacks on their wives and daughters, the Catholic party mustered at about eleven o'clock this day to the number of some hundreds. They were joined by a large band of navvies. They and the Orange party met at Durham Street and a fierce fight ensued. Several houses, in fact, whole streets have been laid almost in ruins. The military have been called out and two troops of hussars are at present patrolling the streets. . . .

Belfast, Monday Night, Seven o'clock, – The riot continues with unabated fury. . . . Several collisions have taken place between the Orangemen and Catholics. The latter are at a disadvantage, having no firearms. The former are abundantly supplied with guns and pistols. Persons have been brought to the hospital severely wounded. The town is in a fearful state. The shops are all closed, the people most excited and everyone trembles for what the next day may produce.

The Catholic bishop of Belfast, Dr Dorrian, appealed for peace, but to no avail. By 29 August Belfast was quiet, but seven people had died and 150 were injured.

The Government set up an inquiry to look into the Belfast riots, but it became increasingly clear that there should be some programme set before the Irish people to alleviate these damaging divisions.

In 1861 John Martin and John Blake Dillon, former young Irelanders, had joined with Moore and the O'Donoghue, the member for Tipperary, in contemplating a National League. This league was intended to be a constitutional society to counteract the activities of the Fenians and was to have as its ultimate aim, the repeal of the Union. It was launched in January 1864 by Martin and the O'Donoghue and was supported by Archbishop MacHale. The main work of the National League was undertaken by John Martin, who like his friend and fellow Young-Irelander, John Mitchell, was a Presbyterian from Newry. He was an honest man, but although he was later elected Member of Parliament for Meath as a home-ruler, his friends admitted that he was not cut out for politics and he became increasingly disappointed by the failure of the League to gain support.

During 1864 there was also an exchange of views between the English Liberation Society, prominent Liberals, and Irish politicians and ecclesiastics. W.J. O'Neill Daunt, a former repealer, who had been living in virtual retirement, had entered into a lengthy correspondence with the Liberation Society as early as 1856. They seemed unlikely bed-fellows for Irish ecclesiastics, as Daunt accepted that their 'anti-Catholic bigotry in theological matters was notorious'.[1] However, they saw the injustice of the existence of the Established Church in Ireland.

On 23 November Cullen presided at a meeting at which MacSwiney and Dillon spoke. The *Nation* reported that 'Alderman Dillon, evidently by previous arrangement, virtually launched the new association'. In December a requisition was put forward for an aggregate meeting:

> For the purpose of forming an association for the following objects – a reform of the law of landlord and tenant, securing to the tenant full compensation for valuable improvements; the abolition of the Irish Church establishment; and the perfect freedom of education in all its branches.

Many people signed the requisition, including twenty-four bishops, several hundred priests and many Liberal MPs.

On hearing about the association John Martin was philosophical: 'Dillon and I are sure not to quarrel. His Association will, I think help the object of the League. If the object be helped I don't care a rush what persons they be who get the credit'.[2]

Dillon sent the requisition to MacHale, who refused to sign it. He stated his reasons in an open letter to the newspapers. He said that he supported the objects of the proposed association but 'it is not so with the agency proposed to carry them into serious and practical effect' and

> to be deceived once was in no way discreditable; it argues only a too generous confidence in the faith and integrity of our fellow-men. But to be deceived again by entering into unconditional fellowship with those who were unfaithful to their trust, would render one liable to the reproach of being a willing party to the deception.[3]

MacHale then referred to the defection of Sadleir and Keogh and finished 'I cannot enter into alliance with any who manifest no regret for the violation of former solemn engagements'.[4]

In a letter dated 18 December 1864 MacHale also wrote to Dr Denvir, the Bishop of Down and Connor, who had written to him asking for his support for the association:

> It is not to the objects of the Association that any objection is made. But I rather fear that, instead of sincerely and earnestly labouring for the attainment of these laudable objects, some will make use of them to forward their own selfish purposes. This fear is founded on recent experience, which has sunk deep into the minds of the people; nor is there any peculiar reason to hope that a similar deception will not be again practised.[5]

The aggregate meeting took place on Thursday, 29 December 1864. The Protestant Vigilance Committee had threatened to set the

Liffey on fire if it was held, and on 28 December the Grand Orange Lodge held a special meeting at which they condemned the proposed popish meeting and reminded MacSwiney that by his oath of office as Lord Mayor he was forbidden to attempt to procure the subversion of the Church Establishment – one of the known objects of the association. The Fenians also attacked the association. The *Irish Leader* said the proposed Association was a trick of would-be place hunters: 'There will be men on the Rotunda platform on Thursday who will haunt the back stairs at the Castle in the evening.'

MacSwiney took the chair and after introductory remarks about the nature of the proposed association, letters were read out from those unable to attend. One of the most notable of these was one written in Rochdale from John Bright:

> I am glad to see that an effort is to be made to force on some political advance in your country. The objects you aim at are good, and I hope you may succeed. On the question of landlord and tenant, I think you should go further and seek to do more. . . . With regard to the State Church, that is an institution so evil and so odious under the circumstances of your country that it makes one almost hopeless of Irish freedom from it, that Irishmen have borne it so long. The whole Liberal Party in Great Britain, will, doubtless, join with you in demanding the removal of a wrong which has no equal in the character of a national insult in any other civilized and Christian country in the world.[6]

Cullen then spoke at some length, dwelling first on education. He advocated the 'right of a Catholic education for a Catholic people'. He then passed on 'merely to glance' at the Land question, saying that it was 'one surrounded by inextricable difficulties'. He concluded by speaking at great length about the position of the State Church. W. J. O'Neill Daunt now demanded the secularisation of the ecclesiastical State revenues of Ireland. After various speeches a resolution was passed for the foundation of a new association. The first of the resolutions was:

> The association shall be called the National Association of Ireland. Its objects shall be – 1st. To secure by law to occupiers of land in Ireland compensation for all valuable improvements effected by them. 2nd. The disendowment of the Irish Protestant Church, and the application of its revenues to purposes of national utility, saving all vested rights. 3rd. Freedom and equality of education for the several denominations and classes in Ireland.[7]

There were, in all, eleven propositions organising the way in which the association was to be run.

After the aggregate meeting in January 1865 O'Neill Daunt wrote to MacHale: 'My Dear lord Archbishop, will you pardon an old friend for expressing his anxiety that you may see your way to confer on us the great benefit of your co-operation?'[8] MacHale would not become involved:

> Your very kind letter reached me in due time. I need not say with what pleasure I read your excellent speech at the late Aggregate meeting, which was true to those sound and equitable principles once universally promulgated throughout the entire land.
>
> You were, I believe, the only one who ventured, in that assembly, to refer to the great injury inflicted by the Union, and to the necessity of repairing it as the only efficient means of repairing the other grievances which engaged the attention of the meeting. You observed fairly that, though a member of the League, you deemed it not incompatible with your duties as such to aid in the present movement.
>
> It does not appear that there was any reciprocal response to the effect that those who would aid that Association would not deem it incompatible with their duties to advocate, through a similar convention, the restoration of a native legislature.
>
> It is unnecessary to enumerate the obvious causes of the deep distrust in the recent movement. They are found in the studied forbearance from any reference to the treachery already practised on the Irish people. One of the deepest; however, is

the restriction of our country's misery to subordinate grievances, without daring even to allude to the prolific parent of wrong, from which all the rest derive their noxious vitality.
. . .

Glad under any circumstances, thus to commune with an old and respected friend, who can recollect those occasions when, under a sincere inspiration for the people's weal, their faith and confidence enabled us to effect what battalions could not achieve, I have the honour to remain, my dear sir, your faithful servant,

John MacHale[9]

Daunt realised that the National Association, unlike the National League, would never consider the abolition of the Union amongst its terms of reference, but he did write again to MacHale, emphasising that he too hated the Union but could still see good in the association. He wrote: 'Conceive the effect upon the public mind if the Archbishop of Tuam appeared in the ranks of the movement as a leader, carrying a resolution against place-hunting'.

MacHale was adamant. He was not joining the association. It was likely that he did not want to join a group so closely allied with Cullen. His own views on political matters were clear, both to himself and to those who knew him. Cullen's were not. He mistrusted Cullen profoundly, after Cullen's support for Keogh and Sadleir. Cullen had no time for MacHale's own political allies, men such as Martin and, formerly, Duffy. It is true that MacHale and his friends had great respect for Daunt and Dillon, who worked with Cullen in the association, but on this occasion MacHale himself preferred to remain on the sidelines. Cullen's motives for political involvement were different from MacHale's. After the aggregate meeting, Cullen wrote to Propaganda:

A few days ago; I profited from a great meeting which was held here in Dublin to elucidate the greatest dangers to the Church and to Ireland. All the people who were gathered, there were about five thousand persons present, greatly applauded my words; so much so, that one may hope that in Dublin evil influence will not make much progress.[10]

The evil influence was, of course, Fenianism. At first the clergy had been content to condemn Fenianism in their pastoral letters, but when it was thought that Fr Lavelle and possibly other members of the clergy, if not Fenians themselves, were sympathisers, Cullen thought that some other initiative was needed. Cullen was also afraid of the threat of Orangeism. He felt that his fears were justified, particularly after the riots following the O'Connell demonstration. MacHale did not appear to share these fears. Although he was never a supporter of violence, he was not afraid of it in the way Cullen was. He continued to support Lavelle, having great admiration for the work done by Lavelle, in his own diocese, against unjust landlords.

However, there did seem to be some effort on Dillon's part to reconcile the two archbishops. He wrote to George Henry Moore, whom he knew to be a good friend of MacHale, to enlist his help for this purpose. Moore wrote to Dillon, saying that he had been to see the Archbishop of Tuam and

> I entirely agree with you in thinking that a sincere and cordial understanding between him and the Archbishop of Dublin would be of incalculable advantage to the Irish Church and the Irish people, and I feel convinced that it will not be the fault of the Archbishop of Tuam if such an understanding cannot be affected.[11]

Moore offered his services to achieve this object, but it soon became apparent that it was not going to be possible because of the 'subtle attempt of the Dublin Prelate to attack the old opponents of Whiggism in a new and disgraceful combination'.[12] Moore had insisted to Dillon that he would not take sides between the two archbishops, but it is evident that his old feelings towards Cullen came to the fore.

In the spring of 1865 Charles Gavan Duffy returned to Europe on a visit from Australia. He attended a public dinner also attended by Moore, Dillon and Isaac Butt. Duffy describes Moore as making a speech 'inflamed with unexpected bitterness'.[13] He says that Moore 'scoffed at the attempt of certain persons, meaning Dr Cullen and his associates, to revive a nationalist movement, after having betrayed and destroyed one of the greatest national movements Ireland ever possessed'. Moore spoke of two men, one, the guest, Duffy, and the other who 'sat in a higher place', meaning Lucas. Duffy says that it needed 'all the sweetness and serenity of John Dillon to prevent an explosion'. Duffy was urged to stay in Ireland. Dillon wanted to nominate him for a popular constituency. Duffy said he would if Moore and the priests of the Tenant League would fall in with the movement. Moore said he would not if Cullen remained in the movement, and Duffy found the old League priests were 'rootedly opposed . . . to any society of which Dr Cullen was a member'.[14]

The National Association began to show signs of divisions early in 1865. The Meath clergy led by the coadjutor bishop, Thomas Nulty, wanted to inaugurate a new Tenant Right Society and the bishop hoped that the National Association would take up the cause of tenant right. However, in his lenten pastoral letter he condemned Irish members of Parliament for 'having prostituted their influence to the Whig government'.[15]

The Meath clergy and various other members of the National Association hoped to change the rules of the association so that it would become nearer in its objects to the Tenant League and Independent Opposition. Some bishops, including MacHale, met at Coffrey's Hotel in Dublin for informal discussions about the rules. It was hoped that MacHale might change his mind and support the association, but nothing short of complete Independent opposition would satisfy him.[16]

The Meath priests also decided that the association did not provide what they wanted. They were disappointed by the results of the 1865 election and withdrew in November. They formed an association of their own, the 'Meath Tenant Right Society', and on 26 November they published an address in which they affirmed that the 'sole question for Ireland is the land question'. They pledged themselves to the prelate who was the most outspoken in condemning place-hunters, 'the oldest and best friend of Ireland – the great Archbishop of Tuam'.[17]

The National Association was dealt another blow on 15 September 1866 with the death of John Blake Dillon. He was the most active and well-liked of its members. Cullen himself seemed to vacillate in his support for the organisation. He was not really happy in politics. He was not confident of the support of Rome for its activities. He felt more secure when campaigning on purely ecclesiastical matters like Church disestablishment than on the land question.

In 1865 the Fenians became more active. In that year, with the end of the American Civil War, a great number of Irish Americans were released from the armies on both sides of the war. These potential soldiers, together with American money, made the British Government nervous. In September 1865 the newspaper the *Irish People* was suppressed and there were midnight arrests all over Ireland in which the known Fenian leaders were taken prisoner. Stephens escaped and made his way to America, but Rossa, Luby and O'Leary were tried. Luby and O'Leary were defended by Isaac Butt and were condemned to penal servitude. Rossa, who conducted his own defence, was sentenced to penal servitude for life.

The Cabinet decided to suspend the Habeas Corpus Act in Ireland and this was carried in both houses on 17 February 1866. In May some Fenians attempted a raid across the Canadian border and in February 1867 there was a raid on Chester Castle. There were various smaller attacks in Ireland, and in September two Fenians who had been arrested were rescued from a prison van in Manchester, and in the course of the struggle, a police officer was accidentally killed when the men were trying to shoot off the lock of the prison wagon. Sullivan states that the life of Sergeant Brett 'was lost by misadventure not sacrificed by design'.[18] However, he says 'panic and passion reigned supreme' and five men were condemned to death. All five men deplored the death of Brett. Thomas Maguire said that he had served the Queen loyally as a marine and was loyal to her still. Edward Condon who was dying said that he was not there and that he did not accuse the jury but prejudice had induced them to convict. He said that he was not afraid to die:

> I only trust that those who are to be tried after us will have a fair trial, and that our blood will satisfy the craving which I understand exists. You will soon send us before God, and I am perfectly prepared to go. I have nothing to regret, or to retract, or take back. I can only say – God save Ireland.[19]

Maguire was pardoned by the Government and Condon was reprieved pending further consideration, but on 23 November 1867 Allen, Larkin and O'Brien were hanged. Sullivan says that there was a feeling in England that the verdict was open to question, but despite this on 22 November large crowds assembled outside the prison. There were shouts of triumph, dances, comic songs and choruses of 'Rule Britannia' for the 'Fenian Murderers' to hear as they prepared for eternity. The bodies of the three men were buried in quick lime in unconsecrated ground within the jail. Funerals for the men were declared illegal. However, many people were impressed by the religious spirit of the men and the Dowager Duchess of Queensbury donated £100 'for the families they would leave behind'.[20] In Ireland the men were known as 'The Manchester Martyrs' and feeling ran high against their sentences. Condon's words 'God save Ireland' became a rallying cry for future generations. In Cork on 1 December there was a funeral procession led by the O'Donoghue. In Dublin a procession of 150,000 was led by John Martin and A. M. Sullivan. Many priests said Masses for the men and as Cullen wrote to Kirby, 'Dr MacHale assisted at High Mass for them'. Sullivan wrote:

> It was the conviction that these men had not had a fair trial, that the cause of Irish nationality was meant to be struck at, and humiliated in their persons; and above all the attempt to class them as vulgar murderers, not political culprits, and to offer indignity to their remains, that led to the wondrous upheaval of Irish feeling which now startled the Empire.[21]

Following this, on 13 December 1867 another attempt was made to rescue prisoners, this time from Clerkenwell jail. A barrel containing gunpowder was used to make a hole in the prison wall. It exploded, killing twelve people from nearby tenement houses and about 120 people were injured. A. M. Sullivan writes:

> It is not astonishing that the latter outrage should leave behind a bitter memory. The slaughter of innocent citizens; little ones maimed and disfigured for life; families decimated and houses ruined – these are things no mind can calmly dwell upon. . . . Gross stupidity on the part of a few miserable Irish labourers – men blindly ignorant of the full power and reach of a gunpowder explosion – not design or thought of hurting life or limb was accountable for that bloody scene.[22]

Sullivan was tried for his writings in the *Nation* and he and three others were convicted of being 'malicious, seditious, and ill-disposed persons, and intending to disturb peace and tranquillity of the realm'. He was sent to prison for three months. Isaac Butt also went to prison for eighteen months for the debts he had built up in defending the Fenians free of charge.

After 1867, despite the increase of sympathy for the Fenians following the 'Manchester Martyrs', Fenianism ceased to be a threat to the Government. The movement was not well organised and the people saw little chance of success.

In 1868 there was a general election. Disraeli, now the Prime Minister, having passed the radical new election reform act of 1867, announced that there would be an election in the autumn with the new register. Earlier that year W. E. Gladstone, the leader of the Liberals on the resignation of Russell, had declared that the time had come when the Church of Ireland must cease to exist as a Church in alliance with the State. A few weeks later he carried resolutions to this effect through the house. This put the question of Church disestablishment firmly on the agenda of the new Government. Disraeli expected the gratitude of the people for the reform bill and the support of the Church party on the question of the Irish Church disestablishment, but the middle classes in the towns were increasingly Nonconformist. Moreover, Gladstone and Bright mounted a great campaign in the country.

In Ireland, George Henry Moore once more gained a seat in Parliament. He had refused to take part in the elections of 1865, being disillusioned with Cullen's National Association. He said he was glad he had kept out as 'Whigs were let in everywhere'. However, in 1868 he sold his precious racehorses to fight once again for a seat in Parliament. In November 1868 he wrote to Sullivan:

> There was not a man in either camp who thought I had a chance three months ago; and without professional agents, without the expenditure of money, with nothing to rely on but the inspiring influence of the clergy, acting under the inspiration of the greatest Irishman in the world, and the pluck and resolution of the people . . . . The glorious old Archbishop won the admiration of all the landlord party by his gentle vigour of expression, and the uncompromising calm with which he pronounced the ultimatum of the people.[23]

The ground for the disestablishment bill had been gradually laid by Daunt, Gray and Bright. O'Neill Daunt, with his association with the Liberation Society, began in 1861 to stir up opinion against the Irish Established Church. The Liberation Society had as their aim not only the disestablishment of the Irish Church but eventually of the English Church also. They never managed to achieve this, but by 1868 the people of Britain could see the injustice and illogicality of the Irish Church establishment.

Bright too had entered the arena with his letter to the emerging National Association. He wanted them to adopt as their policy 'Free land and free Church'.[24] He was invited by Dillon to a National Banquet, but on the event of Dillon's death was entertained by Sullivan. Sullivan himself had stirred up feelings on the disabilities of Catholics in 1862 when, on becoming a Dublin councillor, he had refused to take an oath saying that he would support the Established Church. He was fined £500 and disqualified. The National Association, through Gray, inaugurated a movement against 'obnoxious oaths'. This in turn led to movement for disestablishment. Sullivan, writing on the matter of the Established Irish Church, said that Irish Catholics probably wouldn't have concerned themselves if the Church had been less aggressive. In some parishes where the Protestant Rector had a bona fide congregation of his own and confined his ministrations to them he was frequently popular as a local gentleman. His family were amiable and kindly and good to the poor without invidious object in their charity.[25]

Archbishop MacHale, while sympathising with the objects, did not play a large part in agitation for Irish Church disestablishment. However, in a public letter to Gladstone in 1863 he described the situation as a 'hideous evil'. Perhaps the most influential person in the movement, apart from Gladstone himself, was Sir John Gray, the Protestant Liberal Repealer and editor of the *Freeman's Journal.* He sat on the Irish Church Commission.

On 1 March 1869 Gladstone introduced his bill. On 31 May it passed on the third reading, on 12 July it was passed in the Lords and it received the royal assent on 26 July. The event was seen by many Irish people as symbolising a new spirit of friendship towards the Irish. Sullivan said 'side by side with the New Ireland a New England had arisen'.[26]

Notes

1 W. J. O'Neill Daunt, *A Life Spent for Ireland* (1896), 26 July 1869.
2 P. A. Sillard, *The Life and Letters of John Martin* (1893), pp. 172–3.
3 *Irish People,* 24 December 1864.
4 Ibid.
5 Bernard O'Reilly, *The Life and Times of John MacHale* (1890), II, p. 541.
6 *Freeman's Journal,* 30 December 1864.
7 E. R. Norman, *The Catholic Church and Ireland in the Age of Rebellion* (1965), p. 150.
8 Bernard O'Reilly, op. cit., p. 540.
9 Ibid., 13 January 1865, pp. 540–41.
10 Peadar MacSuibhne, *Paul Cullen and his Contemporaries,* Cullen to Barnabó, 6 January 1865, IV.
11 Maurice Moore, *An Irish Gentleman* (1913), p. 316.
12 Ibid., p. 320.
13 Charles Gavan Duffy, *My Life in Two Hemispheres* (1868), p. 268.
14 Ibid., p. 268.
15 Kirby papers, Cullen to Kirby, 16 March 1865. Quoted in Norman, op. cit., p. 161.

16 Ibid., p. 168. Dorrian to Kirby, June 1865.
17 *Freeman's Journal*, 4 December 1865.
18 A. M. Sullivan, *New Ireland* (1877), p. 193.
19 Ibid., pp. 196–7.
20 Ibid., p. 199.
21 Ibid., p. 202.
22 Ibid., pp. 186–7.
23 Maurice Moore, op. cit., Letter to Sullivan, 25 November 1868, p. 334.
24 A. M. Sullivan, op. cit., 23 December 1864, p. 231
25 Ibid., pp. 219–20.
26 Ibid., p. 276.

20

THE VATICAN COUNCIL

'I have come away from Rome, after having a good opportunity of observing the working of the Council, far more impressed with the deep conscientious love of truth displayed, than the human passions of which so much is said and written.' (Robert Whitty)

ON 26 JUNE 1869 Pope Pius IX announced that a General Council was to be convened. Many of the bishops were initially very pleased. It was felt that there was a need to update an obsolete code of canon law and that something was required to counteract the materialism and rationalism of the age. There also arose the possibility of reunion with the Eastern Orthodox Church and perhaps even with the Anglo-Catholics. However, for some there was also the ominous possibility that the Ultramontane wing of the Catholic Church would push for the definition of the doctrine of papal infallibility.

John Henry Newman, who was naturally anxious for reconciliation between the Anglican and the Catholic Church, welcomed the calling of the Council but feared the doctrine of papal infallibility, as he felt that such a definition might drive a wedge between the Catholic Church and those outside it. However, he refused to be alarmed as he maintained that whatever happened it would be God's will. On 14 October Newman received a letter from Bishop Ullathorne of Birmingham informing him that the Pope had invited him to the Council as a theological advisor. Newman refused the invitation as he was unwilling to undertake a work 'foreign to my talents and among strange persons'. Newman also had an invitation from the liberal Bishop Dupanloup of Orleans to go as his personal theologian. Newman was very touched by the offer but 'I can't accept . . . I am too old for it . . . I think the Roman diet would seriously compromise my health'. He said he was too old to learn the ways of such saints as Athanasius and Augustine – 'They are race-horses – I am a broken-kneed poney'.[1]

The Irish bishops set out for Rome in November 1869 and arrived in time for the opening ceremonies on 8 December. The subjects under discussion were to be – Faith, Discipline, the Oriental Church and the Religious Orders. As yet, papal infallibility was not on the 'Schemata'.

The most controversial aspect of the Council at the beginning was the attitude taken by the civil authorities. The policy of Governments was one of non-intervention, so long as the issues being dealt with were confined to those of a spiritual or religious order. However, they were very wary that there should be no incursions into what the Government considered the domain of civil authority. A document entitled *Ecclesia Christi,* circulated to the bishops in January 1870, was leaked to the German press and caused some controversy. Chapter X 'On the Power of the Church' was one that stirred up the fears of the statesmen:

> . . . The power of the Church is of order or of jurisdiction. This jurisdiction is not only in the realm of conscience (forum internum) and sacramental, but external and public – it is absolute and entire, namely, legislative, judicial and coercive. The Pastors have this power from Christ, and they exercise it freely and independently of any secular dominion. . . .[2]

The publication of the schema at the beginning of February caused consternation in the political and diplomatic worlds. Gladstone was kept informed of proceedings by Lord Acton, who remained in Rome during the Council. Acton, however, was a very liberal Catholic, greatly influenced by the Bavarian church historian, Johan Joseph Ignaz Von Döllinger, who was also a friend of Gladstone. Acton strongly urged Gladstone to intervene against the activities of the Council. The Bavarian Government was influenced by Döllinger and so Gladstone was in favour of a group of Governments turning the Council away from questions of Church and State and in particular to block the Infallibility question.

However, Lord Clarendon, the Foreign Secretary, was being informed by Odo Russell, the British Government's agent in Rome. Russell was not a Catholic but his mother was, and he was sympathetic to the aims of the Council and even to papal infallibility, though he feared its definition might lead to a schism. He was also in communication with Archbishop Manning, who had succeeded Wiseman in 1865. Manning describes the Cabinet meeting at which the matter was discussed:

> The Prime Minister, Mr Gladstone, supported the Bavarian proposal on the grounds and by the arguments supplied to him by Acton; but Lord Clarendon, better informed by Odo Russell, exposed one by one the fallacious statements and wilful distortions of fact. Finally, after a hot discussion, Mr Gladstone was defeated in the Cabinet, the Bavarian proposal was rejected, and the Vatican Council was left to do God's work.[3]

MacHale was kept busy at the Vatican Council. He had the distinction of being the oldest and most senior bishop. He was now in his eightieth year and had been forty-five years a bishop. He was elected to the deputation *de disciplina,* one of four commissions, the others being *de Dogmata, de regularibus, and de Orientalibus et missionibus exteris.* Cardinal Cullen seems to have experienced some chagrin at MacHale's election. He writes in December to Dr Conroy, his chaplain:

> The Irish bishops have elected Dr MacHale as their candidate and have presented him to the French, American and Italian bishops as their choice. Many of our bishops denounced his Grace most heartily for his conduct regarding Lavelle and his conduct towards the propaganda and on the very same day put him forward to represent Ireland in disciplinary matters in *facie universae ecclesia.* I do not know whether this fact will be animadverted on in Rome, but I suppose if the Fenians get hold of it they will proclaim it as a great victory of their sect. It is better not to speak of this unless it be published in the papers.[4]

During this period the Irish bishops had frequent meetings to discuss their own home affairs. Fenianism was often on the agenda. In his letters home, Cullen speaks frequently about a letter written by Fr Lavelle, about which he and all the bishops, except MacHale and Dr Derry, were complaining to Propaganda. Odo Russell also urged the Pope to use the opportunity to condemn the Fenians and encourage the bishops to do so. Pius IX seems to have been wholly sympathetic to Russell and often spoke to him about the Fenians as the 'English Garibaldians'.

MacHale was also active in supporting a petition against bringing before the Council the matter of papal infallibility. Like many of the bishops at the Council MacHale did not dispute the truth of the matter but the 'opportuneness' of the proposal. Like Newman, he feared it would alienate those outside the Catholic Church and would be in danger of being misinterpreted. All through January 1870 there was great activity in the organising of petitions and counter petitions. At the end of the month they were laid before the Pope, who in turn put them before a congregation of cardinals, which included Cullen. The cardinals recommended that infallibility should come before the Council. The Pope then confirmed the decision, and on 6 March it was announced publicly. From then on the question of papal infallibility dominated the Council, bringing forth strong opinions on both sides. The leading opponent of infallibility was Mgr Dupanloup of Orleans. He engaged in prodigious activity, sending letters, pamphlets and appeals all over Europe. The Irish bishops were all for infallibility, apart from MacHale and Dr Moriarty, Bishop of Kerry. Moriarty maintained that as a professor of theology he had taught papal infallibility as a true theological opinion; but he was altogether opposed to its being defined as an article of faith. In a letter to Newman he wrote of the varying opinions of the bishops. There were seven hundred bishops in Rome for the Council and Moriarty estimated that that about two hundred of these were against the definition. They included the bishops of Hungary and Germany, half of France, England (except Westminster and Beverley, perhaps another), all North America. From Ireland I am only sure of one with me. The majority represents the Curia Romana, Italy, Spain, Belgium, Ireland, South America. It is composed of men who have not come into conflict with the unbelieving mind, or into contact with the intellectual mind of the time. When I read the school of theology in which they were trained I am not surprised that they treat every doubter as a heretic. . . .

The greater the majority the better, if it is to be: yet I hope. The Holy Ghost has many ways at his disposal besides votes. My mission is to talk to every man I meet – cardinal, bishop, or monsignore. I try to frighten our opponents and to encourage our friends, for there are many timid. I am the voice of one crying out, not in the wilderness, nor in the Council, but in the streets and the salons.

The pope's blessing to me a few days ago was significant: 'Dominus benedicat *te et dirigat'* – one of his stray sheep![5]

At first the Pope was thought to be entirely neutral in the question of infallibility, but as time went on it became increasingly clear that his sympathies were with the majority. It is likely that with many of the bishops he feared such men as the Dean of the Faculty of Theology at the Sorbonne, Bishop Maret of Sura, and of course the celebrated Dr Döllinger. It was felt that the liberal views of these men were very threatening to the Church.

Back in England, Newman's sympathies lay with Moriarty and MacHale and the majority of the English bishops. He kept quiet but wrote to Ullathorne 'with these thoughts before me, I am continually asking myself whether I ought not to make my feelings public'. Moriarty thought not. On 20 February he wrote to Newman:

I am not in favour of your publishing your views on the great question. If it seems good to the Holy Ghost and the Council that the definition should be made, it would be dangerous to have the public mind prejudiced against it.

Would it not be a difficult task to raise obstacles to the definition, and at the same time to prepare the people for obedience and belief? I fear that Maret and Döllinger have done us harm. Moderate men have said to me that they would never have harboured the idea of definition of Papal infallibility, only for these attacks on the Holy See. I know you could and would write in a different tone and sense; yet the effect would be to render submission more difficult. . . .[6]

During March and April 1870 there were various pamphlets and tracts issued for both sides of the argument. One of the points put by Dupanloup was that the definition of infallibility would not only prevent the returning to the fold of the Protestants and the Eastern schismatics, but also the spread of the gospel among the heathen; 'Let us have pity on all these and not set up barriers and dig gulfs between them and us'. However Mgr Bonjean, Vicar Apostolic in Ceylon, who had been a missionary for twenty-three years amongst the Hindus and Buddhists, replied by saying that the adherents of the ancient Indian religions had such a sense of authority in religion that they would be attracted by the idea of an infallible Pope.

Amidst the sometimes heated discussions, the bishops seemed to have enjoyed their time in Rome. To celebrate St Patrick's Day on 17 March the Irish bishops had a great dinner to which they invited the Irish soldiers of the papal army, the Zouaves. Thomas Canon Pope, a priest of the Dublin archdiocese, describes it in colourful fashion:

The tables were abundantly laden with substantial viands, and their wine goblets were overflowing, in which amid Irish national airs, scintillations of Irish wit and cheering convivialities, was drowned the shamrock in the evening.[7]

During April there was some impatience by many of the majority regarding the delay in bringing forth the question of infallibility, but the opposing side hoped that it would be put off until some further council in another time. Dupanloup wrote to the Pope:

Most Holy Father,
My name is not pleasing to you; I know it, and it is my sorrow.

But for all that I feel obliged, in the profound and inviolable devotion of which I have given many proofs to your Holiness, to open my heart to you at this moment.

The report is confirmed that many are soliciting your Holiness to suspend suddenly our important works and invert the order of the discussions, in order to bring before the Council on the spot, abruptly, before its time and out of its place, the question of the infallibility. Allow me, Most Holy Father, to say to your Holiness: nothing could be more dangerous.[8]

Dupanloup then goes on to warn the Pope of the dangers and begs him to wait and consult with more bishops before taking such a step. The Pope's reply is affectionate and paternal but he warns Dupanloup that he feels compelled 'to warn you not to wish to be wise in your own eyes, or to rely on your own prudence'. He also says 'It is right for the fathers at the Council to put forward clearly difficulties they think stand in the way of definition; but it is not right to strive by all means to bring all over to one's way of thinking'. The public announcement was made on 29 April that the question of infallibility was to come forward forthwith. On 9 May the proposed schema and report on how the subject was to be tackled were given to the bishops and the great debate began on 13 May.

Fr Whitty, now a Jesuit, who had to leave Rome in the middle of May, wrote to Newman. He speaks first of Moriarty:

Poor dear fellow, he is working hard, and the work is for him one of great anxiety, and even one may say of anguish often. Dr Furlong too suffers not a little. I have come away from Rome, after having a good opportunity of observing the working of the Council, far more impressed with the deep conscientious love of truth displayed, than the human passions of which so much is said and written.[9]

The debate considered the past history of the papacy and the past councils of the Church but it was mostly concerned with the opportuneness of the definition. On 19 May Cardinal Cullen gave a long speech for the definition. Thomas Canon Pope says that he spoke for two hours without notes and 'led them captive through all its reasonings, and never liberated them till he concluded amidst an universal burst of applause'.[10]

On the following day most of the speeches were against the definition. MacHale, according to Dom Cuthbert Butler, made 'a long and very good speech'. He first dealt with the theological aspects and then made the point that the simple Catholics of Ireland and, he believed, of other parts of the world, did not think about nor want these definitions; they held the doctrine practically, having sucked it in with their mother's milk. MacHale asked who the definition would benefit, whether it would benefit those outside the Church. He suggested that on the contrary it would be an obstacle to them and raise controversies and troubles. His main theme was that the definition was not necessary and that it opposed scriptural and traditional evidence.

Dr Power of Killaloe, writing home on 20 May, describes the greatness of Cullen's speech, and then 'I am just after hearing Dr MacHale in the Council. He is point-blank against the infallibility of the Pope and made a long rambling speech. He made us sad'.[11] On the other hand, Ullathorne describes 20 May as producing 'very able speakers'.

MacHale was followed by Bishop Darboy of Paris, who suggested that infallibility was introduced by demagogic agitation and that the hands of the bishops were unduly forced. He said the definition would not cure the ills of society or of the world and it should only be enacted with the unanimity of the Council.

On 25 May Cardinal Manning made his speech, introducing himself as the only convert in the Council. He favoured infallibility and the speech was regarded as a great success. He was followed by MacEvilly of Galway, also in support of infallibility. During the next few days there were many speeches for and against, some more serious than others. On 28 May a French bishop then in Florida annoyed many bishops by not appearing to take the question seriously: 'It is true that the Irish believe in the Pope's infallibility; but they also believe in their priests' infallibility – and not only do they believe it, but they beat with sticks any who deny it.' Dr Goold from Australia recalls in his diary that a French prelate opposed the motion and then another French bishop from the United States 'spoke most absurdly on the same side. He had to quit the pulpit. He had outraged the patience of all'.[12] On 31 May Goold records that 'Dr Purcell, Archbishop of Cincinnati addressed the Council feebly and incoherently against, but concluded in favour'.[13]

On 31 May Odo Russell writing home gave his version of the speeches:

> The speeches of Cardinals Schwarzenberg, Rauscher and Mathieu of Archbishops Darboy, MacHale, Ginoulhiac and Simor of Bishops Greith, Hefele, Jussef, Ketteler and Clifford etc. against the definition are said to have produced a deep impression on the assembly, whilst the speeches of Cardinals Patrizi and Cullen, Archbishops Deschamps, Manning, Bishops Pie, Hassoun etc. in favour of the definition are said not to have converted a single member of the opposition.[14]

On 23 June Goold writes that the speakers said nothing new. The speeches were a 'poor repetition of what has been better and more ably said'.[15] If Goold was beginning to feel a certain ennui, Ullathorne writes with great warmth about the conduct of the bishops:

> Free and friendly are the two qualities which more and more distinguish the bishops both in their general and in their particular assemblies. . . . I have never witnessed the least ill-feeling manifested between any two bishops who have spoken even the most strongly against each other's views from the ambo. And you see those who are considered the leading antagonists on even the gravest points, talking as cheerily with each other, and having their pleasant jokes, as those who are most closely allied in sentiments. . . . It is certainly a most edifying assemblage. . . .
>
> Another thing that strikes me is, that whatever criticism

there may be behind the scenes amongst bishops of the same views, they fall upon the policy of the question and not upon persons.[16]

Meanwhile, as the summer wore on, many of the bishops were weary of the heat. Ullathorne writes:

Many bishops are getting leave to go home, unable to stand the heat, or pressed by affairs.

and later:

The weather is sweltering, and all the world is broiling. Bishop Turner has got leave of absence on account of health, and is going. . . . Bishop Clifford has grown very thin.[17]

On 1 June Bishop Grant of Southwark died. After due obsequies the debating continued throughout June. MacHale spoke again, this time about the role of the bishops. He once again argued against the definition, urging that some reference be made to bishops as the successors of the apostles. Dr Power once again did not like MacHale's speech: 'The Cardinal made a most magnificent speech for two hours and created a profound impression. Next day came the "Lion", who made a wretched speech against infallibility.'[18]

The formula for infallibility, finally decided upon 9 July, was:

The Roman Pontiff when he speaks *ex cathedra,* that is, when exercising the office of pastor and teacher of all Christians, he defines with his supreme apostolic authority a doctrine concerning faith or morals to be held by the universal Church, through the divine assistance promised to him in St Peter, is possessed of that infallibility with which the divine Redeemer willed his Church to be endowed in defining doctrine concerning faith or morals: and therefore such definitions of the Roman Pontiff are irreformable of themselves (and not from the consent of the Church).[19]

On 13 July the voting took place. Various points were voted upon and there was a trial ballot on the Constitution as a whole. The voting was vocal, by 'placet' and 'non placet'. The total number of votes was 601, of which 88 were 'non placet'. The Irish 'non placets' were MacHale and Moriarty. After this vote, most of the minority decided to leave Rome. They did not want to spoil the unanimity of the final vote and yet felt unable to vote 'placet' themselves. At the public session on Monday 18 July the result of the final voting was 'placet' 533 and 'non placet' 2. The two 'non placets' were Fitzgerald of Little Rock, USA and Riccio of Cajazzo of Naples. The two men accepted the decree immediately. Most of the bishops signed declarations to say that they accepted the doctrine of infallibility. Neither MacHale nor Moriarty were called upon to make a formal declaration or to promulgate the decrees, but on returning to their dioceses they were obedient to the decrees of the Council, and in 1875 at the Synod of Maynooth, in union with the rest of the bishops, they signed a joint pastoral enforcing the doctrine of infallibility as of the Catholic faith.

The only real rebellion came from Germany, where in March 1871 Döllinger issued a letter withholding his submission. He took a leading part in summoning the Congress of Munich, out of which arose the Old Catholic movement. Döllinger himself wished only for reform and not to create a new denomination. However, the Old Catholics remained only a small sect and Döllinger eventually disassociated himself from them.

MacHale returned to his diocese in July 1870. The people of Tuam were delighted to have him back and meeting him on the Mayo roads they unhitched his carriage and pulled it into the cathedral city, by hand.

Notes

1   Ian Ker, *John Henry Newman* (1988), LD xxiii 396, p. 617.
2   *de Ecclesia Christi*, cited in Dom Cuthbert Butler, *The Vatican Council* (1930), p. 266.
3   E. S. Purcell, *Life of Cardinal Manning* (London, 1896), II, p. 436.
4   Peadar MacSuibhne, *Paul Cullen and his Contemporaries,* Cullen to Conroy, IV, p. 266.

5   Dom Cuthbert Butler, *The Vatican Council* (1930), Moriarty to Newman, February 1870, p. 288.
6   Ibid., pp. 289–90.
7   Thomas Canon Pope, *The Council of the Vatican and the Events of the Time* (1871), p. 187.
8   Mourret, *Concile du Vatican* quoted in Butler, op. cit., p. 300.
9   Whitty to Newman, 15 May, quoted in Butler, op. cit., p. 291.
10   Thomas Canon Pope, op. cit., p. 233.
11   Peadar MacSuibhne, 'The Irish at the Vatican Council', *Irish Ecclesiastical Record* (April 1960), XCII, p. 298.
12   P. F. Moran, *The Catholic Church in Australasia*, p. 806, Dr Goold, Diary,
13   Ibid., p. 808.
14   Odo Russell, *Extracts from Despatches from Rome 1858–70* (1962), p. 437.
15   Moran, op. cit., p. 809.
16   Dom Cuthbert Butler, op. cit., p. 317.
17   Ibid., pp. 327–8.
18   Peadar MacSuibhne, op. cit., p. 300.
19   Dom Cuthbert Butler, op. cit., p. 385.

21

THE PATTERN OF LIFE

'In vain we strive by all the solemnity of divine worship to appease the wrath of heaven, if we refuse to show mercy to our own fellow creatures.' (John MacHale)

DESPITE JOHN MACHALE'S obvious interest in politics and his literary activities, the bulk of his life was spent in the ordinary duties of a bishop. He rose early in the morning and, after saying various devotions, said Mass. He would then have breakfast and usually spend some hours in his library, reading or writing. He read the newspapers and books of meditation or the lives of the saints. In the afternoon he usually took some exercise.[1] In his youth he was quite athletic and enjoyed games, particularly tennis. He would walk for miles, usually very quickly, and also enjoyed riding on horseback. He liked to entertain in the evenings and often invited people for dinner. In the early years Daniel O'Connell was a frequent guest of MacHale. However, at any time he would have the local priests round to dine and would enjoy their conversation and laughter. They would discuss the politics of the day and the affairs of the Church. MacHale was reputed to have tried tactfully to avert open criticism of those who were absent, particularly other clergymen. After dinner there was sometimes music and then the household would say the Rosary and night prayers.[2]

MacHale's household was quite large. As well as servants and priests there probably would have been various members of his family. John MacHale had six brothers. The eldest, Thomas, accompanied the young John to Maynooth in 1807. After that, little is known about Thomas. The next brother, Martin, married and had two daughters. Martin died young and his two daughters were reputed to have been reared by the Archbishop. Myles, the next brother, died in 1816, aged twenty-nine, also leaving a young family.

John's brother James became a priest and he died in 1833. MacHale's older sister, Anne, lived to be eighty-two and died in 1861.[3] The Archbishop was said to be very attached to his sister and was deeply grieved at her death.[4] Anne married and had one son, John. The Archbishop's brother, Patrick, married and died in 1831, leaving two sons, Dominick, who died in 1851 and Thomas, who became a priest and later a professor at the Irish College in Paris. The Archbishop's younger brother, Edward, had a large family who remained at the family district of Laherdane and whose descendants live there still.

The Archbishop's father, Patrick Mór, married again some time after the death of his first wife. He had three more daughters – Ellen, who later married and had a family; Barbara, who did not marry and became the Archbishop's housekeeper, and the youngest, Catherine, who married and lived near the Archbishop in Tuam but did not have any children.[5]

Archbishop MacHale seems to have been deeply attached to his family and very concerned for their welfare. His family were not particularly poor for the west of Ireland, but they were not rich, and many of them went through difficult times. During some periods of his time as Archbishop it would have been a struggle to comply with requests for help and support from them. In this his situation was similar to that of Giusseppe Roncalli, Pope John XXIII, whose family were poor peasant farmers from a remote Italian village and who called on their illustrious relative frequently for financial help and support.[6] MacHale seems to have been generous with his relatives and taken a great interest in his nieces and nephews and in their education and upbringing. One of the Archbishop's cousins, one 'Beezy Barratt', is said to have walked from Laherdane to Tuam, a distance of about forty miles, every month to receive her rent. MacHale's relatives did not always behave in a way that he might have wished. Two of his nephews, John, the son of his sister Anne, and John, the son of his brother Edward, were both expelled from St Jarlath's College for raiding the wine-cellar at night. Another of his nephews, Patrick, was known to be a Fenian. He escaped to America.[7]

The family home at Tubbernavine was bought by the Archbishop, who later added buildings to it. He was said to have done this in order to add to its value and so be able to vote.[8] MacHale bought a small farm in the early 1830s in order to refuse to pay tithes on it. He also purchased lands in the encumbered Estates Court in 1855 with money that he had been loaned. He gave two of these estates to the Presentation Convent in Tuam and kept two, which after his death went to the Vincentian order.[9]

MacHale was known until the end of his life for his generosity, and not just to his own family. During the famine, members of his household were continually baking bread and making soup and the queues to his door were never-ending. Even in later life he would be besieged on his way to and from the cathedral by the poor, and so he always carried plenty of change. There was a tree outside his house which was known as 'beggars' bush', as many used to stand there waiting for him to appear. St Jarlath's College was also in the vicinity of the cathedral and MacHale would often visit the students there, with whom he was very popular.[10]

The sermons of John MacHale were very popular, in both Irish and English. His nephew, Thomas MacHale, published a book of his uncle's sermons after his death. Many of them make powerful reading. He made great use of rhetoric and satire and was particularly drawn to subjects such as charity to the poor and mercy to sinners. In a charity sermon for 'female penitents', in reference to the words of David in the Old Testament, he asks the question: 'What think you was the amount of the crime against which the royal prophet thundered this dire imprecation: May his children be fatherless and his wife a widow?'

MacHale continues with more of David's condemnations: 'Let his children be as vagabonds and be cast out of their dwellings', and then goes further, the evils of one generation not being enough: 'May his posterity be cut off, and in one generation may his name be blotted out.' MacHale says:

> After pursuing his posterity until they utterly disappeared, and finding nothing in the descending series on which to reach his vengeance he returns back on the innocent authors of his existence –

'May the iniquity of his father be remembered in the sight of the Lord, and let not the sin of his mother be blotted out'.

It was not, however, enough that the sins should once experience the anger of the Almighty; but as if they were possessed of fuel for eternal vengeance, he adds –
'May they be before the Lord continually'.

What crime is it of which the prophet wrought up the punishment to such a climax of horror? It must you will say be incest or murder or sacrilege or blasphemy or some dark mysterious combination of sins that are not only unutterable, but from the idea of which the imagination recoils.

No it was . . .
'because he remembered not to do mercy'.[11]

MacHale then talks of the wonderful virtue of mercy, quoting Osee 'I desired mercy not sacrifice', and saying, 'In vain we strive by all the solemnity of divine worship to appease the wrath of heaven, if we refuse to show mercy to our own fellow creatures.'

MacHale says this view of mercy is:

a truth that is so inscribed on the nature of man that it cannot be erased until you tear out at the same time the human heart, with these bowels of mercy which God planted there at the moment of his creation. . . . Mercy, this daughter of Heaven is seen traversing the world, revered by persons of every creed.[12]

He speaks of the beauty of mercy in 'Our Lord's lovely parables' and then of the cause for which he is making the appeal, an 'asylum' that is intended 'for reclaiming the fallen' and so that 'shattered virtue may be repaired'. He says that:

people may say that the girls have strayed through the perverseness of their own will – Perhaps they have – so did Magdalene. They have extravagantly wasted a stock of virtue which a more prudent and reserved line of conduct would have improved. And so did the prodigal son. . . . They have, perhaps, knowingly and deliberately violated the precepts of the law, and incurred all its penalties. So did the woman found guilty of adultery. . . .

Are there really such as are guilty of the sin against the Holy Ghost as to envy God's creatures the pardon of their transgressions? – if there be any who with the ungenerous disposition of the Prodigal son's brother . . . who repined at his father's joy . . . . Let them at once arraign the Almighty for having pardoned the thief on the cross and for having converted the persecuting Saul into a vessel of election.[13]

MacHale quotes Isaiah with reference to the girls: 'they are covered with wounds and bruises which are nor bound up, nor dressed, nor fomented with oil'. He tells his audience: 'To you, then is consigned the merciful task of dressing and binding up the wounds . . . reassuring their fainting spirits.'

He exhorts them that if they are still callous, to at least guard their own homes, and quotes Ecclesiasticus about a 'father waking for the daughter when no man knoweth, and the care for her taketh away his sleep, when she is young . . . lest she should be corrupted in her virginity':

It is incumbent upon you all to raise the broken fences, and to protect the sanctuaries of your own homes against the tide of vice and immorality which is threatening to overflow the most sacred recesses of society. . . . It is then your duty as men and as Christians . . . to rush if necessity demands it, into the flames to rescue the struggling victims from the ruin with which they are menaced, nor to pause in the pious work until you place them in peace and safety on the summit of the holy mountain.[14]

In a sermon on 'The Love of God', MacHale begins by quoting St Matthew, chapter 22:

One of the Pharisees put a question 'Master, which is the greatest commandment of the law?' Jesus said, 'You must love the Lord your God with all your heart, with all your soul, and with all your mind.'

MacHale says that 'Judea exhibited the most signal monument of God's love for his chosen people', yet they seemed ignorant of this first precept of the law and the same is true of many Christians. 'To love God above all things is a duty which flows from the relation that connects the Almighty with his creatures.' There is a propensity in people to love what is excellent and only God is worthy of our unbounded affection. St Augustine said, 'For thee have I been created, O my God, and my soul cannot rest until it rest in thee'. MacHale said that the love of God is a suggestion of the heart and a craving after goodness, but if this did not come naturally to us there are three reasons why we should love God: 1) God commanded it, 2) Because he loved us, and 3) It is only by fulfilling this command that we can fulfil the end of our creation and be crowned with eternal happiness.

With regard to the first reason, MacHale speaks of the rightness and justice of the obligation and says that even an obligation out of fear can ripen into charity, but the second reason appeals to us as 'the soul of man is generous and gratitude one of the finest feelings of the human heart'. The love of God for us is beyond the comprehension of the human mind. St Paul has difficulty in expressing it:

> For this cause I bow my knees to the Father of Our Lord Jesus Christ . . . that Christ may dwell by faith in your hearts, that being rooted and founded in charity, you may be able to comprehend with all the saints what is the breadth and length and height and depth; to know also the charity of Christ which surpasseth all knowledge that you may be filled unto all the fullness of God. (Eph 3: 14–19)[15]

MacHale says he will not dwell on the natural gifts of God, such as the gifts and wonders of creation, but on the Christ who offers himself as propitiation to his eternal Father to redeem a guilty world:

He descends from heaven; and clothes his divinity in the form of sinful man. He lives in obscurity and privation; he diffuses blessings around him . . . heals the sick, the lame and the blind . . . his return is ingratitude. His apostles desert him in his hour of distress – one of them requites him with foulest treachery – sinks in a garden under the load with no-one to comfort him, is nailed to an ignominious cross and resigns his life with prayer and forgiveness for his enemies.

This is the astonishing prodigy of love that made the psalmist say:

What is man that thou art mindful of him or the son of man that thou visitest him? Thou hast made him a little less than the angels; thou hast crowned him with glory and honour. (Ps 8:5, 6)

The charity of God is incomprehensible, and equally incomprehensible is the insensibility of the human being:

If my enemy had reviled me I would verily have borne with it; but thou a man of one mind, my guide and my familiar who dost take sweetmeats together with me. (Ps 15)

Christ not only suffered but left us the fruits of his suffering in the Eucharist as permanent memorial of his affection.

The third reason why we should love God is our own happiness:

If anyone love me he will keep my word and my Father will love him, and we will come to him and make our abode with him.

Even in this world we can achieve 'cheerfulness of mind' and 'calm tranquillity not disturbed by pride in his prosperity'. St Paul said: 'I am filled with comfort; I exceedingly abound with joy in all our tribulations.' (II Corinthians 7:4). Jesus said:

Come to me all you that labour and are burthened and I will refresh you; take up my yoke upon you, and you shall find rest to your souls.

MacHale says that if you have been seeking pleasure, ambition or riches, return to the 'only true source of happiness' and 'divide not your hearts between God and the world'. He suggests that we should beseech the Almighty 'to purify our affections that they may be entirely centred on Him'. We should ask the Holy Spirit to 'kindle in us the fire of divine love':

> Spirit of Charity which proceeds from mutual affection of Father and Son take possession of our souls, that we may feel at length thy heavenly influence . . . draw . . . our erring affections towards thee . . . that we may have eternal repose in thy love and enjoyment hereafter. Amen.[16]

Notes

1 Bernard O'Reilly, *The Life and Times of John MacHale* (1890), II, p. 657.
2 Ibid., p. 657.
3 This information was obtained from the MacHale family in Laherdane.
4 Ulick Bourke, *The Life and Times of the Most Reverend John MacHale* (1883), p. 148.
5 MacHale family, op. cit. There appears to be some confusion here, as O'Reilly states that Catherine was the housekeeper and that the information he gives about the Archbishop's private life is from Catherine's notes. MacHale also states in his will that Barbara was the housekeeper.
6 Lawrence Elliot, *I Will be Called John* (1973), pp. 120, 129.
7 MacHale family, op. cit.
8 Ibid.
9 This information is taken from a letter from a Bishop Joseph Walsh, dated 28 February 1947, that is in the Tuam archives.
10 E. A. D'Alton, *History of the Archdiocese of Tuam* (1928), p. 99.
11 John MacHale, *Sermons and Discourses,* ed. by Thomas MacHale (1883), Charity sermon for female penitents, pp. 309–10.
12 Ibid., pp. 310–11.
13 Ibid., p. 415.
14 Ibid., p. 316.
15 Ibid., p. 113.
16 Ibid., p. 117.

22

LAND AND HOME RULE

'The point d'appui rests not in Ireland but in America. Either from political electioneering purposes, or from patriotism, or more corrupt motives, skilful hands will play to the impulsive Irish heart.' (Sylvester Malone)

DURING HIS TIME as Archbishop of Tuam, John MacHale played a prominent role in the politics of the age. His concerns were twofold: he wanted the Irish people to be able to practise and be educated in their Catholic religion freely, and without hindrance; he was also concerned with the material welfare of the people, especially the people of his own diocese, who were the poorest in Ireland.

His early involvement in these matters led him to support O'Connell, firstly with regard to Catholic Emancipation and then in the agitation for the repeal of the Union. In the 1850s, when repeal seemed no longer possible, he turned to the land question and tenant right, believing that these much needed reforms might be brought about by political movements, in particular, Independent Opposition. After the defection of Keogh and Sadleir, he retired from the political scene to some extent, refusing to be involved in the National Association. However, he maintained his support both for Repeal and for the Tenant League, supporting John Martin's National League and keeping in close contact with such political allies as O'Neill Daunt and George Henry Moore.

During this period, MacHale's influence in the Church in Ireland waned. This was largely due to his differences with Cullen. Cullen was always highly regarded in Rome, wielding much influence there, and Cullen also succeeded in having his own candidates and supporters elected as Irish bishops. During the 1860s, Irish affairs were dominated by the activities of the Fenians and, largely through Cullen's influence, MacHale was seen as a Fenian supporter. This was

clearly not the case, but it was based on the fact that MacHale refused
to condemn one of his much respected parish priests, Patrick Lavelle,
and because he took the Fenian journal, the *Irish People*. However,
although MacHale was not so influential in the Church, despite his
advancing years his influence in the country at large and also abroad
was as great as ever.

To many visitors to Ireland and even to many of the Irish
themselves, Ireland seemed relatively prosperous and MacHale's
continual, sometimes lone agitation for tenant right seemed to be the
rantings of an old man stuck in a rut. But seeing the never decreasing
flow of immigrants and the continuing practice of eviction, MacHale
was convinced that the welfare of the country lay in the plight of the
tenant farmers and that there would be no investment in industry in
Ireland until these questions were solved. He did not support the
violence of the Fenians but he recognised their frustration.

The situation that MacHale saw in the west of Ireland is well
illustrated in a pamphlet published in the form of a letter to
Gladstone, by the Reverend Sylvester Malone, in 1867.[1] Malone
describes the events that took place in Kilkee in County Clare. The
lands round Kilkee were owned by the Marquis of Conyngham and
were managed for him by a middleman, Mr Studdert. These 'lands
of Druagh', originally, were waste lands, many parts of which were
'quaggy bog'. There was no vegetation, some long grass and heaps of
sand. The middleman let much of this land to squatters, who over
the years began the long work of cautious draining. The work was
dangerous and hard as the squatter could easily drown and was
constantly wet. Nevertheless, work went on, the husband digging
and draining while the wife carried baskets of sand and seaweed from
the seashore. The seaweed was used for manure and often the people
would spend the night on the beach during a storm, when large
quantities of seaweed were thrown up. By degrees several patches of
bog were brought into cultivation. Some parts were converted to
meadowland, some for the cultivation of potatoes. Constant
manuring was necessary to prevent the land from returning to the
wild. There was a very fine, beautiful beach at Kilkee and it became
popular for visitors, who would journey there on a turf-boat. At first
there were just a few sheds nearby but gradually the residents began

to build more solid and tasteful houses. Every year their profits from summer visitors were ploughed back into improvements: one year a new floor, the next a cast-iron grate, and so on. The ground rent charged by the middleman was quite high, as he had no other income and he had a life interest in the property. As the middleman neared the end of his life the tenants invested more in their property, thinking that they would get better terms from their 'noble landlord'.

In 1859 Studdert died and the first thing the landlord did was to claim all the property as his own. He ignored all the work and expenditure of the tenants and advertised in public journals for the unreserved auction of their property. The tenants were invited to bid for their own homes and their fears often made them bid more than they were worth. Bailiffs were supplied with proposals for rents far higher than the tenants could afford. The rents increased by 700 per cent. Under the middleman, Widow Marnan had paid £1.15s. Under the Marquis she had to pay £10. W. Hennessy paid 10s under the middleman and was required to pay £24 under the Marquis.[2] The Government valuation was ignored and even that had not taken into account a penny of what the tenants had spent. The tenants were told that only thirteen of the 250 buildings of Kilkee were going to be left to stand, and the thirteen included churches and schools. Malone speaks of Sergeant Landers who 'grew grey in her majesty's service' whose house was a model of cleanliness, one wall of which was a lovely mosaic of sea-shells, which he was always arranging and polishing.

In 1861 there was a public meeting and a memorial was drawn up and signed by 248 tenants. It was thought that the Marquis who was residing in Canterbury was unaware of the situation. It was decided that the Catholic and Protestant clergymen should go as a deputation bearing the memorial to the Marquis. They set off in June 1861, taking with them a legal agent, Mr Benton. In Canterbury Mr Benton argued the case well and the Marquis said 'the prayer of the memorialists is granted'. Everyone was overjoyed. When the Limerick steamer arrived at Kilrush Quay, a carriage decked with boughs was ready for the reverend gentlemen. Bonfires were lit and everywhere gratitude to the Marquis was expressed. Before long, however, their hopes were dashed. A letter came from the Marquis in which he stated that rents were only to be reduced on houses recently built and unless the rents were paid in full the demolitions would continue. Malone tells of one young man who was determined to defend the home of his parents against eviction with force if necessary. The police heard of his intentions. He was arrested but forced to emigrate or his parents would be homeless. Malone speaks of the feelings of the boy on that emigrant ship and proclaims 'Behold the spirit of Fenianism'.[3]

In the census of 1860 there were 1,879 people in the area. By 1867 there were 950 and many of these were now existing on a patch of potato bog that they had been lucky enough to receive. Mr Keane, the representative of the Marquis, now occupied 136 out of 200 acres of arable land. In January 1865 there were 131 people evicted at one sweep. Malone speaks of the absolute necessity of tenant right:

> While I hold that nothing short of autonomy or, in its old familiar language, repeal of the Union can ultimately satisfy the Irish people, there need be no hesitation in asserting that fixity of tenure will dry up the source of discontent among nine-tenths of the agricultural population . . . . We have only seen the beginning of trouble. The base of troublous operations cannot be touched. The point d'appui rests not in Ireland but in America. Either from political electioneering purposes, or from patriotism, or more corrupt motives, skilful hands will play to the impulsive Irish heart.[4]

One writer and politician who supported MacHale and took up the cause of the Irish tenant at this time was John Stuart Mill. He tried to influence English opinion but was continually amazed at the ignorance in England about the problems of Ireland. There was no lack of discussion in England about 'The Irish Question'. Thousands of articles and pamphlets were written. When the phenomenon of Fenianism arrived on the scene, hours of parliamentary time and columns of newspapers were taken up in analysing its causes. Mill wrote:

> If there is anything sadder than the calamity itself, it is the unmistakable sincerity and good faith with which numbers of Englishmen confess themselves incapable of comprehending it.[5]

Mill says that the English rulers thought that rebellion in Ireland was not for a grievance or for suffering but for an idea, the idea of nationality, and consequently asked the question 'What can England do?'

> Unhappily, her offence is precisely that she does not know, and is so well contented with not knowing, that Irishmen who are not hostile to her are coming to believe that she will not and cannot learn.[6]

Mill speaks about the history of English rule in Ireland. He describes the land as being confiscated three times over, part to enrich the powerful English and their Irish adherents, part for the endowment of a hostile hierarchy and the rest given to English and Scottish colonists to hold as garrisons against the Irish. Manufacturing industries were crushed for the purposes of making room for English products, apart from the manufacture of linen, which was carried on by colonists. Added to this, the vast majority of the Irish, the Catholics, were despoiled of their political and civil rights. Mill asks the question: Can a nation that treats its subjects like this expect to be loved by them? The English seemed to think that because political disabilities were taken away from the Irish and the spectre of the starving had been removed by 'the angel of death', the Irish no longer had grievances.

> What seems to them the causelessness of the Irish repugnance to our rule, is the proof that they have almost let pass the last opportunity they are ever likely to have of setting it right. . . . Rebellions are never really unconquerable until they become rebellions for an idea.[7]

Mill points out the differences in the attitude to land that have grown up in different countries. He says that before the Norman conquest the Irish knew nothing of the 'absolute property in land'. Land belonged to the entire clan and the chief was little more than the managing director of the association. Feudalism and the idea of the landlord was associated with foreign domination and was never recognised by the moral sentiments of the people. In Ireland as in many countries, land was regarded as the inheritance of all and it was felt that it was 'manifestly just that he who sows should be allowed to reap'. If this were not to be the case, then the landlords must be well thought of, rooted in the traditions of the country, identified with the religion and nationality of the country, which was not so in Ireland. The unsuitability of this English system of capitalist farming for Ireland was aggravated by the fact that only a third of the people of England lived by agriculture, whereas in Ireland the system of land tenure was 'all in all'. Mill says that the system in Ireland was the worst in Europe as 'farm-labourers are entirely without a permanent interest in the soil. . . . In Ireland alone the whole population can be evicted by the mere will of the landlord'. Mill maintains that nothing else will do but to give the Irish tenant all that he requires or he will be supported in a revolution by hordes of prosperous countrymen from across the Atlantic – 'The English Nation will have to decide whether it will be that just ruler or not?'. Mill continues that if not:

> We shall be in a state of open revolt against the universal conscience of Europe and Christendom, and more against our own. And we shall in the end be shamed, or, if not shamed coerced, into releasing Ireland from the connexion; or we shall avert the necessity, only by conceding with the worst grace, and when it will not prevent some generations of ill blood, that which, if done at present may still be in time permanently to reconcile the two countries.[8]

Mill's ideas on land were supported by John Bright and many of the more radical clergy, including not only MacHale but Nulty and the priests of Meath. Nulty later described Mill as 'the deepest thinker of his day'[9] and Fr Lavelle in his writings cites Mill to show that 'the land of Ireland, and the land of any country, belongs to the people of that country'.[10] Manning too was influenced by these ideas. In his *Letter to Earl Grey* he wrote:

> There is a natural and divine law, anterior and superior to all human and civil law, by which every people has a right to live on the fruits of the soil on which they are born, and in which they are buried.[11]

In June 1868 Lord Malmesbury said that Manning's writings on the Irish land question were 'nothing but pure communism'.[12] Cullen was more cautious in his opinions. He did desire to see the gradual creation of something like a peasant proprietorship but his respect for existing property rights kept him away from the ideas of men like Bright and Mill. In Parliament in 1868, when Mill elaborated his schemes, Gladstone said that any government headed by him would never entertain such ideas but he would allow 'frank recognition of the principle of perfect security to the tenant for the proceeds of his capital and industry expended on the soil'.[13]

In his first ministry between 1868 and 1870 Gladstone did attempt to do something about the land question. After passing the Irish Church Bill he recognised that in his attempts to pacify Ireland he must look to the land. He spent some time in 1869 studying the intricacies of land tenure and the Irish Land Act was passed in 1870. The bill was largely Gladstone's own work and was drafted without any reference to the Irish bishops or the National Association. John Morley in his *Life of Gladstone* says that it was 'almost a point of honour in those days for British cabinets to make Irish laws out of their own heads'.[14] The bill was passed easily as it did not interfere with property rights and was merely designed to protect tenants from unfair treatment. It recognised the custom of tenant right that existed in Ulster. It limited the landlord's powers of arbitrary eviction, and enforced compensation. It allowed loans of public money for tenants to buy their holdings and a 'scale of damages' was established for eviction. No payment for disturbance was made in cases of eviction due to a failure to pay rent, but all tenants, including those evicted for failure to pay rent, received compensation for improvements.[15]

Despite its drawbacks, the bill was well received by the Irish bishops, including MacHale. Manning wrote to Gladstone from Rome that he had heard that MacHale spoke favourably of the bill and 'The other bishops spoke most warmly of it; which was not affected by one or two expressions of doubt whether in the scale for computing compensations the outgoing tenant is sufficiently protected'.[16] Even Fr Lavelle seemed pleased with it, saying in a letter to Moore 'It is something better than I expected'. In between sessions of the Council, the bishops did peruse the bill further and sent via Manning a memorandum detailing its faults. However, although they said that it could not be regarded as a 'settlement of the question' they did regard it as 'the beginning of a new and happier state'.[17]

The Irish Land Act was not very successful as it did not include security of tenure and there was nothing to stop landlords putting up their rents to force tenants into arrears and so be evicted, but it did save tenants from the worst kind of eviction and included some compensation. The land bill was also supported by George Henry Moore but he refused to share the belief that Gladstone could make the Union palatable by reform.

Irish politics suffered a severe setback, and John MacHale lost a good friend, on the sudden death of Moore in April 1870. A rather sad incident occurred whereby a ribbon society was founded on one of Moore's estates. Moore had never evicted a tenant in his life but had unwisely taken in those evicted by his neighbours. The ribbon society demanded large reductions in rent from Moore to embarrass him in Parliament. He asked his friends to arbitrate, Sullivan, Fr O'Shea, Fr Lavelle and John Martin, and agreed to abide by their decision. This worked for a while and then trouble arose again, requiring Moore to leave London hurriedly and return to his estate. He wrote to his wife on Saturday 16 April to tell her that he had arrived safely: 'The climate and air are delicious, and it seems to me as if it were "good for us to be here", and that if we could build tabernacles for ourselves in this world we could find a paradise for ourselves here.'[18] Moore died on Tuesday 19 April. Lavelle wrote to Sullivan: 'Our poor Country! How badly you could spare your son at this juncture! . . . He died of cerus apoplexy – heartbreak I call it.'[19]

Moore's funeral oration was delivered by Isaac Butt, who described Moore as a 'high-minded, generous, Irish gentleman'.[20] From now on it was Isaac Butt who became the leader of the Irish Members of Parliament. At first sight Butt would have appeared an unlikely champion of Irish rights. He was the son of a Church of Ireland minister and in his youth had been a disparager of 'popery' and imbued with a fiery orangism. However, in the 1840s Butt joined with O'Connell in his attempts to stimulate native industries and despite his Protestant conservatism he won O'Connell's admiration and support. During the years of the famine, his pity and indignation at the human misery drove him to espouse the cause of Irish nationalism. Butt never supported armed insurrection as, apart from a dislike of violence, he knew that it would fail, but like MacHale he did sympathise with its causes and was willing to use all his powers as a lawyer to defend the rebels. Terence Bellew MacManus said of him:

> If I had ten thousand lives and ten thousand honours I would be content to place them under the watchful and glorious genius of the one and the high legal ability of the other.[21]

After Butt's defence of the Fenians and of the staff of the *Irish People*, during his subsequent period of imprisonment he laboured at the work of the regeneration of the *Irish People*. He produced many pamphlets, in particular, one on land tenure in Ireland – *A Plea for the Celtic Race*. He had many replies. Lord Lifford described Butt's schemes as 'Communistic' and 'intended, or at least adapted, for the purpose of depriving the Protestant proprietors of all influence over the people'.[22]

After the 1868 General Election, Butt joined with Moore in agitation for the release of the Fenian prisoners and over the fact that political prisoners were incarcerated alongside convicted murderers. In March 1870 Butt produced a pamphlet appealing for amnesty for the Irish political prisoners. This was too soon for Gladstone, but he did appoint a commission of inquiry to look into allegations of ill-treatment, and in January 1871 some prominent prisoners, including O'Leary, Luby and Rossa, were released on condition that they served the remainder of their sentences in exile. Gladstone's promises of justice for Ireland produced a new feeling of hope, which for many meant that self-government for Ireland now seemed a possibility.

On 19 May 1870 a meeting was held in Bilton's Hotel in Dublin. Here Butt outlined his plans for a federation of England, Scotland and Ireland, each with a parliament subordinate to Westminster. Butt hoped that by suggesting a House of Lords for Ireland with the power of veto, he might rally Protestants to his cause, as in that way the Protestant landowners could prevent further assaults on their interests. The new group, called the 'Home Government Association', were a mixture of Catholic and Protestant, Liberal and Conservative. A resolution was passed 'that it is the opinion of this meeting that the true remedy for the evils of Ireland is the establishment of an Irish Parliament with full control over our domestic affairs'.[23] The group, which included Professors of Trinity College, Galbraith and Haughton, was eventually joined by John Martin and A. M. Sullivan and then by members of the Fenians.

The new movement did not have an enthusiastic reception from the press and it was generally ignored by the clergy. The Liberal press said it was an 'Orange plot' and the Conservatives 'a Jesuit conspiracy'.[24] However, there were four by-elections in Ireland in 1871 and they all returned Home Rule candidates. Amongst these was Butt himself who was returned for Limerick and John Martin who was elected for Meath. The Galway by-election was won by Mitchell Henry, a very rich Protestant Home-ruler who was able to be of great assistance to the ever penniless Isaac Butt. Another candidate for Galway, a Captain Nolan, on MacHale's request had stood down so that the seat would be undisputed. Many of the Home Rule candidates were opposed by the clergy, especially the bishops, who felt that they were going too far. Dr Moriarty said that any party led by Butt would be a 'sham'.[25] Cullen, having worked for an alliance between the hierarchy and Gladstonian Liberalism, did not want to see it disappear in favour of Home Rule. In a letter to Manning inquiring as to his position on Home Rule he says:

> I have determined to have nothing to do with the home rule movement for the present. The principal leaders in the

movement here are professors of Trinity College who have never heretofore manifested any good feeling towards the people of Ireland, and Orangemen who are still worse. . . . The other leaders are editors of half-Fenian or anti-religious newspapers, and some few wrong-headed or disappointed Catholics who are ready to engage in any new project whatever it may be. Very few, perhaps ten or twelve priests, have taken a part in this agitation, but I think all the bishops and the great mass of the clergy seem determined to keep aloof.[26]

Cullen was wrong in his assumptions. Many bishops, including Nulty, worked for the success of Home Rule candidates and O'Hea of Ross and MacHale declared early for Home-rule. O'Hea gave only informal support but MacHale was completely behind Butt and his name was on the governing body of the Home Government Association. A. M. Sullivan believed that many bishops kept aloof from the movement because they were grateful to Gladstone for the Church Act. Sullivan's brother, T. D. Sullivan, wrote to Daunt saying that he ascribed the small number of priests to a fear on the part of the clergy 'that if they came more numerously into it, they would frighten the Orangemen and Protestants from joining it'. Daunt believed that many priests supported Home Rule but would not allow the publication of their names to that effect, for various reasons. He thought that they were held in check by the bishops, who hoped to receive an endowment for their university out of Gladstone. He also speaks of a certain priest who was kept back by 'the number of Tory names on the committee. Miserable jealousies and fears!'[27]

In his biography of Butt, *The Road of Excess,* De Vere White says: 'The Roman Catholic Church was always regarded by the British Government as a parent of treason, but a few Protestants . . . have done more harm to English interests than all the hierarchy of that Church put together with the notable exception of Dr MacHale – a very great Irishman'.[28] However, the Home Rule party now inherited the remnants of the Opposition Party, with MacHale and the former Callan curates, O'Shea and Keefe, declaring for Butt and Home Rule. The new candidates for Home Rule also followed Butt in supporting denominational education. Butt wanted Trinity College to remain Protestant but wanted the Catholics to have an educational establishment that was its equal. He also disapproved of the national education system, saying 'I believe that an education from which religion is excluded is at best an imperfect education'. In May 1871 MacHale published an open letter to Gladstone in which he said:

> English statesmen feel, or affect to feel, much surprise at the growing and wide-spreading demand among the Irish people for the restoration of their native legislature. This demand is second only to their demand for perfect freedom and independence of Catholic education from all alien political influence. . . . The longer educational justice is denied us, the louder and more pressing will be the demand for our own parliament.[29]

In February 1872 another vacancy occurred in Galway. This time Captain Nolan put his name forward and was opposed by the Honourable William le Poer Trench, who though liberal in his views was unpopular because of his family's proselytising activities. Archbishop MacHale let it be known that he was voting for Nolan, the Home Rule candidate, and the clergy threw themselves into the campaign in support of Nolan. Nolan won overwhelmingly, getting 2,823 against Trench's 658. Trench petitioned against the result, saying that there had been undue influence by the Roman Catholic clergy on Nolan's behalf. The case was tried by William Keogh, now a judge, in Galway, the following year. The case excited enormous interest and a great number of witnesses were heard. The clergy who were most involved were the Archbishop and Frs Lavelle, Loftus and Conway. MacHale, now eighty-two years of age, gave clear and concise evidence. When asked whether he approved of Captain Nolan's principles with regard to Home Rule and the repeal of the Union he replied: 'Decidedly; and especially, as you mention, repeal of the Union. That Home Rule I do not understand so well; it is a very ambiguous phrase; but I understand repeal of the Union and that I approve of.'[30] MacHale was questioned by Serjeant Armstrong, one of the ablest cross-examiners of his time. When Armstrong said that MacHale was often spoken of as the 'most influential potentate in Connaught', MacHale replied that Armstrong was often described as 'the light of the bar', but he added 'these are childish compliments'. MacHale was able to use the trial as a plea for the secret ballot. When asked the opinion of the clergy he said:

> I have not the least doubt but that the clergy would hail it, on two accounts; first, because it would secure the complete freedom of the tenant-class and the immunity from landlord coercion; and secondly, it would screen the clergymen themselves from what is sometimes to them the very unenviable position of being obliged to come forward to defend the freedom and rights of the tenantry.[31]

Judge Keogh, as expected, found against the priests and the Archbishop, and Trench was given the seat. It was likely that there was some truth in the charge of improper influence of clergy. D'Alton describes Fr Loftus as 'not a man of much culture'. He was reputed to have called someone a 'drunken blackguard' and said that the local landlord was ruled by his wife who 'wore the breeches'. Loftus later apologised to the landlord's wife, saying that he deeply regretted the expression about Mrs Griffith but did not repent of his insults to the landlord.[32]

The case caused a great outcry in Ireland, not just because of the verdict but because of Keogh's handling of the case. Keogh used the occasion to deliver a nine-hour speech of invective against the Irish clergy, described by Butt as being 'rabid', 'partisan', 'unbalanced', 'abusive' and 'vulgar'. He called one priest 'an insane disgrace to the Catholic religion' and said that Fr Lavelle was trying to 'pollute the diocese'. The case was debated in the House of Commons. Keogh spoke with great sarcasm about Nolan's description of MacHale as 'the great Prelate of the West', at which Butt reminded the House that a certain William Keogh, when appealing to the voters of Athlone, had said 'the illustrious Archbishop of Tuam who, like a lofty tower which rises on the banks of the Tiber, is the pride and protection of the city and the glory and guardian of its people'.[33] The Irish newspapers poured forth torrents of condemnation of Judge Keogh, who for some time had to go around Ireland with an armed guard.

In June 1872 the *Freeman's Journal* printed a letter from MacHale, which cautioned the people against taking too much notice of Keogh's remarks and stated that the trial had been unusual as matters 'Totally irrelevant to the simple issue raised' had been called in evidence. The trial had some good effects for Home Rule, however, in that it helped to speed up the passing of the Ballot Act in the same year, 1872. In February 1872 at the Kerry by-election the Catholic Liberal, J. A. Dease, supported by Cullen and Moriarty, was defeated and the Protestant landlord, Rowland Ponsonby Blennerhassett, succeeded as a Home-ruler, getting 62 per cent of the vote. Despite the setback of the 1872 election, the Home Rule movement went from strength to strength. In November 1873 a conference was held in Dublin where the Home Government Association was replaced by the Home Rule League. In the general election of 1874, of the 103 Irish seats, 60 went to Home-rulers, 33 to the Tories and 10 to the Liberals.

MacHale played little part in this election. This was probably due to his age, but the leaders kept him informed of events and he gave his support where he could. When Daunt visited him in September 1873 he found the Archbishop in a fine state of mental agility, 'his intellect is still strong, and his shrewd sharp eye is as vigorous as ever'.[34] In 1875 Butt submitted his proposals for establishing a federal union between Great Britain and Ireland to the Archbishop, saying: 'There is no approbation I would value more highly than that of your Grace'. The correspondence resulted in a Home Rule meeting being held in Tuam. When welcoming Butt at this meeting MacHale said that the 'mantle of O'Connell' had fallen on Isaac Butt. Butt wrote that Dr MacHale's sanction was 'more than an equivalent for any discouragement which could meet us in that which I am sure is the path of duty'. However, Butt and the Home-rulers had a difficult time. Butt had tried to introduce a land bill in 1874 but it came to nothing, and once again in 1876 he introduced a bill that was defeated at its second reading. There were also disagreements amongst the members. Sullivan wanted the movement to be a popular one with local branches, whereas Butt had no feeling for popular mobilisation.

In 1875 John Martin died, leaving a vacancy in Meath. Some people wanted Duffy who was visiting Ireland to accept the seat but he refused and the seat went to a tongue-tied young squire, Charles Stewart Parnell. Butt welcomed the young recruit, believing that the recruitment of Protestant landed gentry would heal the divisions in Irish society. Divisions began to grow in the parliamentary party as Butt disapproved of Parnell's 'obstructionist tactics'. At this time Butt was becoming ill and increasingly unpopular and in August 1877 at the Home Rule Confederation Butt was dropped from the presidency and Parnell appointed. In January 1879 MacHale urged the necessity of working together:

> It is to be hoped . . . that this first month of the new year shall witness in the Capital of our country an assembly of our faithful, devoted, and experienced sons of Ireland, judiciously framing wise and efficient rules for the future direction of our members of parliament, regardless of the contending parties of the British nation. Let the existence of Home Rule be vigorously insisted upon.

The eighty-seven-year-old Archbishop went on to urge the necessity of a 'steady, united, and, when prudent, an aggressive parliamentary form of action'.[35]

Notes

1 Sylvester Malone, *Tenant Wrong Illustrated in a Nutshell*, in a letter to the Rt. Hon. Mr Gladstone MP, 1867.
2 Ibid.
3 Ibid.
4 Ibid.
5 J. S. Mill, *England and Ireland* (1868), pp. 6–7.
6 Ibid., p. 7.
7 Ibid., p. 7.
8 Ibid., p. 44.
9 Thomas Nulty, *The Land Agitation in Ireland* (Letter to the clergy and Laity in the Diocese of Meath, 1881), p. 5.
10 Quoted in E. R. Norman, *The Catholic Church and Ireland in the Age of Rebellion* (1965).

11   Henry Edward Manning, Cardinal Archbishop of Westminster, *Ireland: A Letter to Earl Grey* (1868).
12   Parliamentary Proceedings published under the superintedance of T. C. Hansard, 25 June 1867.
13   Ibid.
14   John Morley, *Life of Gladstone* (1868), I, p. 926.
15   Llewellyn Woodward, *The Age of Reform* (1938), pp. 362–3.
16   Gladstone Papers, Manning to Gladstone, 24 February 1870.
17   Ibid.
18   Maurice Moore, *An Irish Gentleman* (1913), p. 375.
19   Ibid., p. 376.
20   Terence De Vere White, *The Road of Excess* (1946), p. 237.
21   Ibid., p. 139.
22   Ibid., p. 219.
23   Ibid., p. 240.
24   Ibid., p. 241.
25   Ibid., p. 251.
26   Manning Papers, Cullen to Manning, 13 October 1871. Quoted in Norman, op. cit., p. 417–18.
27   W. J. O'Neill Daunt, *A Life Spent for Ireland: Selections from Journals* (1896), 15 July 1870, p. 274.
28   Terence De Vere White, op. cit., pp. 251–2.
29   *Freeman's Journal,* 11 May 1871.
30   *Report of the Commisioners appointed to inquire into corrupt practices at the last election for Galway with judgement and papers,* Parliamentary Papers, XLVIII, 1872.
31   Ibid.
32   D'Alton, *History of the Archdiocese of Tuam* (1928), p. 83.
33   De Vere White, op. cit., p. 271.
34   W. J. O'Neill Daunt, *A Life Spent for Ireland: Selections from Journals* (1896), p. 308.
35   Bernard O'Reilly, *The Life and Times of John MacHale* (1890), II, pp. 666–7.

23

THE WRITINGS OF JOHN MACHALE

'Were there no other monument to attest the early and superior civilization of our nation, it is indelibly impressed on its truly philosophical language.' (John MacHale)

DURING HIS LIFETIME John MacHale wrote a great deal. In the early 1820s the letters of Hierophilos were printed in national papers and caused much controversy and debate. In 1828, realising that there was a great need for theological books to be written in English, MacHale published his *Evidences and Doctrines of the Catholic Church*. This was well received in England, Ireland and on the Continent and brought notice and recognition to the young priest.

Despite the success of his English writings, however, MacHale felt it was very important to write for the Irish-speaking population. Although the English language was fast becoming the main language of Ireland as a whole, many people in the west spoke only Irish, and for most people of that area Irish was their first language, as it was for MacHale himself. It was also necessary for him to counteract the activities of the proselytisers who became active early in the century. The Hibernian Bible Society and the Religious Tract and Book Society in a period of ten years were said to have distributed over four and a half million tracts, texts, pamphlets and Bibles. In 1840 MacHale published an Irish Catechism, *An Teagasg Críosdaighe,* and shortly afterwards a little manual of prayer, *Craobh Urnaighe Cráibhighe*. These works were small and cheap and included morning and evening prayers that contained litanies. In the second edition of this prayerbook, which was published in 1857, the Archbishop added penitential psalms and translations of the *Dies Irae* and the *Stabat Mater*. He translated these so they could be set to music. During this period he also published Irish editions of the Way of the Cross and devotions on the Rosary.

311

While recovering from an illness, MacHale first began to translate *Moore's Melodies,* poems of which he was particularly fond and which were immensely popular. In the nineteenth century, the poet Thomas Moore was highly regarded and considered to be on a par with Moore's good friend, Lord Byron. It was during this time that MacHale learnt to play the piano and the harp so that he could set the melodies to Irish traditional music. He wrote to Moore in 1841:

> For some time back I have been occasionally engaged in translating into a corresponding Irish metre some of your exquisite melodies. Of the selections about thirty are now ready for publication. They have been indiscriminately chosen from the first to the tenth number, as they seemed to me best suited to the sentiments of the Irish people and the spirit of that ancient language, which, with the inhabitants of extensive districts, is yet the native tongue.[1]

Moore replied

> That these songs of mine, should be translated into what I call their native language, is in itself a great triumph and gratification to me; but that such a tribute should come from the pen of your Grace considerably adds to the pride and pleasure I feel in it.[2]

These translations of *Moore's Melodies* were very popular and many new issues were brought out. The London publishers would not allow the Irish version to appear with the English version, but when, after Moore's death, the copyright ran out in 1871, an edition with the English on one side of the page and the Irish on the other was brought out by a Dublin publisher. In March 1844 Moore wrote to a friend:

> I see my friend John of Tuam, the 'Lion of the Fold of Judah', as he is called by repealers, continues to publish in monthly numbers his translations into Irish of Homer and the Irish

melodies. My latest newspapers from Dublin contain specimens of the work, together with remarks on the version of the melodies, of which here are some specimens; 'To all who are acquainted with Irish literature it is well known that the Archbishop of Tuam has for some time past snatched an occasional moment from the little leisure which the onerous cares of his pastoral duties allow him, for the purpose of rendering into our own ancient and harmonious tongue those sweet melodies of our glorious Moore. . . . Of the fidelity and beauty of the translation, it is impossible to speak in terms too eulogistic. Irish scholars are already aware of the exquisite manner in which the songs published in the two former numbers have been rendered into Irish.[3]

Moore himself, though Irish, was born in Dublin and did not understand Irish. He regrets that he cannot appreciate MacHale's translation, but:

There is one curious circumstance, however, which I did understand, namely, that 'in the Irish version the metre of the original is accurately adhered to in each song'. I sung them over to myself (as far as I could decipher the words), and found this to be the case.[4]

MacHale's translation of the first book of Homer's *Iliad* came out in 1844 and the second in 1845. MacHale considered the Irish language particularly suitable for the task:

There is no European language better adapted than ours to a full and perfect version of Homer. It is true that in radical structure the Irish bears a stronger resemblance to Hebrew than to the Greek language. But in the happy flexibility of the latter to the most varied and harmonious combinations there is such an analogy between it and the Irish language as to render one of the fittest medium for the transfusion of the other. Of this easy pliancy of our language to those kindred forms of compound adjectives, in which the Greek, especially that of Homer, abounds, the remains of our ancient poetry, furnish copious illustrations.

If a language, almost a wreck, long abandoned without improvement to the humbler classes of society, be distinguished by such rare excellence, we may judge of its power when it was the exclusive instrument of communication throughout the entire kingdom; nor is it difficult to fancy its capability of indefinite improvement if enriched with all the treasures with which genius and industry, stimulated by the rewards of learned professions. . . .[5]

The third book of the *Iliad* did not appear until 1851 because of the famine. The fourth book was published in 1857, the fifth in 1860, the seventh in 1869 and the eighth in 1871. In 1861 MacHale published an Irish translation of the Pentateuch, a work that took precedence over his translations of Homer and Moore. In March 1871, with the completion of eight books of the *Iliad*, MacHale, then in his eighty-first year, writes:

It is probable that the labours of my translation of the Iliad shall close, and that I shall resign to some other worthy hands the task of enriching further our Irish literature with a translation of the remainder of Homer's magnificent Iliad, and, perhaps, I may hope, of his no less charming poem of the Odyssey.[6]

Throughout his life, MacHale was consistent in his upholding of the Irish language. He believed that it was important in the first place, as it was the language of the poor. He felt that it was incumbent upon him to educate the people of his diocese in their religion in their own language, and in addition to his writings he preached in Irish every Sunday in the cathedral. In this he differed from O'Connell, who, though fluent in his native language, regarded the Irish as an encumbrance and thought that in the modern world English was the language of progress. The Young Irelanders, in particular Thomas Davis, stressed the importance of the Irish language. Davis said 'a people without a language is only half a nation' and he held the view that the essence of nationality was implicit in language. MacHale, too, thought that the Irish language was part of the nationhood of the Irish people and regretted the decline of the language, particularly in the National School system. MacHale also felt that the Irish language was a beautiful language worth preserving for its own sake:

> Even in its present condition, the Irish language is one of the most effective instruments of oratorical persuasion, by which the feelings of a religious and sensitive people could be roused and regulated to any pitch. Were there no other monument to attest the early and superior civilization of our nation, it is indelibly impressed on its truly philosophical language. For if as is universally confessed, language be one of the most unequivocal standards by which you can ascertain the degree of refinement reached by any people, the sententious and expressive aphorisms that give such a complexion to ours, prove that those, to whom it is familiar even only as a spoken dialect, must necessarily be a highly intellectual people.[7]

The Works of John MacHale in Irish

Togha Abhrán air Eireann ro chan Tomas Ua Mórdha (Dublin: John Cumming, 1842)

A Selection of Moore's Melodies (Dublin: James Duffy, 1871)

A Selection of Moore's Melodies, ed. by T. O. Russell, with an appendix in English & Irish. p. 75. (Dublin: Gill; London: Nutt, 1899; 2nd edn, 1901)

An t'Iliad.

An Chéad Leabhar (Dublin: John Cumming, 1844)

An Deara Leabhar (Dublin: John Cumming, n.d.)

An Ceatharmadh Leabhar (Dublin: John Cumming, 1857)

An Seisseadh Leabhar (Dublin: John Cumming, 1860)

An Seachmhadh Leabhar (Dublin: John Cumming, 1869)

An t'Octuiliadh Leabhar (Dublin: John Cumming, 1869)

An Teagasg Críosdaighe (Dublin: T. Coldwell, 1839)

An Teagasg Críosdaighe (Dublin: Warren, n.d.)
An Teagasg Críosdaighe (Dublin: T. Coldwell, 1859). With this is bound *Craobh Urnaighe Cráibhighe* (Dublin: Duffy, 1857) and *Toras na Croiche* (Dublin: Duffy, 1861). The Catechism and Prayer-Book were original works, the English being a translation.
Toras na Croiche. Aistrighth[e] (Dublin, 1873)
Aisdrughadh Gaoilhilge Leabhar na nGeiniolach (Dublin: James Duffy, 1868). The Preface is dated 1858.
An Irish Translation of the Holy Bible. Vol. I Genesis to Joshue, from the Latin Vulgate, with a corresponding English version, chiefly from the Douay, accompanied with notes from the most distinguished commentators, pp. viii. 388. (Tuam, Dublin: James Duffy, 1861)

The Works of John MacHale in English
Letter of Hierophilos (Dublin, 1822)
Letters from James Warren Doyle (J. K. L) and John MacHale to Lord Farnham (Dublin: T. O'Flanagan, 1827)
Evidences and Doctrines of the Catholic Church, 2nd edn (London, 1842)
Dr Mac Hale's letter to Earl Grey, exhibiting the principles of the Church of Rome by R. J. M'Ghee (Dublin: R. M. Tims, 1832)
Letter to the Protestant Bishop of Exeter in vindication of the principles of the Catholic Church. p. 12. [1833].
Pamphlets on the Catholic Emancipation in England, 1829 by John Mac-Hale-Hierophilus (San Francisco, 1940)
The Letters of J. Mac Hale, under their respective signatures of Hierophilos; John, Bishop of Maronia; Bishop of Killala, and Archbishop of Tuam. (Dublin: John Duffy, 1847; 2nd edn, Dublin; 1847, repr. Dublin: M. H. Gill & Son, 1888)
The splendid oration delivered by the Most Reverend Dr MacHale at the opening of the second session of the National Synod of Ireland, on 29 August 1850. Dublin: printed by C. M. Warren [1850]
Sermons and Discourses, ed. by T. MacHale (Dublin: Gill & Son, 1883)
Speech when presiding at the Connaught Provincial Home Rule Meeting, 21 October, 1875, p. 7. Dublin: Irish Home Rule League, [1875].

Notes

1 Bernard O'Reilly, *The Life and Times of John MacHale* (1890), MacHale to Moore, 22 November 1841, II, pp. 632–3.
2 Ibid. MacHale MSS. 18 December 1841, p. 633.
3 Thomas Moore, *Memoirs, Journals and Correspondence* (1853–6), March 1844.
4 Ibid.
5 Bernard O'Reilly, op. cit., II, p. 636.
6 Ibid., p. 637.
7 Quoted in Nuala Costello, *Life of John MacHale,* MacHale's preface to the *Iliad,* p. 144.
8 With acknowledgements to Nuala Costello and The British Library.

24

THE GOLDEN JUBILEE

'As the eagle may gaze on the sun, so may the eye of John of Tuam look into the whole of his past life, and find no inconsistency there to dazzle or dim his vision, no public act which he can regret or wish blotted out.' (A. M. Sullivan)

IN JUNE 1875 John MacHale celebrated his Golden Jubilee. He had been fifty years as a bishop of the Church. This was an unusual event in the Church as not many priests become bishops at so early an age and not many live to such a great age. The preparations for the event had begun some years earlier, as the priests of Killala decided that a marble statue would be a fitting tribute to the Archbishop. They did not want to ask the poor people for money, so it was collected from subscriptions from clergy all over Ireland and even further afield. A London Catholic Journal, the *Weekly Register,* joined the movement for the memorial fund, saying:

He has . . . enjoyed the confidence, the love, and the veneration of the people of Ireland to a greater extent than any of his contemporaries, ecclesiastical or lay, except his illustrious friend and admirer, O'Connell. . . . Who has shown more ardent love of country? more unswerving devotion to the Holy See? . . . more indomitable courage in asserting the rights of his country and denouncing the wrongs under which she laboured and still suffers? more tender regard for the condition of the poor? more constant watchfulness for the preservation of the young against the insidious wiles of perverters? or a more unshaken resolution to keep clear of the blandishments of power, in order to be free upon all occasions to do battle for the cause of his native land in its civil, social, and religious aspects, than the illustrious Archbishop of Tuam?[1]

The Archbishop had said that he did not want any money to be given to him and that all the festivities on 8 June were to be at his own expense. His actual enthronement as bishop had been on 5 June but he chose a Tuesday for the celebrations to enable priests to travel on the Monday so as to be able to get to Tuam. There was great merry-making in the city of Tuam and the streets were decked with garlands, flags and banners and in the evening after a great banquet there were bonfires and fireworks.

MacHale received many letters of congratulation. There were some from past pupils, now themselves in their eighties, and letters from old friends who could not come to the celebrations. Many came from America, including the Archbishop of Cincinnatti and the Bishops of Rochester, in New York, Chicago, and Little Rock, Arkansas. MacHale received letters from many English people, particularly English priests, some of whom he had never met. One from a young priest from Birkenhead is typical:

> Most Reverend and Dear Father in Christ:– Will you allow me, although so far off and so little known to your Grace, to offer you my most earnest and heartfelt congratulations on this most solemn and magnificent occasion, the Episcopal Jubilee of your Grace?
>
> My dearest father, who died three years ago, once received two beautiful letters from you, at the time of the Irish famine, and which my dear mother treasures among her household relics. They are letters of thanks for some contributions which he had gathered together. . .
>
> I believe he sent your Grace my likeness a short time before he died. I have been a priest for now two years. May I beg your Grace to pray God to give me the apostolic spirit and fervour in that ministry of which your Grace is the most glorious and brightest ornament in these realms? . . .
>
> Will your Grace kindly bless me, my dearest mother, and my brothers and sisters?
>
> With the greatest respect and esteem,
> Your Grace's servant
> Wilfrid Dallow[2]

He also received tributes from many Irish Protestants, even those of a very anti-Catholic nature. William Kennaghan wrote:

> My Lord Archbishop:- Though a Conservative, an anti-repealer, an anti-Home-Ruler, and a member of the Disestablished Church, I still must honour the distinguished Prelate who, through evil report and good report, stood by and to what he finally believed to be right. . . .
>
> Accept, my Lord Archbishop, the good wishes of one who has admired you for your liberality and your love of our common country; and may your Grace live long to enjoy the friendship of your own body and the respect of those differing from you in creed and politics.[3]

Mitchell Henry, the Protestant Home-ruler MP, had promised to attend the celebrations on 8 June but was not able to come on account of the death of his friend. After explaining the reason for his absence he says:

> Well, your Grace will receive tomorrow every variety of expression of respect and attachment; and I had hoped to add mine in person.
>
> One thing only I will say: You must live for your country. She requires your influence and example; and I pray God that He may long spare your great intellect and disinterested love for what is right and just to Ireland.
>
> Believe me my dear Lord, with great respect and esteem,
> Your Grace's faithfully and truly,
> Mitchell Henry.[4]

The Irish newspapers announced the coming festivities, not least the *Freeman,* who printed a short biography of the Archbishop on 5 June. Sir John Gray, who had been a great friend of MacHale, had died the previous April, but the paper remained friendly to MacHale:

> During more than fifty years of the century which is passing away, the history of the Archbishop of Tuam is, in great part,

the history of Ireland. Many of the pages that tell of our country's struggles, its trials, its disasters, and also, but too seldom, its triumphs, are pages which he himself has contributed to it. . . . And whenever the effort was to be made, whenever the longing was to find utterance in hot and earnest words, the people were always sure that John of Tuam would be ready for the work.

Therefore it is that he has always held so cherished a place in the people's heart; and therefore it is that they rejoice with him so affectionately today. . . .

One of the noblest features of his Grace's character is his more than Spartan independence of soul, and his abhorrence of anything like begging for public favour. Few of us can forget the incident of his appearance in the witness-box at Galway, to give evidence in reference to the famous Election Petition tried there a couple of years ago. It was a memorable display. . . . After so long a life, – it was a proud thing for the venerable man to be able to say, in reply to an insolent taunt, that during the entire of it he had never, either directly or indirectly, asked public favour, or the minutest portion of public patronage for himself or for any one, even the most remotely connected with him.[5]

Not just the Irish papers recorded the event. Once again the London *Weekly Register* wrote at length about MacHale:

His reputation is dear to the Catholics of England, as well as to his own compatriots. We are all proud of him, for he has held the banner of the Church aloft unfalteringly during many a troublesome season.[6]

At the celebrations, more than two hundred clergy took part in the religious ceremonies, which were attended by a huge congregation, and thirty-two addresses were presented to MacHale from various groups, including Members of Parliament. The Reverend Joseph Galbraith, a Protestant professor of Trinity College, read the address of the Home Rule League, saying that the name of the Archbishop stood first on the published list of those who convened the national conference on Home Rule.

> The history of your life records, indelibly printed in the hearts of the Irish people, the proofs of your devotion to our country. Even in the grand scholarship, by which, among all the claims upon your time, your Grace has created a rich and living literature, of the old and too-much forgotten language of our land, we trace the indications of that passionate love for Ireland, which has associated your name with all that is pure and exalted in patriotism.[7]

Another address was from the young men of the Medical School of the Catholic university. They also commended MacHale on his cultivation of the Irish language and said that he should be enrolled among 'the Princes of the Church'[8] as a Cardinal, not an ambition entertained by MacHale.

The Wednesday was organised by the clergy and began with a Mass in the cathedral. After that, MacHale went with Mr Biggar MP and Professor Galbraith to the Presentation Convent where the girls showed them their handiwork and sang for their guests.

On the Wednesday afternoon the statue of MacHale was unveiled by Bishop Nulty of Meath. The Archbishop was not present on this occasion. The address was given by A. M. Sullivan. He went through the life of the Archbishop, saying that his was 'the grandest name in Irish history during the nineteenth century'. He spoke about how MacHale was 'the right arm' of Daniel O'Connell and about his work for Catholic education.[9]

> But we saw him under another aspect when famine was mowing down the people in Ireland. There are at this day present in the homes in the west old men and women who could tell a tale, otherwise unheard by human ear, or unseen by human eye, of the great Archbishop's labours during those dreadful years. If he had no other title to our love, it would be found in his heroism and devotion during the famine time. . . .
> As the eagle may gaze on the sun, so may the eye of John of

Tuam look into the whole of his past life, and find no inconsistency there to dazzle or dim his vision, no public act which he can regret or wish blotted out. . . . And here will come in future years, to find new strength, whosoever, battling in the cause of public right and justice, faints or grows weary, or desponds in the face of dreadful odds.[10]

The Times reported the unveiling of the statue the following day:

The statue of Archbishop M'Hale, which is of Carrara marble, was unveiled today in presence of about 5,000 persons. . . . The unveiling was performed by Bishop Nulty, who pronounced a warm panegyric upon the great Archbishop of the West, the pride and glory of the Irish Church, and the best and noblest of Irishmen.[11]

There was a great banquet in the evening, where the guests were entertained with music and children's choirs. The massive silver cup presented to MacHale by the students of Maynooth on the day of his consecration as Bishop on 5 June 1825 went round the table as a 'loving-cup'. The guests included the Lord Mayor of Dublin, MacSwiney, as well as many priests and Members of Parliament. As the Tuam clergy were the hosts, the chair was taken by Dean MacManus. He proposed the health of the Archbishop, who rose to speak. After prolonged cheering he began by telling a story about a renowned Irish lawyer, Curran:

His client had been indicted for a crime of which he strenuously protested he was not guilty, having no recollection of ever committing it. But this could avail him but little before the immaculate judges of that day, and their mode of administering justice.

Curran, however pleaded the case so successfully, and drew such a picture of the man and his sufferings, that the supposed culprit could not acknowledge his own identity. 'I knew I had been badly treated' he afterwards said; 'I endured a great deal at the hands of my persecutors. But hang me, if I ever had to bear a hundredth part of what Mr Curran said I had to suffer'.

Well, now I have all my life been only fulfilling the ordinary duties of my office,– as well as I could to be sure; but you must not give me credit for doing more. . . .

In the fulfilment of the highest duties, when we all have done our very best, what are we but useless servants? In saying this I must not be understood as undervaluing the public homage, the testimonies of respect and esteem, which you have been kind enough to pay to me.

That I have had a long life is no merit of mine. This is God's gratuitous gift, for which I humbly thank him.[12]

MacHale then went on to praise the generosity of the people of the diocese and the zeal of the clergy in setting up convents, monasteries and schools.

I have received congratulatory letters from several clergymen who were, I cannot say my fellow students, but my disciples and pupils in years long gone by. Of all the students of Maynooth who contributed towards presenting me with that cordial cup that has just passed round, only one, I believe, is now living. I could not think of a more appropriate occasion for bringing forth and exhibiting to you this memorial of the affectionate feelings of the dear companions of my youth. . . . I am glad to see that divisions are being healed; that henceforth diocese shall not be set against diocese, nor province against province. It is my rule that we shall have Home Rule in Church and State.[13]

In his note on the speech O'Reilly is at pains to point out that just as MacHale does not want complete separation from Britain and is content to have an Irish Parliament under the Queen, in the same way MacHale is not talking about separation from Rome but more independence for the provinces. In any interpretation, it probably did not go down well in Rome.

A poem was composed by the brother of Alexander Sullivan, T. D. Sullivan, especially for the occasion and was sung at the banquet.

> Ah, men will come and pass away
> Like rain-drops in the sea,
> And thrones will crumble to decay,
> And kings forgotten be;
> But through all time in every clime,
> The children of the Gael
> Will guard the fame and praise the name
> Of glorious John MacHale.[14]

Despite the happiness of MacHale's Jubilee celebrations and the obvious esteem that he was held in by many disparate groups, the divisions created by earlier political disagreements remained. Every diocese in Ireland was represented and the dioceses of the west sent numerous contingents, but the Bishop of Galway, Dr MacEvilly, did not attend the celebrations and chose those particular days to send the secular clergy of his diocese on a retreat. However, the clergy from the religious orders of Galway, especially the Jesuits and the Dominicans, were there in force. On numerous occasions Dr MacEvilly had shown his disapproval of MacHale, particularly with regard to the Fenians.

In a letter to Rome on 10 June 1875 Cullen wrote rather peevishly 'Dr MacHale's Jubilee, I have heard was a poor concern'. On 29 June Cullen wrote again talking about MacHale's speech, which expressed his wish for 'home rule in spiritualibus et in temporalibus'.[15]

Later in July 1875 MacHale wrote to Cullen telling him that he had written to the Pope asking him if his nephew, Thomas MacHale, who was at that time the Vicar-General of Tuam, could be a coadjutor bishop to help him in his work. Dr Thomas MacHale had had a distinguished career, winning the highest honours in his youth, gaining doctorates in both Philosophy and Divinity. He was well known to Cullen as he had studied at the Irish College in Rome and in earlier times Cullen had written to MacHale with warm praise of his nephew. He had been suggested as a possible bishop on two previous occasions but had let it be known that he did not wish it. It was not unusual for an ageing bishop to ask for a particular person to help him in his final years, as it was felt to be important that they could work well together. In his letter to Cullen MacHale seemed confident of his support:

> From your Eminence's position, as well as your early college relations with him, you will be naturally consulted on the important business, and I have every reason to think that I do not miscalculate in assuming that those relations were so satisfactory as to encourage the hope of his having your eminence's valuable support.[16]

Cullen finally replied to MacHale's letter at the end of August 1876 to tell him:

> As the election of your coadjutor is in the hands of Propaganda, it would not be proper for me to interfere.[17]

At the subsequent election, Thomas MacHale got twelve votes as against MacEvilly's sixteen. The majority of the Tuam priests did not want Dr Thomas MacHale. He was regarded as 'a doctrinaire and theorist rather than a practical administrator'[18] who had lived most of his life in a college and had no understanding of the secular mission. D'Alton writes:

> Dr MacEvilly was not a man of much amiability, and not such as could attract personal popularity. But he knew more of the world and of the lives of secular priests than Dr MacHale.[19]

MacHale was at first determined to go to Rome to plead his case as he was aware of MacEvilly's hostility towards him, but in the end he sent his nephew, who renounced all pretensions to be a bishop and just asked for someone other than MacEvilly. It was thought by many that the Pope would allow Thomas MacHale to help the Archbishop during his lifetime but appoint MacEvilly after his death.

In 1877 MacEvilly went to Rome, accompanied by two other bishops. This resulted in a letter from Propaganda making various charges against MacHale concerning the proselytism within the diocese and the behaviour of the clergy. MacHale vigorously refuted the charges and, after the death of Pius IX in 1878, the new Pope, Leo XIII, asked Daniel McGettigan, the Archbishop of Armagh and Primate of Ireland, to go to the diocese of Tuam to investigate. In October 1878 Cardinal Cullen also died. McGettigan obviously felt great embarrassment at the task. He writes to MacHale:

> The Holy See has expressed a wish that I should visit your Grace. Without the request of the Holy Father, it would be an intrusion on my part to ask for a personal interview relevant to that business.[20]

McGettigan visited MacHale and wrote to Rome with a favourable report of the diocese and advising them not to send MacEvilly to Tuam as Coadjutor, but in January 1879 Cardinal Simeoni of Propaganda wrote again to McGettigan, saying that several bishops had written to him advising that a coadjutor should be sent to Tuam, otherwise:

> greater injuries must accrue to the spiritual welfare of the same from the single efforts of the Protestants, the Sacred Congregation, having solely in view the salvation of souls in that diocese, cannot put away all anxiety on that subject.[21]

McGettigan was asked once again to look into the matter and send more detailed accounts. In a letter to a fellow clergyman McGettigan is clearly angry at the turn of events:

> I was led to believe that there was an end to every attempt at annoying his Grace in the government of his diocese. You will however see from the letter which I forward, and which reached me a few days ago, that the busy-bodies are sending unfounded statements to Propaganda, and endeavouring to disturb the peaceful state which now exists in Tuam. . . . That there is no ground for anxiety about the state of religion in Tuam, and that there is nothing to be feared from the assaults

of the 'Soupers', – are two things I am firmly convinced of already.[22]

In February 1879 McGettigan sent his report to Propaganda. In it he says:

Everything is progressing most edifyingly in the diocese of Tuam. I quite lately saw one of the suffragen bishops of Tuam, one in no wise favourable to the Archbishop, the most Rev. Dr Gillooly of Elphin, who, in answer to my query as to how things were getting on in the diocese of Tuam, answered 'quietly and satisfactory to everybody'. What is still more important, I could gather from the conversation of that Prelate, that he did not at all approve of the proceedings of those who are persistently and not edifyingly endeavouring to force, *vi et armis* the B– of G– into the Church of Tuam.[23]

McGettigan then went on to answer all the queries in detail, concluding:

Moreover the diocese of Tuam is blessed by the presence of an archbishop still in the enjoyment of bodily vigour and possessed of a wonderful energy of soul. He is quite able to fulfil all his episcopal functions. He has also a vicar-general of great perspicacity and courage, who is not the man to suffer tamely any injury to be done to religion. . . .

No spiritual detriment can arise from the present condition of things in that archdiocese: and nothing but the most serious evils could result from forcing the Bishop of Galway into the Church of Tuam against the consent of the Archbishop.[24]

In the event Rome took no account of McGettigan's advice. Reports continued to come in about MacHale's diocese. In September 1879 MacEvilly wrote to the Irish College in Rome:

> Clifden is in a horrible state. The P.P., Dean McManus fighting with his curates and the curates with one another and the Soupers with all. I don't know what to do.[25]

MacEvilly was asked to go to Tuam and MacHale was forced to comply. MacEvilly seems to have been fairly tactful in his administrations and kept out of MacHale's way. O'Reilly states that MacHale never showed any lack of charity towards MacEvilly or 'sovereign respect' towards the Pope:

> even when studied and persistent misrepresentations had obtained from the apostolic authority acts which wounded the deepest sentiments of a soul devoted to the Church and to Ireland.[26]

The incident is a strange one and unfortunate for the memory of John MacHale. D'Alton writes: 'It would have been better for his fame as well as for his peace of mind had he passed away a few years earlier'.[27] It seems odd that the Holy See would wish to cause unnecessary stress to an Archbishop who was already eighty-eight years old. If, as seems likely, there was some disorganisation in the diocese, it could have been sorted out without appointing MacEvilly. However, it probably indicates the fears they felt about a prelate of the Church whom they felt had Gallican tendencies, who had rebels and Protestants for his friends and talked about Home Rule 'in spiritualibus'.

Notes

1   Bernard O'Reilly, *The Life and Times of John MacHale* (1890), II, pp. 351–2. *Weekly Register*, 7 October 1875.
2   Ibid., June 1875, pp. 565–6.
3   Ibid., pp. 567–8.
4   Ibid., p. 569.
5   *Freeman's Journal*, 5 June 1875.
6   Bernard O'Reilly, op. cit., II, p. 571. *Weekly Register* 1875.
7   Bernard O'Reilly, op. cit., II, p. 577.
8   Ibid., p. 577.

9   Ibid., p. 588–9.
10   Ibid., pp.589–90.
11   *The Times,* 9 June 1875.
12   Bernard O'Reilly, op. cit., II, pp. 593–4.
13   Ibid., p. 595.
14   E. A. D'Alton, *History of the Archdiocese of Tuam* (1928), pp. 87–8.
15   Pádraic Ó Tuairisg, *Árd-dheoise Thuama agus Cartlann Choláiste na nGael sa Róimh sa naoú haois déag,* unpublished thesis, Tuam archives, K/75/304, 13 June 1875, p. 477.
16   Bernard O'Reilly, op. cit., 23 July 1875, II, p. 602.
17   Ibid., 26 August 1876, p. 604.
18   E. A. D'Alton, op. cit., p. 91.
19   Ibid.
20   Bernard O'Reilly, op. cit., II, p. 620.
21   Ibid., p. 621.
22   Ibid., Armagh, 8 February 1879, p. 621.
23   Ibid., p. 622.
24   Ibid., p. 624.
25   Ó Tuairisg, op. cit., K/79/374, p. 525
26   Bernard O'Reilly, op. cit., II, p. 628.
27   E. A. D'Alton, op. cit., p. 100.

25

THE LAST YEARS

'Didn't he love the poor just like Our Lord himself?'
(Presentation sister)

IN 1862 IT WAS DECIDED, largely through the influence of Sir John Gray, to celebrate the centenary of the birth of Daniel O'Connell by erecting a statue to him in Sackville Street, Dublin. Consequently, a committee was set up to collect subscriptions and to organise the affair. It was at first proposed to inscribe the statue with the words 'The Liberator', referring to O'Connell's great achievement in securing Catholic Emancipation for Britain and Ireland. However, Archbishop MacHale objected to this as it did not take into account O'Connell's other achievements, particularly that of his involvement in the Repeal movement. The committee listened to MacHale's advice and the statue eventually just bore O'Connell's name.

In 1875 MacHale journeyed to Dublin to join in the centenary celebrations. There was a great banquet in the evening with the Lord Mayor presiding and MacHale sat next to his old adversary, Cardinal Cullen. After proposing the toast, the Lord Mayor said that he was to be followed by one whose voice and pen had been constantly used in defence of O'Connell's principles. The Lord Mayor reminded the assembly of O'Connell's title for MacHale, 'The Lion of the Fold of Judah'.[1] At this, the assembled company rose to their feet and cheered. In his speech MacHale once more raised the subject of repeal:

> It is on account of his extraordinary and heroic exertions to procure the blessings of self-government for his native country that O'Connell has so endeared himself to the Irish people. And they, on their side, have given proof of the immense value

331

they set on such self-government, by thus honouring its devoted champion with such a magnificent national celebration.[2]

MacHale kept up his passion for repeal by keeping in close contact with Isaac Butt and the Home-rulers. In 1875 a fund was started for Isaac Butt who, in abandoning the practice of his profession in the service of Ireland, was finding great difficulty in supporting his family. His problems were increased by certain irregularities in his personal life and the existence of an illegitimate son, William. Professor Galbraith and Mr Parnell asked MacHale for permission to put his name on the committee for the fund. He replied promptly:

> In recognition of the great talents of Mr Butt hitherto devoted to the service of Ireland, and in the hope that his countrymen will give their countenance to the same noble object, I beg to forward my subscription of £5 to your committee. If the labourer is worthy of his hire, it cannot be expected that one who sacrifices the ample emoluments of a lucrative profession to the promotion of his country's interests should be left without grateful recognition and remuneration.[3]

After the demise of Butt, the new Home Rule Party under Parnell became the first paid political party at Westminster. This enabled men of all social classes to be elected and began to change the nature of Parliament. The newly organised Home Rule Party became increasingly confident and demanded rather than requested reforms. This political development coincided with economic distress in Ireland. In 1878 agricultural prices fell dramatically and for three years there had been a poor potato crop. Tenants were unable to pay their rents. In many cases landlords granted voluntary abatements as they did in England, but many others did not. Evictions for non-payment of rent rose considerably in late 1878, and violence in 1878 and 1879 was a direct response to this. Despite the violence there had been a rapprochement between old Fenians and parliamentarians and men like John O'Connor Power and Joseph Gillis Biggar became Members of Parliament. In November 1878 there was a Tenant Right meeting at Ballinasloe in County Galway. This was attended by Parnell and O'Connor Power. At this meeting letters of support were read out from Archbishop MacHale and Bishop Duggan of Clonfert. MacHale was particularly anxious that there should not be divisions in the Irish party between those who had supported Butt and those who favoured the more aggressive tactics of Parnell and Biggar, and between those who were primarily concerned with the land question and those who were interested in Home Rule. In January 1879 MacHale wrote to the *Freeman's Journal* urging unity upon the Home Rule MPs:

> It is high time that a term be put to the disheartening divisions that prevail in the ranks of the Irish popular representatives in the British House of Parliament. The evils of discord, existing for some time past, have been aggravated by recent manifestations as senseless as the worst enemies of Ireland could desire. . . . Let the errors of the past be generously forgiven and forgotten; . . . Let the existence of Home - Rule be vigorously insisted upon. Let unity of action among the members, as far as possible, be insured by summoning them in due time for seasonable deliberation in London, whenever great measures for the benefit of Ireland or of the British dominions are about being introduced into Parliament, as well as during the progress of such measures through both Houses.[4]

In June of that year, a rather uncharacteristic letter from MacHale appeared in the *Freeman's Journal*. In it he condemned a meeting that was to be held the following day in Westport. He said that he was in sympathy with the aims of the meeting:

> But night patrolling, acts and words of menace, with arms in hand, the profanation of what is most sacred in religion – all the result of lawless and occult association eminently merits the solemn condemnation of the ministers of religion, as directly tending to impiety and disorder in Church and in society.[5]

It was thought that the letter was probably written by MacHale's nephew, Thomas MacHale. Michael Davitt in his book, *The Fall of Feudalism in Ireland,* says that at the time rumour asserted that although 'the name was that of John of Tuam . . . the spirit and composition were of another and lower order'.[6] This may have been the case, but it is also likely that MacHale was concerned about the emerging violence in the country. After the death of Sir John Gray, MacHale once again found an opportunity to encourage the Irish people in their striving for Home Rule and to deplore violence. This occurred at the celebrations for the unveiling of a statue in Gray's honour. By this time Cullen was dead and MacHale himself was eighty-nine. This occasion was also marked by a national celebration and all areas of Ireland were represented. MacHale and his nephew were given the use of the High Sherriff's carriage and the streets were lined with cheering people for his drive from Coffey's hotel to the unveiling, many people realising that they were unlikely to see the famous Archbishop in Dublin again. MacHale was invited by the Lord Mayor to perform the unveiling ceremony. This he did and then stood up to say a few words. He spoke, first of all, about his friend, the late Sir John Gray. He spoke about his work as a Member of Parliament and how he had striven unstintingly for the interests of Ireland. He stressed that the evils that still beset Ireland could only be removed by 'constitutional agitation' and

> Of this wholesome agitation there can be no fear of our having too much, until the conviction grows on the minds of Englishmen that Ireland is to be governed according to the convictions of Irishmen, and not according to the crude notions of the Saxon or the Saxon garrison in our land.[7]

The crowd broke into applause, but the Archbishop reiterated his theme of the importance of constitutional agitation:

> Immoral and illegal combinations, disowned by right reason and reprobated by religion, cannot be enlisted in the service of our country.

He finished by once again repeating the

> deep sense of our obligations for the invaluable assistance extended to our country, and, above all, to the West of Ireland, in the dreary years of famine and pestilence, by the late laborious, upright, and patriotic proprietor of the *Freeman's Journal*.[8]

Despite his fears of violence, MacHale was once again involved in the great Tenant Right meeting in Ballyhaunis in 1879. In October 1879 the Irish National Land League was set up for the protection of tenant farmers and the eventual achievement of a peasant proprietorship. This was controlled by Parnell and Davitt, who was himself a former Fenian. This partnership and the involvement of the Irish Parliamentary Party showed that the land issue was clearly linked to the demand for Home Rule.[9] The League was largely funded from America. It had an efficient organisation and a central office in Dublin. As the evictions and subsequent violence spread, the 'land war', as it was called, was blamed by the Liberal Government on the Land League, and speeches of its leaders were cited as incitements to violence. Parnell's famous speech in the west of Ireland in which he said 'keep a firm grip of your homesteads' was represented as giving direct orders to rebel. However, the government accepted that there was near starvation in the west and tried to build on the work of the earlier Marlborough Relief Committee to relieve distress. The Conservatives in 1880 saw the Land League as an attack on property but established a commission to look into the problems of agriculture in Britain and Ireland. Gladstone, on regaining office, appointed a separate commission to inquire into the nature of tenurial relations in Ireland. This resulted in the Land Act of August 1881, in which Gladstone was assisted by T. M. Healy, an Irish lawyer. The Land Act, according to Davitt, 'completely revolutionised the system of land tenure in Ireland'. It did indeed give tenants many of the things they had been fighting for: the right to sell tenancies at the best price they could get; the right to have fair rents fixed by the land courts at intervals of fifteen years; security of tenure – as long as the rent was paid and conditions of tenancy observed, the tenants could not be evicted; and what was known as the 'Healy clause' – no rent shall be allowed or made payable in respect of improvement made by the tenant or his predecessors. Davitt describes the bill as 'the language of common sense' and:

> It was the result of a kind of guerilla social warfare . . . moulded to some extent, upon the recommendations of the Bessborough commission, and these were, in a large measure, influenced by the work of the land-League agitation, and grounded upon the economic facts which both the Isaac Butts movement and that led by Mr Parnell had driven into the public mind.[10]

The Land Act coming at the end of MacHale's life must have been a great source of satisfaction to him, embodying as it did many of the items for which he had campaigned so vigorously.

Throughout the closing years of the 1870s Archbishop MacHale continued with his religious duties, setting himself a heavy schedule despite his advancing years. During the year 1878 he conducted his annual pastoral visitations in the months of July, August and September. At these visitations he confirmed 5,417 persons, sometimes confirming as many as four hundred on one day. He also found time to continue to write vast numbers of letters. In September 1878 he wrote to a Mrs O'Connor:

> Though its acknowledgement is somewhat tardy, your kind letter of the 23rd of August reached in due time. In stating that you have great trials it will no doubt affect your consolation to reflect that none of the saints, the faithful friends of God were without their share of them. And if seen in the spirit in which they received them they will become consoling occasions of merit. Although any chapter of that admirable book – *The Imitation of Christ* – could be read with great fruit, I would recommend to you on this occasion the 12th or last chapter of the second book, *The King's highway of the Holy Cross.* . . .

> Wishing you a large share of the grace with which our divine Redeemer bore his Cross, believe me my dear Mrs O'Connor
>
> Your very faithful servant
> John MacHale.[11]

MacHale's health remained good and he was able to continue with all his usual offices until late in October 1881, when he seemed to become weaker, and after some days it became apparent to members of his household that the end was near. His breathing became very difficult. He received the last sacraments, and on the evening of 7 November, his household was summoned, and his relatives, servants and local priests from the town and from the college remained at his bedside praying. His sister has described how, holding candles, they knelt before a crucifix and prayed that John MacHale might receive the grace of a happy death. He died later that evening and the chaplain and other clergymen prepared his body to be laid out in the diningroom. Outside, the bells tolled from the cathedral towers and the Town Hall, which announced to the people that John MacHale was dead. After the morning Mass the people came to pay their last respects, to pray and look at their Archbishop for the last time.

The news of MacHale's death quickly spread around the world. There were many obituaries to John MacHale. His friends in the *Freeman's Journal* wrote:

> A pillar has fallen in the temple. A tower has tottered to the ground in Israel! John, Archbishop of Tuam, breathed his last at St Jarlath's yesterday evening. . . . His Grace was the senior prelate of the Catholic Church: and in his person were most remarkably conjoined the purest attributes of priest and patriot. . . . In his learned leisure, or in the fierce arena of polemics or politics, John of Tuam was an Agamemnon, king of men, and stood towering head and shoulders over the crowd.[12]

The *Irish Times* was a newspaper that had continually opposed MacHale on religious matters and in politics, but their tribute was generous:

A leading Irishman of a long past generation, who had retained his marvellous intellectual and physical vigour to the age of ninety passed yesterday out of life. The Archbishop of the West, as he was most often styled, expired during the evening, after a brief struggle with no definite disease. . . . Dr MacHale never lost his quick interest in affairs, and to the close was an intense Irishman. . . . Though all his life he hoisted his flag, he never drove the people into extremes by rash counsels, and confined his agitation to changes which he desired in tenure of land. The roar of the LION never failed to arouse the English journals. . . . Dr MacHale is a name to be added to the roll of eminent powers and unquenchable activity in the use of them for such ends as were commended to his judgement. To young men he presents a unique example of a buoyant nature and highly cultivated mind, the one conserving and inspiring the other, and carrying him on, in defiance of time, to a patriarchal longevity in unbroken health and impulse.[13]

The Times of London devoted two long columns on the death of their old adversary on 8 November 1881. After describing his distinguished education and literary achievements it continued:

Dr MacHale toiled at his ecclesiastical duties like the youngest and most active of his priests, never refusing to share with them the burden of their parochial cares. He preached, he heard confessions, he administered the sacraments, he attended the dying, and no severity of weather or other impediment was allowed to stand in the way of the discharge of his pastoral duties. . . . With an independence of spirit that savours of the old Spartan he steadily refused during his long life to ask a favour from any ministry for himself, or for anyone in any way connected with himself and it is said that for the large sums disbursed in the County Mayo during the famine and the next few years of distress, by far the largest portion was collected by his forcible and touching appeals to the 'faithful' in every part of the world.

In another part of the newspaper:

> His Grace belonged to a different class of prelates from those who have for a long series of years been appointed to fill the Irish sees. He had no sympathy with the Ultramontanists, and often withstood them to their faces. His love of liberty was shown in ecclesiastical as well as in political matters.[14]

For a week the city of Tuam was draped in mourning. From the mast of the Town Hall there hung a flag with the words, 'Ireland's greatest son, John, is dead.' On the Sunday, a procession of schoolchildren, students and various societies and groups went to the Archbishop's house, where they were met by the clergy and Town Commissioners. From there a long procession, which included the Right Rev. Dr Bernard, the Protestant Bishop of Tuam, went round the streets of Tuam and then brought the body to the cathedral. The funeral took place on Tuesday, 15 November. The ceremonies were led by the Archbishop of Armagh and the Bishop of Meath, both good friends of MacHale, but there were many hundreds of bishops and priests who took part. There was a large contingent from Maynooth and the huge congregation included Catholics and Protestants, rich and poor. The Office for the dead was recited before the Pontifical Mass. There was no funeral oration and the service ended with the chant, *Libera me, Domine, a morte aeterna*.

Thus ended the life of John MacHale, who, in his actions, in his writings and in his struggles, personified the life of nineteenth-century Ireland. His name became legendary in Ireland. He symbolised the struggle of the poor to survive and to maintain their survival by having some control over their land. After being convinced that Ireland would be better off being ruled by Irish people, he supported the people in their nationalist aspirations, both in government and in their language. MacHale was a loyal priest and bishop. He fought hard for independent Irish education and particularly for religious education. Above all, John MacHale was a man of the people, a pastor of his flock. A very old sister of the Presentation order, on being asked whether she thought MacHale was a 'holy man', replied: 'Didn't he love the poor just like Our Lord, himself.'

Notes

1   Bernard O'Reilly, *The Life and Times of John MacHale* (1890), II, p. 648.
2   Ibid., p. 649.
3   Ibid., p. 674.
4   *Freeman's Journal,* January 1879.
5   Ibid., June 1879.
6   Michael Davitt, *The Fall of Feudalism in Ireland* (1904), p. 153.
7   Bernard O'Reilly, op. cit., II, p. 652.
8   Ibid., p. 653.
9   Desmond McGuire, *History of Ireland* (1987), p. 139.
10   Michael Davitt, op. cit., p. 321.
11   Tuam Archives. K/78/275, p. 514.
12   *Freeman's Journal,* 8 November 1881.
13   *Irish Times,* 8 November 1881.
14   *The Times,* 8 November 1881.

BIBLIOGRAPHY

Acton, John Emerick Edward Dalberg Baron, *Selections from Correspondence* (London: Longmans and Co., 1917)

Bagehot, Walter, *Biographical Studies* (London: Longmans, Green & Co., 1881)

Beck, G. A., *English Catholics 1850–1950* (London: Burns and Oates, 1950)

Bourke, Ulick, *Life and Times of the Most Reverend John MacHale* (New York: P. J. Kennedy, Excelsior Catholic Publishing House: 1883)

Broderick, John F., *The Holy See* (Apud aedes universiatis Gregorianae Romae, 1851)

Brynn, Edward Garland, *The Church of Ireland in the Age of Catholic Emancipation* (New York, 1982)

Butler, Dom Cuthbert, *The Vatican Council 1869–70*, ed. by Christopher Butler (London: Collins and Harvill Press, 1930)

Butt, Isaac, *The Irish Deep Sea Fisheries: A Speech Delivered to a Meeting of the Home Rule Association, October 1871* (Dublin, 1874)

Corish, Patrick J., *A History of Irish Catholicism* (Dublin and Melbourne: Gill and Son, 1967)

Costello, Nuala, *John MacHale* (Dublin: The Talbot Press Ltd; London: Gerald Duckworth and Company Ltd, 1939)

D'Alton, E. A., *History of the Archdiocese of Tuam*, II (Dublin: Phoenix Publishing Co., 1928)

Daunt, W. J. O'Neill, *A Life Spent for Ireland: Selections from Journals by his Daughter* (London: T. Fisher Unwin, 1896)

Davis, T., *Letters of a Protestant on Repeal* (Dublin: The Irish Confederation, 1847)

Davitt, Michael, *The Fall of Feudalism in Ireland* (London and New York: Harper and Brothers Publishers, 1904)

Denieffe, Joseph, *A Personal Narrative of the Irish Revolutionary Brotherhood* (Shannon: Irish University Press, 1969)

De Vere White, Terence, *The Road of Excess* (Dublin: Browne and Nolan, 1946)

Dickens, Charles, *Little Dorrit* (London: Penguin Books, 1857)

Donohoe, Tony, *Local Songs, Poems, and Ballads from the Shadow of Nephin* (Ballina Printing Co., n.d.)

Duffy, Charles Gavan, *My Life in Two Hemispheres* (London: T. Fisher Unwin, 1868)

League of North and South (London: Chapman and Hall, 1886)

Edwards, David L., *Christian England* (London: William Collins, 1981)

Elliot, Lawrence, *I Will be called John* (1973)

Fitzpatrick, W. J., *Correspondence of Daniel O'Connell: The Liberator*, 2 vols (London: John Murray, 1888)

Greville, Charles, *The Greville Memoirs: a journal of the reign of Queen Victoria, 1837–1851*, ed. by Christopher Lloyd, 3 vols (London: Roger Ingram, 1948)

Griffin, A., *Meagher of the Sword* (Dublin: M. H. Gill and Son, 1916)

Gwynn, Denis, *Daniel O'Connell: The Irish Liberator* (London: Hutchinson & Co., 1947)

Hall, S. C., *Achill Mission* (1844)

Hansard's parliamentary debates, LXXII–LXXXVII (London: T. C. Hansard, 1844–1846)

Hayles, E. E. Y., *Pio Nono* (London: Eyre and Spottiswoode, 1954)

Healy, J., *Maynooth College: Its Centenary History* (Dublin: Browne and Nolan, 1895)

Heron, R. M., *The Irish Difficulty* (London, 1868)

House, Humphrey, *The Dickens World* (Oxford: Oxford University Press, 1941)

Keenan, Desmond, *The Catholic Church in Nineteenth Century Ireland* (Dublin: Gill and Macmillan, 1983)

Ker, Ian, *John Henry Newman* (Oxford: Oxford University Press, 1988)

Kerr, Donal A., *Peel, Priests and Politics 1841–1846* (Oxford: Clarendon, 1982)

Lane, Peter, *British History 1760–1914* (London: John Murray, 1978)

Lathbury, D. C., *Letters on Church and Religion of William Ewart Gladstone* (Dublin: John Murray, 1910)

Lavelle, P., *The Irish Landlords Since the Revolution* (Dublin, 1870)

Lucas, Edward, *The Life of Frederick Lucas MP*, 2 vols (London: Burns and Oates, 1886)

McGrath, Fergus, *Newman's University: Idea and Reality* (London, New York, Toronto: Longmans, Green and Company, 1951)

McGuire, Desmond, *History of Ireland* (Twickenham: The Hamlyn Publishing Group Ltd, 1987)

MacHale, J., *Letters of Hierophilos* (Dublin, 1822)

Evidences and Doctrines of the Catholic Church, 2nd edn (1828)

Letters (Dublin: James Duffy, 1847)

Sermons and Discourses, ed. by Thomas MacHale (Dublin: M. H. Gill and Son, 1883)

Letters (Dublin: M. H. Gill and Son, 1888)

MacSuibhne, Peadar, ed., *Paul Cullen and his Contemporaries, with their Letters from 1820–1902*, 5 vols (Naas, County Kildare: Leinster Leader, 1961–77)

Malone, Sylvester, *Tenant Wrong Illustrated in a Nutshell* (Dublin, 1867)

Manning, Henry Edward, *Ireland: A Letter to Earl Grey* (London: 1868)

Meagher, *Speeches on Legislative Independence of Ireland* (New York, 1853)

Mill, J. S., *England and Ireland* (London: Longmans, Green, Reader and Dyer, 1868)

Moore, Maurice, *An Irish Gentleman* (London: T. Werner Laurie Ltd, Cliffords Inn, 1913)

Moore, Thomas, *Memoirs, Journal and Correspondence*, ed. by Lord John Russell, 8 vols (London, 1853–6)

Moran, P. F., *The Catholic Church in Australasia* (Sydney: Oceanic Co., 1897)

Morley, John, *Life of Gladstone*, I (1868)

Mozley, Thomas, *Letters from Rome* (London: Longmans & Co., 1891)

Murray, Daniel, *Correspondence between Dr Murray and Dr MacHale*, (Dublin: M. H. Gill and Son, 1885)

Nangle, Edward, *Dr MacHale's Letter to Bishop of Exeter Dissected* (Dublin: J. Robertson and Co., 1874)

Newman, John Henry, *The Letters and Diaries of John Henry Newman,* ed. by Charles Stephen Dessain et al (London: Thomas Nelson and Sons, 1961–1977)
Discussions and Arguments (London: Basil Montagu Pickering, 1872)
Autobiographical Writings, ed. by Henry Tristram (London and New York, 1956)

Nicholls, David, *Church and State in Britain since 1820* (London: Routledge and Keegan Paul, 1967)

Norman E. R., *The Catholic Church and Ireland in the Age of Rebellion* (London: Longmans, 1965)

Nulty, Thomas, *The Land Agitation in Ireland* (Manchester: Heywood & Sons, 1881)

O'Keeffe, R., *Report of the Action for Libel against His Eminence, Cardinal Cullen* (London, 1874)

O'Reilly, Bernard, *The Life and Times of John MacHale,* 2 vols (New York and Cincinnati: F. Pustett, 1890)

Parker, Charles Stuart, ed., *Sir Robert Peel, from his Private Papers,* 3 vols (London, 1899)

Pearson, Hesketh, *The Smith of Smiths* (Harmondsworth: Penguin Books, 1934)

Pope, Thomas Canon, *The Council of the Vatican and the Events of the Time* (Dublin: James Duffy, 1871)

Purcell, Edmund Sheridan, *Life of Cardinal Manning* (London: Macmillan & Co., 1896)

Russell, Odo, *Extracts from Despatches from Rome 1858–1870,* ed. by Noel Blakiston (London: Chapman and Hall, 1962)

Seddall, Henry, *Edward Nangle: The Apostle of Achill* (London, Edinburgh: Hatchards, 1884)

Senior, N. W., *Journals, Conversations and Letters relating to Ireland* (1868)

Sillard P. A., *The Life and Letters of John Martin* (Dublin: James Duffy and Company, 1893)

Stanley, E., *Religion and Education in Ireland* (London, 1835)

Sullivan, A. M., *New Ireland* (London: Sampson, Lowe, Marston, Searle and Rivington, 1877)

Swift, Jonathan, *Journal to Stella* (London and Toronto: J. M. Dent and Son, 1924)

Thackeray, W. M., *The Irish Sketchbook* (Gloucester: Alan Sutton Publishing Ltd, 1842)

Trevelyan, G. M., *Life of John Bright* (London: Constable and Co., 1913)

Tuke, James, *A Visit to Connaught* (1847)

Walpole, Sir Spencer, *The Life of Lord John Russell,* 2nd edn, 2 vols (London: Longmans & Co., 1891)

Whately, Jane, *Life and Correspondence of Richard Whately* (1866)

Whately, Richard, *Christian Evidences* (1864)
    Romanism, ed. by E. J. Whately (London,1878)

Whyte, J. H., *The Tenant League and Irish Politics* (Dundalk: Dundalgan Press, 1963)

Wiseman, N. P. S., *Impression on a Visit to Ireland: A lecture delivered in London, November 1858* (Hobart Town: Mercury Office, 1859)

Woodward, Llewellyn, *The Age of Reform 1815–1870* (Oxford: Clarendon Press, 1938)

Irish Political Tracts
Oxford History of England
Oxford History of Ireland

Newspapers and Magazines

The Edinburgh Review	*The English Historical review*
The Examiner	*Fraser's Magazine*
The Freeman's Journal	*The Illustrated News*
The Illustrated Police News	*The Irish Ecclestiastical Record*
The Irish People	*The Irish Times*
The Kilkenny Journal	*The London Illustrated News*
The Manchester Guardian	*The Morning Chronicle*
The Nation	*The Pilot*
Punch	*The Tablet*
The Times	*The Weekly Register*
The Westminster and Foreign Quarterly Review	

INDEX